FOREWORD

The story of the city of Atlanta is an extraordinary account of a small southern town that evolved into a brilliant global city. It is the story of a courageous community that struggled to lay down the burdens of race and embrace the richness of human diversity, the cornerstone of our strength and our prosperity.

From her earliest inhabitants to her most recent newcomers, Atlanta has always been a place of spectacular vision, social progress, and economic success. This powerful book, *Atlanta: An Illustrated History*, tells the story of the people and events that have shaped this beloved city we call home.

In order to understand the significance, the essence and the soul of Atlanta, one must know her history. Atlanta is more than the state capital of Georgia, more than the "Gateway to the South," even more than the "Next Great International City." She is more than her airports, super-highways, majestic skyline, historic southern architecture, and beautiful gardens.

Atlanta is a marvelous idea. She is an innovative concept. She is the best of the Old South and the New South. She is the fulfillment of our greatest hopes, dreams, and aspirations.

Thoughtful reflection reminds me that even during periods of great uncertainty and social transformation, Atlanta showed a potential for change unmatched in other parts of the Deep South. The ability to manage change, to adapt, to rise to the challenges of the times—for the benefit of all—THIS IS ATLANTA.

From the very beginning, Atlanta distinguished herself as unique. Unlike her neighbors in the antebellum South, Atlanta earned renown not for her agriculture, but for her industry—her railroads, marketplaces, and commercial buildings.

Like the phoenix rising from its ashes, Atlanta emerged in the aftermath of the Civil War to become Georgia's premier transportation and commercial center. The pride, the optimism, and the sheer energy that emanated from Atlanta's citizens soon became known throughout the South as the Atlanta Spirit.

From Henry Grady, newspaperman who first declared Atlanta "the New South" and Alonzo Herndon, Atlanta's first black millionaire, to Joel Chandler Harris and Margaret Mitchell, two of Atlanta's most revered storytellers, the Atlanta Spirit knew no boundaries.

At the turn of the twentieth century, the diversity that would become the hallmark of Atlanta society began to blossom. Former planters and freedmen and their descendants flocked to the city from surrounding cotton fields in search of opportunity.

However, Atlanta's path to racial harmony was riddled with obstacles. Jim Crow laws emerged to enforce racial segregation and to keep the spirit of slavery alive. Signs that read "colored only" and "whites only" divided every aspect of Southern life.

The irony is that despite the burdens of race, all the people of Atlanta took part in the city's progress. The fortitude and the talents of the people, *all the people*, would not be denied.

Business flourished on Peachtree, Broad, and Forsyth streets, as it did on "Sweet Auburn" Avenue, the heart of Atlanta's black business district. Institutions of higher learning for both whites and blacks, both men and women, were established.

The city's explosive population growth led to the development of Atlanta's suburbs. Atlanta built her first airport, Candler Field, the forerunner of the renowned Hartsfield International Airport. And Atlanta's preeminent product, Coca Cola, became the world's favorite soft drink.

But Atlanta had yet to achieve her greatest triumph. She had yet to create what we call the Beloved Community, a community at peace with itself, a colorblind society rooted in the fundamental principles of equality, freedom, and justice for all.

It is true, black Atlantans had established their own thriving community of churches, businesses, and universities. Yet the limitations of Jim Crow prevented blacks from fully exercising their citizenship. Blacks lived separately from whites, were barred from using the same public facilities as whites, were denied the same quality of education as whites, and were refused the most essential expression of democracy—the right to vote.

The 1954 Supreme Court decision in *Brown* v. *Board of Education* and the success of the Montgomery Bus Boycott two years later—led by Atlanta's son and my dear friend and brother, Dr. Martin Luther King Jr.—signaled that an unstoppable change was coming to the South. The Civil Rights Movement became the powerful catalyst that tore down the walls of racial segregation and brutality that had dominated the South since the days of slavery.

Atlanta's leaders took heed. Cooperation between the city's black and white leadership enabled Atlanta to avoid much of the violence that marked the desegregation of other cities. As early as 1961, Atlanta had begun to peacefully integrate public facilities throughout the city. It was this effort to nonviolently bridge the racial divide that established Atlanta as a beacon of progressive Southern living.

From this point forward, the city soared to achieve record-setting accomplishments. Among her triumphs, Atlanta became the first major Southern city to elect an African-American as its mayor. Atlanta Hartsfield Airport became the nation's largest and busiest airport. And Atlanta hosted the 1996 Summer Olympics, the centennial celebration of the modern Games. What a phenomenal city! What a phenomenal citizenry!

Andy Ambrose's book is so important because it tells the story of our collective past, it forces us to face our history and ourselves. It reminds us of the great distance we have traveled and inspires us to continue to forge new frontiers. Page after page you will be encouraged and you will be persuaded to believe that Atlanta is a city in the process of becoming the capital of the twenty-first century.

It is my hope that as you read the words and view the illustrations in this book, the famed Atlanta Spirit will touch you. It is a spirit fueled by our love of Atlanta. It is a spirit emboldened by a sense of compassion for our fellow man. It is a spirit driven by a common goal to create a better city, a good city and a beloved city.

REPRESENTATIVE JOHN LEWIS
UNITED STATES CONGRESS

ACKNOWLEDGMENTS

"South of the North, yet North of the South" is the way that W. E. B. Du Bois once described Atlanta. As this insightful quote suggests, Atlanta occupies a unique position in southern history—a city linked by religion, race relations, the Civil War, and rural influences to the region and yet separated at times from the South by an aggressive, opportunistic boosterism that has frequently sought support and models for growth and development outside the region. Throughout its history, Atlanta has continually remade and reinvented both its image and its aspirations—at times connecting itself to the history and cultures of the South and at other times separating itself from the region to align with northern, national, and even international trends and resources.

It is these characteristics that, in my opinion, make Atlanta such an interesting city and metropolitan region to study. In this book, I try to present a historical overview of the city's development, paying particular attention to the ways in which certain forces—namely changes in transportation, race relations, and the city's particular form of civic boosterism (known as the "Atlanta Spirit")—have shaped its growth and history.

I am indebted to many for their help and advice in bringing this project to fruition. The staff of the James G. Kenan Research Center at the Atlanta History Center is due much credit, including Director Michael Rose, Betsy Rix, Paul Crater, and Helen Matthews, who undertook the difficult task of selecting and identifying the many photographs, illustrations, and maps that accompany the book's narrative. Former AHC Executive Director Rick Beard also deserves recognition (or blame) for encouraging me to take on this project. I also wish to thank Darlene Roth—colleague, co-author, and collaborator (or, as she has often described it, "co-conspirator") in many museum and public history projects. Others, deserving mention and thanks are Karen Leathem (managing editor of *Atlanta History: A Journal of Georgia and the South*) who helped with editing and indexing; Charles Smith, who volunteered his time and efforts to produce the book's index; Craig Pascoe (editor of the journal); Catherine Lewis; the senior staff at the Atlanta History Center (who suffered through this process with me); and all the other wonderful staff and volunteers of the Atlanta History Center, who continue to explore and present through the center's exhibits, programs, historic houses and gardens, archives, and publications, the fascinating stories of this city and region.

Similarly, I want to acknowledge my debt and gratitude to the many talented historians and scholars who have researched and written about Atlanta over the years, including my mentor and advisor at Emory University, Dana White, who first steered me to the Atlanta History Center. Others, whose research and publications I drew upon, are listed in the bibliography to this book.

Any acknowledgments of those who assisted in this process would be incomplete, however, without mention of the three people who have contributed the most to my career and life—my wife Terry and my two children, Kalin and Madison. They are the loves of my life and the center of my universe.

CHAPTER I

Beginnings: 1800–1865

The Richard Peters House, southwest corner of Mitchell and Forsyth streets. Peters (1805–1888) owned the house from 1847 to 1881.

A magnificent inland city will at no distant date be built here.

—Alexander H. Stevens,
vice president of the Confederacy and
governor of Georgia, 1839

WHEN ATLANTA WAS FOUNDED IN 1837, there was little in the occasion or in the resources of the surrounding area to suggest that this tiny outpost at the end of a proposed railroad line would one day be Georgia's state capital, its largest city, and one of the most important commercial, financial, and transportation centers in the nation. The city was located above the fall line—the end point of easy river navigation—in the last portion of the state to be settled by non-Native Americans. (Savannah, for example, had been founded over a century earlier.) Cotton, the staple cash crop of southern agriculture, could be grown in this section of the Upper Piedmont, but even at this early date, it was clear that King Cotton would never be produced as abundantly or profitably as in regions further south. For many, the tiny community's first name—Terminus—appeared to describe both its most salient feature and its likely future as a modest, end-of-the-line railroad stop. When Stephen D. Long, chief engineer for the Western Atlantic Railroad, was offered an interest in the tiny community, he refused it, commenting that Terminus was "a good location for one tavern, a blacksmith shop, a grocery store, and nothing else." Even Richard Peters, a Western & Atlantic Railroad executive who is credited with giving Atlanta its name, advised an associate in 1846 that "the place can never be much of a trading city, yet may be important in a small way."

By the outbreak of the Civil War fifteen years later, however, Atlanta was a trading and transportation center of key importance to the state and the South. With a population of over 9,000, Atlanta in 1861 was the fourth-largest city in Georgia. During the next three

The French explored the southeastern coastline with an eye to colonization. This map names the rivers after French rivers. (Left to right) the Charente, now the Newport River; the Garonne, now the Ogeechee River; the Gironde, now the Savannah River; and the Grande, now the Broad River.

years, the city's population would soar to more than 22,000, making Atlanta not only the largest city in the state, but also the third-largest city in the South (behind only New Orleans and Richmond). Two forces were primarily responsible for spurring this rapid, early growth—the city's strategic and expanding rail connections and the equally famous Atlanta Spirit—a brash, opportunistic, and, at times, exaggerated view of the city and its potential shared by many of Atlanta's civic, business, and political leaders. In less than three decades, these forces would manage to transform Atlanta from a tiny railroad village to the self-proclaimed Gate City of the South.

THE NATIVE AMERICAN PRESENCE

Long before Atlanta was founded and white settlers and black slaves first moved into the northwest portion of the state, indigenous people occupied the region. In fact, evidence suggests that Native Americans may have been present in the area for thousands of years preceding the arrival of Europeans and Africans. Little is known of the earliest occupants of the region, but archaeologists believe that Paleo-Indians were well established in the Upper Chattahoochee corridor by 5000 B.C. and that bowls carved out of soapstone in the Stone Mountain area of present-day DeKalb County were part of a trading system that extended as far as the Mississippi River and the Gulf of Mexico.

During the Mississippian era (stretching roughly from A.D. 900 to 1600), Native American communities developed and expanded along the rich river valleys of the Southeast. These inhabitants were accomplished farmers, cultivating substantial crops of corn, beans, squash, sunflowers, tobacco, and gourds that, in turn, supported the development of increasingly large towns (whose populations at times numbered between ten thousand and twenty-five thousand).

The political and spiritual centers of these Mississippian communities were large, earthen mounds built by hand on which rulers—considered to be the earthly representatives of the sun—lived. These mounds were often massive, covering several acres and rising over a hundred feet in the air. One of the mounds at Etowah (near present-day Cartersville, Georgia), for example, extended over 3 acres of land and contained an estimated 4.3 million cubic feet of dirt. The rulers who resided at the summit of these mounds played a critical role in Mississippian society—directing the planting of crops, conducting important religious ceremonies, commanding large armies, and exacting tribute from the towns under their authority. Despite the complexity and size of these communities, they were no match for the Spanish explorers and conquistadors, who invaded the region in the early 1500s. Thousands of Native Americans died in battle or from exposure to foreign diseases. By the 1600s, most Mississippian societies had collapsed, and the surviving populations had spread across the land. Many of their mounds remained behind, however, and can still be seen at Georgia sites such as Etowah or the Ocmulgee National Park near Macon—silent monuments to a once-vast civilization.

THE GROWING CONFLICT

By the time the English settled along the coast of Georgia in 1733, two groups of Indians occupied most of the present-day state—the Creeks and the Cherokees. The Native Americans that the English referred to as the Creeks were actually a loose political confederation of tribes of differing backgrounds and languages. (At least ten different languages and dialects were spoken among this group.) The Creek Confederation had a sizeable nucleus of towns in middle Georgia around the present-day Columbus area, but their lands and communities also extended westward into Alabama, south to the coast, and northward toward the mountains. Each town in the Creek Confederacy was an independent and autonomous unit, possessing its own town square where all the important governmental and ceremonial activities took place. For purposes of the confederacy, however, Creek towns were usually designated as either white (*Hathagalgi,* or populated by people of peace) or red (*Tcilokogalki,* led by warriors). Leaders of white towns traditionally negotiated peace, while red towns took the lead in war.

(Top) *Naturalist Mark Catesby (1682–1749) explored the wilderness in the Carolinas, Georgia, and Florida for five years taking notes and making drawings, including this rendering of a red bird. From 1731 to 1743 Catesby published* The Natural History of Carolina, Florida and the Bahama Islands.

(Center) *Naturalist William Bartram (1739–1823) made a journey through the American southeast from 1773 to 1776 taking notes and making sketches of the flora and fauna, including this detail of a* Franklinia altamaha *tree. He published* Travels through North and South Carolina, Georgia, and East and West Florida *in 1791.*

(Bottom) *John Abbot (1751–c. 1840), an English-born naturalist and painter, spent most of his life in Virginia and Georgia. His paintings, such as this one of the short-billed marsh wren, influenced many naturalists.*

This map of Carolina by H. Moll shows Azilia where the state of Georgia is today.

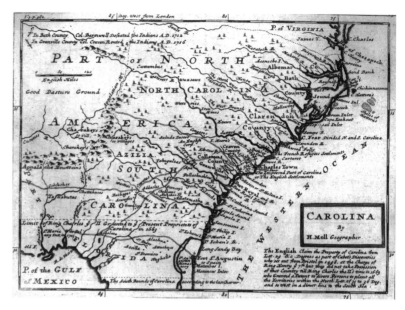

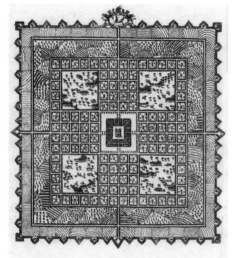

A Plan representing the Form of Setling the Districts, or County Divisions in the Margravate of Azilia.

Sir Robert Mountgomery (1680–1731) proposed setting up a colony between the Savannah and Altamaha rivers under the name of the Margravate of Azilia. The plan was represented in his promotional pamphlet A Discourse Concerning the Designed Establishment of a New Colony to the South of Carolina, in the Most Delightful Country of the Universe (1717).

The second largest Indian presence in Georgia was the Cherokee or *Chalakee* as they were called by other Native Americans and Europeans or the *Ani-yunwiya* (meaning Principle People) as they preferred to call themselves. The Cherokees resided primarily in the southern Appalachian Mountains, and, unlike the Creeks, were members of a single tribe with a common history and language. Until the mid-1700s, the Creeks and Cherokees remained bitter enemies and frequently engaged in war. Following the Cherokee defeat of the Creeks in the Battle of Taliwa in 1755, the Chattahoochee River became the established boundary line between the two nations—with the Cherokees to the north and west of the river and the Creeks to the south and east.

Such agreements and established boundaries between Native American nations meant little to foreign settlers hungry for land however, and pressure on Creeks and Cherokees to relinquish their holdings within Georgia continued to grow throughout the eighteenth and early nineteenth centuries. Land was procured from the Creeks and Cherokees in Georgia through a variety of means and approaches, including continual encroachment on Indian lands by white settlers, secret agreements with individual Indians, foreclosure on tribal lands to pay individual trade debts, negotiated cessions following wars, and outright bribery of various Native American leaders. In 1763, for example, the colony of Georgia negotiated with the

In the original establishment of Georgia by General James Oglethorpe (1696–1785) in 1733, the western boundary extended to the Mississippi.

This drawing was one in a sketchbook executed by Philip Georg Friedrich von Reck (1710–1798) during a 1736 trip to Georgia.

Creeks for the territory between the Savannah and Ogeechee rivers, and ten years later Georgia gained additional lands along the coast through a similar treaty with the Creeks.

Following the Revolutionary War, Creek alliance with the British and Cherokee attacks on both the British and American colonists were used as justifications for the seizure of additional Native lands in Georgia. Another important cession of land took place in 1814 after an unusual alliance of Lower Creek villages, the Cherokees, and the U.S. Army joined forces to defeat the Red Sticks—a conservative rebellious faction of Upper Creek Indians (in the Alabama territory) that was engaged in a bitter civil war with the Lower Creeks. In the resulting treaty, all of the Creeks, regardless of their position on or role in the war, were essentially punished for the actions of the Red Sticks. About thirty million acres of Creek land in Alabama and Georgia were surrendered to the federal government, including some of the lands belonging to Creek villages that had fought alongside Jackson.

(Another interesting historical result of Jackson's war on the Red Sticks was the construction of Fort Standing Peachtree in 1814 at the confluence of the Chattahoochee River and Peachtree Creek. This

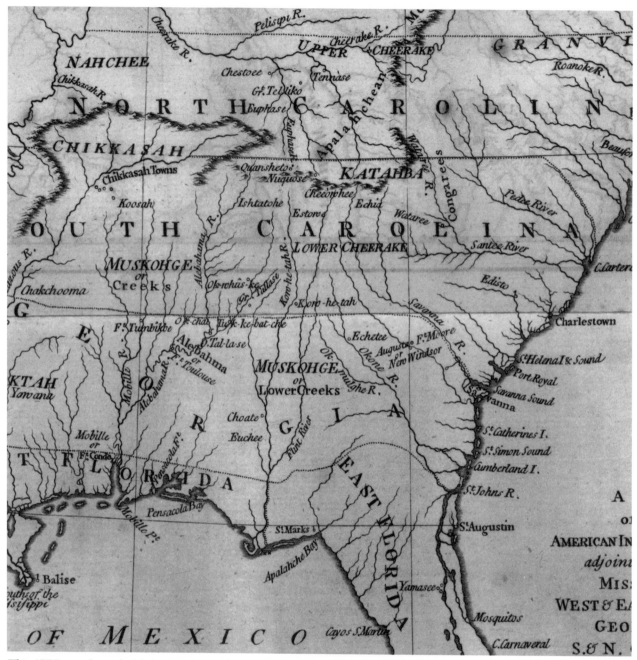

This 1775 map shows the Native American nations at the time of the English settlement of Georgia. Note the Lower Cherokee in north Georgia and the Lower Creeks in south Georgia.

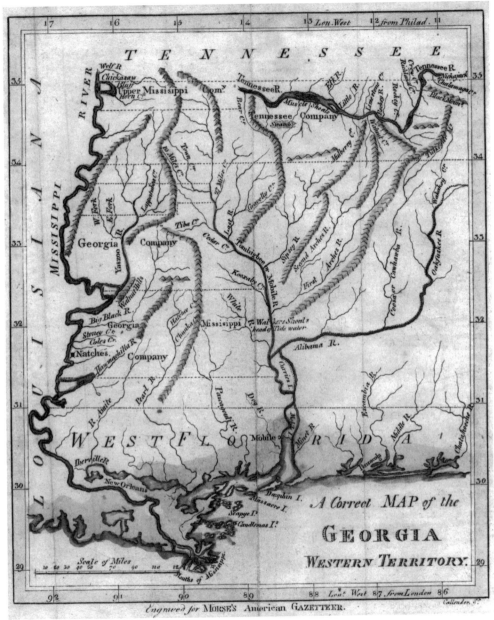

*After independence removed British restrictions on settlement in these western lands, a wave of land specu-
lation broke out. The most infamous of these was the Yazoo Land Fraud, the name given to the 1795 sale
by the Georgia legislature of vast holdings in the Yazoo River country to four land companies following the
wholesale bribery of the legislators. The territory comprised most of present-day Alabama and Mississippi.*

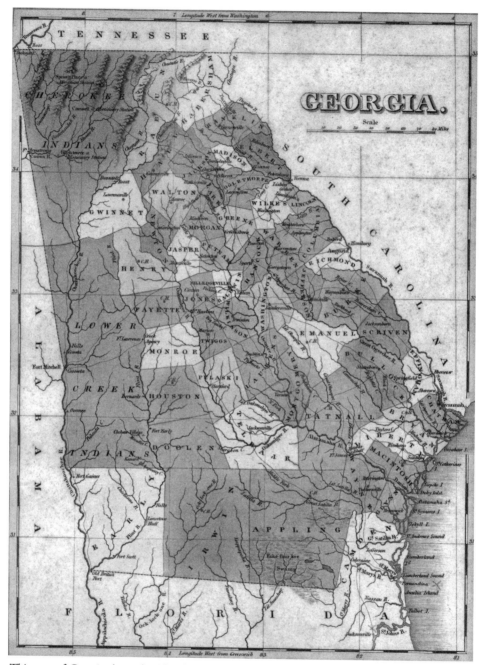

This map of Georgia shows the Cherokee and Lower Creek lands. Buzzards Roost (near the site of present-day Atlanta) appears on the Chattahoochee River.

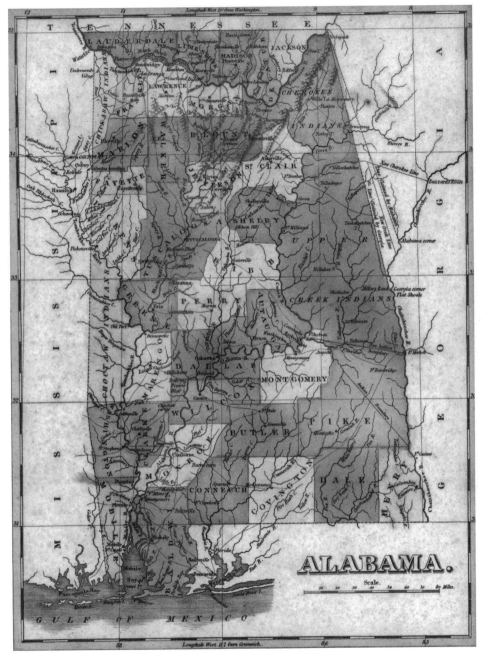

This map of Alabama shows the Cherokee and the Upper Creek lands.

Although William McIntosh (c. 1775–1825) was the chief of only a small faction among the loosely confederated Creeks, he negotiated many treaties between his people and the federal government, many of them with only partial support of the Creeks. From a lithograph by J. T. Bowen from Thomas McKenney's and James Hall's History of the Indian Tribes of North America, *1854.*

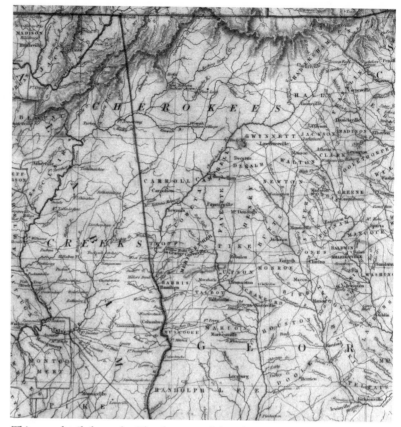

This map detail shows the Cherokee west of the Chattahoochee River after the Creeks were forced out. The names New Echota Indian Town and Etowah Indian Village appear in their territory. East of the river, Atlanta is not yet founded but Rock Mountain (present-day Stone Mountain), Decatur, Campbellton, and Campbell County are shown.

fort, which stood where the Atlanta Water Works are now located on Hemphill Avenue, was one of a series of forts erected along the western edge of white settlement in Georgia.)

As pressure for more land for white settlement grew, the state and federal governments pursued disparate and, at times, contradictory approaches to Native acculturation and land acquisition. In the late eighteenth century, the federal government under the direction of George Washington introduced a "civilization program" for Indians that called for their gradual assimilation into American society through the adoption of English literacy, Christianity, private—rather than

The Western and Atlantic Railroad from Chattanooga, Tennessee, to Atlanta, where it meets the Georgia Railroad and the Macon and Western Railroad. Atlanta was built around the terminus of the Western and Atlantic.

Chief Menawa (c. 1765–1836) led the Upper Creeks against federal forces under Tennessee Militia Major General Andrew Jackson during the Creek War of 1813–1814. From a lithograph by J. T. Bowen from Thomas McKenney's and James Hall's History of the Indian Tribes of North America, *1854.*

tribal—land ownership, and patriarchal, nuclear households. Under this plan, Indians were also expected to abandon hunting economies and their traditional gender roles. Any lands that the Indians did not use for private farms would eventually be distributed to white settlers. Beginning in 1790, the federal government began distributing livestock and plows to Indian men to encourage farming and giving spinning wheels and looms to Indian women to foster European concepts of domesticity. In Georgia, the civilization program among Creeks and Cherokees was begun by Indian superintendent Benjamin Hawkins, who established his headquarters along the Flint River.

While Creeks and Cherokees did adopt some of these prescribed practices, often blending both European and Native customs, by the turn of the century, an alternative approach to solving the so-called Indian problem (and gaining Indian lands) was fast gaining popularity at the state and federal levels. This approach called not for the "civilization" of Indians and their assimilation into mainstream American society, but for their complete separation and removal to lands further west. In 1802, Georgia signed a unique compact with the federal government that set this process in motion and assured the eventual removal of all Creek and Cherokee Indians from the state. According to the 1802 Compact, the federal government settled Georgia's debts from the infamous Yazoo land frauds, and Georgia in turn sold to the federal government all its lands west of the Chattahoochee River. To further compensate Georgia for the loss of these lands, the federal government pledged to work toward extinguishing all Indian claims to land within the chartered limits of the state. (The following year, the Louisiana Purchase made lands available for this proposed Indian resettlement.)

The Creek and Cherokee nations responded to these increased pressures and calls for removal in a variety of ways. The Creeks attempted to resist the sale or confiscation of their lands by establishing a National Council that would speak for and represent the entire nation. They also created a written code of laws, delineated the nation's boundaries, and stipulated, under penalty of death, that only the National Council could approve the sale of Creek lands.

These efforts notwithstanding, Creek lands in Georgia continued to disappear at an increasing rate. In 1819 the Creeks ceded land to the federal government in northeast Georgia that was then divided into the state counties of Hall, Walton, Habersham, and Gwinnett. Two years later, the Creeks surrendered one-half of their remaining land in Georgia through another treaty with the federal government. At the center of these land deals was William McIntosh, the son of a Creek mother and a Scottish father. After commanding Andrew Jackson's Creek allies during the war with the Red Sticks, McIntosh had become the speaker of the Lower Creek Council. By 1821 he was already a wealthy man, with a store, plantation, and ferry on the Chattahoochee River and a thriving hotel at Indian Springs. In addition to these riches, McIntosh had accumulated additional property and perhaps as much as forty thousand dollars from the federal government for his efforts in negotiating the 1821 treaty. While McIntosh may have sincerely felt that he had the best interests of the Creek Nation in mind when he negotiated this treaty, his actions ran counter both to Creek law and to the wishes of the National Council. The council promptly denounced McIntosh and threatened him with death, but eventually relented because of his prominence and because the nation sorely needed the money generated by the treaty to settle old debts.

In 1825 McIntosh negotiated his final land deal at the Treaty of Indian Springs, which acceded to the sale of all of the remaining Creek land in Georgia and two-thirds of their holdings in Alabama. The treaty ran against both Creek and federal guidelines. Not only had the treaty not been approved by the National Council as required by Creek law, it also violated federal law requiring that treaties be formally approved by the heads of sovereign nations. Even President James Monroe's explicit instructions to the treaty commissioners not to negotiate without the entire council received no heed.

The Creek National Council once again declaimed the actions of McIntosh (and the five other Creek headsmen who had signed the document). This time, however, the council went further, stripping McIntosh of his rank and ordering his execution as a traitor. On April 30, 1825, Creek warriors surrounded McIntosh's home on the Chattahoochee River, set it on fire, and shot and killed him as he tried to escape. The following year, President Monroe negotiated a new treaty with the Creeks that formalized the sale of all remaining Creek lands in Georgia, though still allowing them to retain some of their lands in Alabama. In 1836, the federal army began the forcible relocation of the remaining Creeks in Alabama to Indian Territory further west. More than one-third of the Creek Nation perished during and immediately after their removal.

The Cherokees in the northwest portion of the state adopted a somewhat different approach than the Creeks in their attempts to maintain their land holdings in Georgia. In 1819 the Cherokees relocated their national capital from East Tennessee to New Echota (near present-day Calhoun, Georgia). Here, they established a national constitution with provisions for legislative, executive, and judicial branches of government and a national press, which utilized the Cherokee syllabary—invented by Sequoyah—as well as the English language to publicize their cause, not only among the Cherokee people, but also with their sympathizers and supporters in New England. The Cherokee leaders also welcomed Christian missionaries into their midst—some of whom became staunch advocates for the nation—and adopted many of the same practices earlier advocated by the federal government in its civilization program. These Cherokee lands in north Georgia contained many, if not most, of the "hallmarks of civilization" found in other prosperous southern communities of the time: sturdy houses, large farms, schools, grist and saw mills, and small household industries. Some Cherokees also adopted the growing southern practice of enslaving Africans and African Americans. (Of a total population of about fifteen thousand residents in Cherokee Georgia at this time, over twelve hundred were enslaved African Americans. Another two hundred residents were white settlers, living on the lands with Cherokee permission.)

Despite all these efforts, the push to remove the Cherokees continued and accelerated at both the federal and state levels. In 1828 Andrew Jackson was elected president on a platform advocating Indian removal, and in 1830 Congress passed the Indian Removal Act, which

Sequoyah, inventor of the Cherokee alphabet. From a lithograph by J. T. Bowen from Thomas McKenney's and James Hall's History of the Indian Tribes of North America, *1854.*

Cherokee chief Major Ridge (left)*; his son John Ridge* (middle)*; and editor of the* Cherokee Phoenix *Elias Boudinot were leaders of the faction urging removal to the west. In 1835, the three signed the Treaty of New Echota giving away all the remaining Cherokee land in Georgia and agreeing to remove west. However, like most Cherokees, Principal Chief John Ross* (right) *opposed the treaty. From lithographs by J. T. Bowen from Thomas McKenney's and James Hall's* History of the Indian Tribes of North America, *1854.*

authorized Jackson to negotiate removal treaties with all remaining Indian tribes in the Southeast. The same year, the Georgia legislature passed a bill providing for the surveying and distribution through a lottery of all Cherokee lands in Georgia. The discovery of gold on Cherokee land near Dahlonega increased the pressure to confiscate and distribute remaining Indian lands, and white settlers began pouring onto the territory, searching for gold and destroying or appropriating the property of Cherokee residents. In 1832, the U.S. Supreme Court under the leadership of Chief Justice John Marshall ruled in *Worcester* v. *Georgia* that the Cherokees were a sovereign nation and that Georgia laws regarding removal of Indians and the confiscation and distribution of their land and property were invalid. Unfortunately for the Indians, the state of Georgia and the executive and legislative branches of the federal government largely ignored this ruling.

Concerned that the Cherokee nation would lose its lands in Georgia and gain nothing in return, a group of Cherokee leaders,

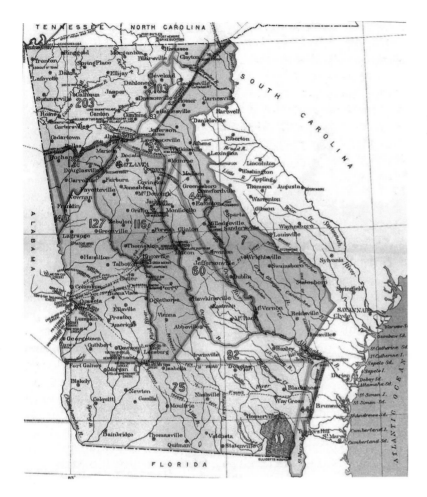

including The Ridge (or, as he was often called, Major Ridge), his son John Ridge, and his nephew Elias Boudinot, began to negotiate with the federal government regarding removal. Principal Chief John Ross and the majority of Cherokees, however, opposed these efforts and refused to participate. When the Treaty of New Echota, which surrendered for sale all of the remaining Cherokee lands in the Southeast, was signed in Boudinot's home on December 29, 1835, not one of the signers was a member of the Cherokee National Council, a fact which made the treaty void under Cherokee law. Chief John Ross continued his efforts to overturn the treaty, but in May 1838 the federal government and Georgia state militia established fifteen removal stations and stockades in Georgia, and three weeks later, virtually all Cherokees in the state had either been rounded up and placed in

In 1836 Yoholo Micco (also known as Chief Eufaula) led the last of the Lower Creeks from Alabama to the federal reservation in Oklahoma. His fight against the loss of their land and their forced removal lasted for years. From a lithograph by J. T. Bowen from Thomas McKenney's and James Hall's History of the Indian Tribes of North America, *1854.*

these stockades or had been marched to embarkation points in Tennessee. In the resulting forced march westward to the Indian territories, at least one-fourth of the Cherokee nation died en route or soon after their arrival. This tragic journey is known to surviving Cherokees as the Trail of Tears.

Like McIntosh before them, Boudinot, The Ridge, and his son John later paid with their lives for their part in the treaty negotiations surrendering Indian lands in Georgia. One year after the Trail of Tears began, all three men were executed, in accord with Cherokee law prohibiting unauthorized land sales. Those who carried out this judgement were never identified, and no formal charges were ever brought.

The departure of Creek and Cherokee Indians from Georgia ended one important period of the Atlanta region's history and ushered in another. The removal of these Indian nations, however, did not completely erase all reminders of their earlier presence. The Indian Springs Hotel owned by William McIntosh, for example, is today the home of the Butts County Historical Society, and Cherokee Chief Joseph Vann's 1799 house operates as a museum in a state park outside Chatsworth. Other Creek and Cherokee connections to north Georgia are suggested in local city, county, and river names such as Chattahoochee, Oconee, and Coosa (from the Creek) and Kennesaw, Tallulah, and Dahlonega (from the Cherokee). Allusions to earlier Indian trails that once traversed the entire region can be found in the names of metropolitan-area roads and streets, such as Sandtown, Hightower, Shallowford, and Peachtree. These roads and others still follow portions of routes and pathways established by Native Americans hundreds, if not thousands, of years ago.

EARLY WHITE SETTLEMENT

Even before the final removal of the Creeks and Cherokees from northwest Georgia, white settlement in the area was already on the rise. Gwinnett County, for example, the oldest of the Georgia counties in the immediate Atlanta metropolitan area, formed shortly after the Cherokee Land Cession of 1817 and the Creek Cession of 1818. Fayette and Henry counties followed a couple of years later after the Creek Cession of 1821—as did DeKalb County (which was created in 1822 from sections of Fayette, Henry, and Gwinnett counties). When the Creeks surrendered additional lands in the area four years later, two more counties—Coweta and Carroll—joined the state roster, and in 1828, Campbell County was created by carving out and combining sections of DeKalb, Fayette, Coweta, and Carroll. Cherokee County, which originally contained all of the remaining

Cherokee lands in northwest Georgia, was brought into being in 1831. And the following year, Cobb, the last county to be formed in the Atlanta region during the 1830s, emerged from a section of Cherokee County.

Settlements, such as Lawrenceville (1821), Decatur (1823), and Fayetteville (1827) sprung up throughout these new counties, and by the early 1830s, the populations of these towns and their respective counties were growing rapidly. Gwinnett County, for example, had a population of over thirteen thousand in 1830—more than three times its figure just ten years earlier. DeKalb's residents in 1830 numbered over ten thousand, and Fayette County boasted about five thousand—almost double its population five years earlier. Most of these early residents were male and white. In Gwinnett County, for example, men outnumbered women by almost a thousand. African Americans, the vast majority of whom were slaves, made up about ten percent of the population in most of these counties.

Settlers came to the region for a variety of reasons, but Georgia's land lottery system was one of the most popular. The state lottery system divided available public land into sections (which were composed of 3 districts), districts (9 square miles), and land lots (202-1/2 acres). The state reserved parcels of land in these offerings for a county seat (situated in the center of each county), schools, cemeteries, and other governmental uses. Churches also had ready access to land although they could not procure an entire land lot. Individual ticket holders whose numbers were drawn in these land lotteries received a lot that that could be as much as 202-1/2 acres; also available were 100-acre farm lots and 40-acre gold lots (only distributed during the 1831 lottery following the discovery of gold in the Cherokee Indian territory).

While the Georgia land lottery system was intended as a way to ensure the equitable distribution of public land, participation in the lottery was nevertheless restricted. Enslaved African Americans, for example, were prohibited from buying tickets, as were women other than Revolutionary War widows and speculators. Land speculators, however, still found ample opportunities to purchase lots from cash-poor individual lottery winners. From 1830 forward, all confiscated or ceded Indian lands were divided and distributed to Georgia settlers via this system.

Many of the early settlers in the Atlanta area in the 1820s and 1830s made their livings, in part, by providing accommodations and services to the cattlemen, traders, stagecoaches, and farmers who traveled through the region. Some of these early residents established inns or

Cherokee Chief David Vann (1800–1863). From a lithograph by J. T. Bowen from Thomas McKenney's and James Hall's History of the Indian Tribes of North America, *1854.*

Pioneer settlers in the Atlanta area, Thomas (1809–1884) and Temperance (1818–1896) Connally stand before their homestead near East Point with their granddaughter Electa and domestic servant Aunt Martha.

Isaac Green Mitchell (1810–1881) was a farmer and later a Methodist minister in early Atlanta. He was the son of pioneer citizens William and Eleanor Mitchell, the brother of Alexander Weldon Mitchell, and great-grandfather of novelist Margaret Mitchell.

taverns along existing roads and stagecoach routes. Charner Humphries, for example, an early settler from South Carolina, constructed White Hall Tavern (or Whitehall House as it was sometimes known) at the present-day intersection of Lee and Gordon streets in West End. This structure was situated along a stagecoach route that led westward to Alabama, and during its three decades of existence, White Hall served not only as a tavern and a way station for stagecoaches, but also as a militia post and a post office.

Other settlers established ferries to cross local rivers or provided blacksmithing, livery, milling, and other services to travelers and area residents. James McC. Montgomery, a DeKalb resident who also served as the county's postmaster, census taker, clerk of the Court of the Ordinary, and its first state senator, is another good example of this type of early settler/entrepreneur. Montgomery moved to the Fort Standing Peachtree area, still Indian land at the time, during the 1820s. In 1833 he finally received legal title to the property he was occupying, and over the next couple of years, he established both a store and a ferry that crossed the Chattahoochee River. With bridges in short supply and rivers that could not be easily navigated by steamboats, ferries such as Montgomery's provided a much-needed transportation service. Some of these ferry operations survived and were still in use well into the twentieth century. None are still present today, but their earlier existence and importance is suggested in surviving city street names, such as Paces Ferry, Nelsons Ferry, Powers Ferry, and Johnson Ferry roads. Other existing Atlanta street names such as Moores Mill, Howell Mill, and Houston Mill suggest another important industry and service provided by Atlanta's early settlers—grist and saw mills.

THE COMING OF THE RAILROADS

The building of new public and private roads, ferries, and stagecoach lines in northwest Georgia in the 1820s and 1830s helped fix the Atlanta area as part of an early transportation nexus. It also began the realization of the state's goal to facilitate travel in the area and to draw revenue and increased commerce and trade from those passing through on their way to the nation's interior. But another mode of transportation altogether, the railroad, would ultimately bring this dream to reality and, in the process, spur the founding and the early growth and development of Atlanta.

In 1825 the Georgia Legislature created a Board of Internal Improvements to promote the establishment of a state transportation network and to determine whether turnpikes, canals, or railroads (or a

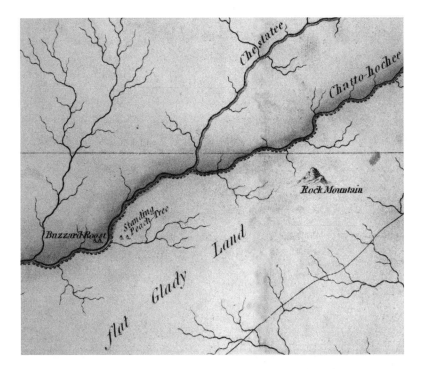

This detail of an 1818 map by surveyor Daniel Sturges shows the Chattahoochee River with the two Indian villages Buzzards Roost and Standing Peachtree near the site of the future Atlanta.

mixture of all three) would be the most effective means to this end. Much of the early focus was on turnpikes and canals (given the success of the Erie Canal in New York in 1825), but eventually the state and the board began to realize the enormous potential of railroads. Surveys were begun under the direction of Chief Engineer of the Board, Hamilton Fulton, and Wilson Lumpkin in 1826 to determine the best routes and locations within the state for a canal or rail system. Both men eventually came to support railroads over canals, and Lumpkin, in particular, became a very strong advocate and voice for the railroads. As Indian Commissioner, state senator, and finally as governor, Lumpkin focused his power and influence on removing all obstacles (including the Creeks and Cherokees) to a statewide rail system.

In 1833 the first state railroad was completed, connecting Charleston, South Carolina, with Augusta, Georgia. That same year, the Georgia legislature, at Governor Lumpkin's urging, chartered three new railroad lines—the Central of Georgia, the Georgia Railroad Company, and the Monroe. The Central connected Savannah with Macon, while the Georgia Railroad intended to start from Augusta and head west toward an undesignated point in the state's interior. (After that phase of construction was completed, the Georgia Railroad

(Top right) *Howell's Mill was located on Peachtree Creek and Howell Mill Road crossed the creek on this covered bridge.*

(Bottom right) *Mayson and Turner Ferry, established in 1844 at the present site of the bridge on Bankhead Highway (formerly Mayson Turner Ferry Road), made possible travel across the Chattahoochee River. The importance of ferries in the early economic life of the area is evidenced by the continued existence of Montgomery Ferry Road, Johnson Ferry Road, and Paces Ferry Road. Likewise, the name Shallowford Road shows the importance of places where the river could be easily forded.*

(Above) *The presence in Atlanta of so many streets incorporating the word* mill—*Howell Mill Road, Moore's Mill Road, etc.—attests to the economic importance of mills of various types located on the many creeks in the area.*

This Map of the Southern States shows Georgia with the counties in almost their modern-day locations and shapes. Atlanta is not on this map but the railroad lines to which it owes its existence are in place.

The Western and Atlantic freight depot was located where the Macon and Western splits off on its way south. Notice also the roundhouse just beyond it.

The car shed built for the Western and Atlantic Railroad by Edward A. Vincent was completed in 1854. It was large enough to accommodate the four rail lines that entered the city in the 1850s.

was given permission to establish branch lines to Eatonton, Madison, and Athens.) The Monroe Company obtained the right to build a road from Macon northward to Forsyth. With the key cities of Savannah, Augusta, and Macon joined in an emerging system of state railroad lines, all that remained was to connect these three lines to a central railroad trunk that would head north to Tennessee and, by extension, to the rich farmlands of the Tennessee Valley and the Ohio and Mississippi rivers. The ultimate goal of state leaders and railroad promoters to join Savannah on the Atlantic Ocean with Memphis on the Mississippi River and thereby gain access to all the major foreign and domestic trade routes of that era demanded this connection.

In 1837 engineers for the Western & Atlantic Railroad (a state-funded enterprise) staked out the southern endpoint of a railroad line

The Western and Atlantic car shed is seen from the first bridge to be built over the tracks. The wooden bridge spanned the rail lines between Broad Street on the north of the tracks and Market Street running south. The other streets all crossed the tracks at street level and were thus very dangerous.

they hoped to build northward to Ross's Landing (Chattanooga) on the Tennessee border. The point the engineers chose was roughly seven miles east of the Chattahoochee River on the summit of a 1,000-foot ridge. This inauspicious act marked the official founding of Atlanta, or Terminus as it was then known.

As noted earlier, there was little in the founding and creation of Terminus to suggest that this small community would ever be of great size or of significant importance to the state or the region. Construction of the Western & Atlantic (W&A) railroad, which began in 1838, proceeded slowly northward from Terminus, handicapped by labor disputes and financial problems. In 1839 a disturbance among railroad workers in Terminus resulted in the deaths of two women and the imprisonment of thirty-four men. A financial depression that began in 1837 and lingered until the mid-1840s also hurt the W&A's construction efforts, as did the cost of early construction. By 1843 the W&A had already spent $2.5 million of the state's money on grading and surveying without any substantial amounts of track being laid. In response, the state legislature authorized the sale of the road for $1 million, but there were no takers. Finally, on May 9,

Railroad engineer Lemuel P. Grant (1817–1893) designed the Civil War fortifications of Atlanta.

The 1858 Lemuel P. Grant House still stands on St. Paul Avenue in Grant Park.

1850, (some twelve years after construction of the line began) the first Western & Atlantic train ran between Atlanta and Ross's Landing.

Fortunately for Atlanta, its railroad connections (and its future) were not solely limited to the Western & Atlantic, but included several other expanding rail lines that would eventually join the town with cities and markets throughout Georgia and the Southeast. By 1850, not only was the W&A connected to Atlanta, but so too was the Georgia Railroad (from Augusta), the Macon and Western (from Macon, but also from Savannah via the Central of Georgia Railroad), and the Atlanta and West Point (from middle Alabama through West Point, Georgia). In 1857, a rail line from Chattanooga to Memphis completed the original Georgia dream of linking the Atlantic Ocean with the Mississippi River, and a delegation of railroad officials and Memphis businessmen passed through Atlanta on their way to a symbolic celebration of the new trade route in Charleston. The delegation invited Atlanta mayor William Ezzard to accompany them to Charleston, where he took the opportunity to raise a toast to Atlanta as "the Gate City—the only tribute she levies is the affection and gratitude of those who partake of her unbounded hospitality." Atlanta's claim to being the Gate City of the region was a bold statement for a town only twenty years old and dwarfed in size by older port cities such as Charleston, New Orleans, and Savannah. But while Ezzard's boast featured the exaggerated claims that would prove to be a key element of the "Atlanta Spirit," his pronouncement also contained a visionary recognition of the role that Atlanta would soon come to play in the region and the important part that railroads connections would have in this transformation.

LIFE IN EARLY ATLANTA

The railroad's central role in the founding and development of early Atlanta was evident in the layout, naming, and political and economic makeup of the community. The geographical center of Terminus, for example, was the zero-mile post—the end line of the Western & Atlantic Railroad. In 1842 the zero mile post moved about a quarter-mile southeast from Land Lot 78 to Land Lot 77 after Samuel Mitchell donated five acres of land to the state of Georgia to be used for railroad purposes. State Square, a rectangular parcel of land bounded by Central Avenue and Pryor, Alabama, and Decatur streets, thus became the location for a passenger terminal (the city's first), a few railroad shops, and a roundhouse. Mitchell had the remainder of his property surveyed into town lots, as did the adjacent land lot owners Judge Reuben Cone of Decatur, Lemuel P. Grant (who

In this 1853 map drawn by E. A. Vincent, the city limits are in a perfect circle one mile in every direction from the Zero Mile Post.

Martha Lumpkin (1827–1910), the daughter of Governor Wilson Lumpkin for whom present-day Atlanta was named Marthasville 1843–1845.

would later develop Atlanta's Civil War defenses and create Grant Park), and Hardy Ivy (the first resident to settle within the original city limits of Atlanta). These town lots and the streets that divided them were aligned, not along the original land lot divisions or pre-existing roads and pathways, but instead along the railroad lines. Mitchell's activities and the similar actions of other property owners along with the two rail lines that would merge with the W&A to form Atlanta's famous "steel triangle" literally and physically positioned the railroad at the center of the city's early life and commerce.

The names by which the community became known—Terminus, Marthasville, and finally Atlanta—further illustrate the railroad's central importance to early life in Georgia's present-day capital.

Edward Everett Rawson (1818–1893) moved to Atlanta in 1857 and started a hardware business. He was also involved in city politics and civic activities, particularly the advancement of education. Rawson typified the spirit which built commercial Atlanta.

Terminus, the first, unofficial name for the settlement, was a reference to the community's location at the southern terminus of the W&A line. Six years after its founding, the town officially changed its name to Marthasville, in honor of the youngest daughter of Governor Wilson Lumpkin (who had done much to bring railroads to Georgia and Atlanta). Finally, in 1845, the town once again adopted a new moniker—this time incorporating itself as the town of Atlanta. (Supposedly a feminine version of the word *Atlantic*, the name had first been used by chief engineer John Edgar Thompson of the Georgia Railroad to designate his railroad's local depot.)

The railroad brought rapid growth to the young city's commerce and trade and provided civic and political power and influence to local railroad men. Additionally, the livelihoods and successes of Atlanta merchants were increasingly tied to the railroads. In 1849, Atlanta's annual trade was estimated at only $200,000. Two years later, after the W&A line from Atlanta to Ross's Landing was complete, the city's trade total jumped to over $1 million. By the time Memphis businessmen and railroad leaders, along with Atlanta Mayor Ezzard, traveled to Charleston to celebrate the completion of railroad lines to Nashville and Memphis in 1857, annual business in Atlanta stood in the range of $3 million. Included in this economic growth were emerging Atlantan industries, including railroad shops and metal-working factories. The largest of these was the Atlanta Rolling Mill—the biggest producer of railroad tracks in Georgia (second in the Southeast behind the Tredegar Iron Works in Richmond, Virginia).

As trade expanded between the nation's interior and Georgia's coastal cities via the rail lines, Atlanta merchants and businessmen benefited as well, and soon assumed positions of civic and political leadership in the young city. In many antebellum cities and communities of the South, the planter elite dominated. In Atlanta, it was merchants, businessmen, real estate speculators, and railroad people.

The rapid growth of the community's population and businesses began Atlanta's transformation from frontier town to city. In 1847 the state officially recognized Atlanta as a city and authorized an expanded form of municipal government. The new charter provided for a mayor and a city council, as well as other municipal offices, such as clerk, treasurer, and marshal. In many ways, however, Atlanta was still a city in name only. The city council, which met for the first time in 1849, for example, often had to focus its early energies and attentions on issues more associated with a frontier town than a growing metropolis—unlimed and unsanitary privies, dangerous (even deadly) potholes, and continuing problems of hogs and uncollected refuse in the street. The city streets themselves were largely unpaved and extremely dangerous. Deaths and accidents occurred frequently at railroad crossings, and once, in 1852, a man was killed when he fell into an open pit on Loyd Street and broke his neck. In 1858 the city finally adopted a paving ordinance, requiring that all streets in the business area be paved with "smooth flagstone or burnt brick." The vast majority of city streets, nevertheless, remained unpaved.

Slowly, however, some of the hallmarks of city life, including new religious and educational institutions, began to appear in Atlanta. In 1847 the community's first house of worship (a non-denominational church) was erected on Peachtree Street. Wesley Chapel, a Methodist church, followed the next year, as did Sandy Springs Methodist Episcopal Church (on present-day Mt. Vernon Highway). By 1850 a number of denominations and their churches could be found throughout the city. Public schools were still nowhere to be found in early Atlanta, but a few private academies for white citizens formed, including the Atlanta Medical College and the Atlanta Female Academy. Other urban firsts during this period included Atlanta's earliest newspapers—the *Luminary* (later the *Tribune*) and the *Enterprise* —both of which were established in 1846. (The first newspaper of any permanence, however, and the only one to survive the Civil War was the *Atlanta Intelligencer*.)

The decade of the 1850s marked an important turning point for Atlanta in its transition from a small frontier settlement to a young, vibrant city. One of the first steps toward urban respectability was the election victory in 1851 of the Moral and Reform party's candidate for mayor, dry good merchant Jonathan Norcross, over the aptly-named Rowdy party. Mayor Norcross promised to collect taxes and to enforce city laws on cockfighting, the discharging of firearms, and prostitution. He also made clear his intention to clean up notorious sections of the city like Murrell's Row (named for the infamous Tennessee thief and murderer John A. Murrell and located along Decatur Street) and Snake Nation (a shantytown situated in the area between Peters Street and the W&A railroad). The Rowdies responded with threats against Norcross and his store, but the mayor refused to back down and instead organized a volunteer police force to help enforce the laws. Two years later, during the tenure of his mayoral successor John F. Mims, both Murrell's Row and Snake Nation were razed.

Other important events that occurred in Atlanta during the 1850s included the creation of the city's first municipal cemetery— Oakland—and the establishment of Atlanta's first (and only) antebellum park in an open square just north of the railroad passenger

Dr. Benjamin F. Bomar (1816–1868), Atlanta's second mayor (served 1849–1850). Daguerreotype attributed to Chauncey Barnes, Mobile, Alabama, 1850s.

(Top right) *City authorities chartered Atlanta Fire Company No. 1 on February 23, 1850. City firefighters are shown here c. 1850–1854.*

(Bottom right) *Built in 1848 by a Methodist congregation, Wesley Chapel was the first Atlanta church built by a denomination, but the second church overall as the first was nondenominational. The chapel was located at the corner of Houston and Peachtree streets, just south of the present site of the Candler Building.*

ATLANTA MEDICAL COLLEGE.

(Above) *The Atlanta Medical College, established in 1854 and built in 1855, was located on the northwest corner of Butler and Jenkins (now Armstrong) streets. Slated for destruction by General Sherman, the college was saved by the quick wits of Dr. Pierre-Paul Noel D'Alvigny and stood until 1906 when it was razed to make way for an expansion of Grady Memorial Hospital.*

WESLEY CHAPEL.
FIRST CHURCH ERECTED IN ATLANTA.

depot. In 1854 Atlanta's selection as the county seat for newly-created Fulton County (which was carved out of the existing boundaries of DeKalb County) demonstrated the city's growing local importance. Not content with this political status, city leaders also lobbied the Georgia legislature to drop Milledgeville as the state capital and select Atlanta instead. The city's bid (like that of rival Macon) was unsuccessful, but over a decade later (1868) Atlanta achieved its dream of becoming the political center of Georgia. By 1860 Atlanta had emerged as a rapidly growing railroad city of strategic transportation and commercial importance to the state and region. With a population of 9,554, it already ranked as the fourth-largest city in the state.

SLAVERY

Adding to Atlanta's population numbers during the 1850s were a growing number of enslaved African Americans. In 1850, 512 slaves lived in the city; ten years later the number had grown to 1,914. In both years enslaved African Americans made up about twenty percent of the total Atlanta population. These numbers and percentages were

(Left) *Alexander Welden Mitchell (1812–1891) was a cotton dealer active in politics. He played an important part in the victory of the Moral and Reform party over the Rowdy party in city politics.*

(Middle) *This advertisement appeared in the first city directory published for Atlanta,* Williams' Atlanta Directory, City Guide, and Business Mirror, *1859–1860.*

(Right) *The Atlanta City Hall and Fulton County Courthouse built by Columbus Hughes 1853–1854. The building stood until 1884 when it was demolished to make way for the current state capitol.*

much smaller than those found in many of the other large cities of the South (where, in some cases, there were black majorities), but the growing slave presence in Atlanta would play an important role in tying the city more closely to the region and to the Confederacy when the Civil War broke out.

Atlanta had two slave markets located in the downtown area along the rail lines, where African Americans could be bought and sold as property and shipped elsewhere in the South. Those involved in agriculture made use of some of the slaves. Most slaves, however, worked as general laborers, domestic servants, or in skilled labor positions, such as brickmasons, carpenters, blacksmiths, and mechanics. Ephraim Ponder, a former cotton planter and slave trader, was by far the city's largest slaveholder with sixty-five slaves, but most of his slaves were hired out, especially those trained as mechanics and tradesmen, and allowed to retain some of their wages. One of Ponder's slaves, Festus Flipper, was a shoemaker and the father of two sons who would achieve local and national prominence—Henry O. Flipper, the first black cadet to graduate from West Point and Joseph S. Flipper, a bishop in the African Methodist Episcopal Church and chancellor of Morris Brown College in Atlanta.

The presence of a growing number of slaves in the city—some of whom lived outside the daily supervision and control of owners and overseers—increased white concerns about the possibility of slave insurrections and violence. Some white laborers also resented the competition caused by skilled slave labor. The city council passed numerous ordinances restricting the movement of slaves and even tried to outlaw the hiring-out system. Such efforts were ultimately unsuccessful. After nine slaves were charged with insurrection in 1853, the slave codes were tightened even further.

African Americans, free and enslaved, had to observe strict curfews within the city and carry permits when passing into or out of the city limits. They had no right to assembly—even for purposes of religion, entertainment, or amusement—without special permission from the mayor. Even seemingly trivial actions, such as walking on the street with a cane or smoking in public, carried punishments for African Americans.

Free blacks, or "free persons of color" as they were known during this period, also had to follow the slave codes, as well as additional restrictions on their movements and freedoms. They could not live within the Atlanta city limits, for example, without written permission from the city council. The city saw fit to tax any goods these blacks sold and any services they bought. Punishments for crimes or offenses were also much harsher for free blacks than whites. When the

The Crawford, Frazer & Co. slave market in 1864 was located at No. 8 Whitehall Street, between Alabama and Hunter (now Martin Luther King Jr. Drive) streets. Photograph by George N. Barnard.

city council passed a law, for example, in 1854 to prohibit crossing a bridge too quickly, whites found guilty received a $25 fine. African Americans, free or enslaved, found guilty of the same offense received twenty-five lashes. Small wonder that the 1860 census found only twenty-five free persons of color residing in Atlanta.

THE CIVIL WAR

As the debates over secession heated up and the 1860 presidential election approached, opinions in Atlanta regarding which path the city and the region should take varied widely. Many citizens were advocates of seceding from the Union while some Atlanta businessmen, who were concerned that rash action could hurt their economic interests, counseled patience and advised against secession. In the 1860 election the majority of voters in Atlanta selected Unionist candidates Stephen A. Douglas and John Bell (Lincoln was not on the ballot in Georgia) over secessionist candidate John C. Breckinridge. But, by the time Georgia seceded from the Union in 1861, Atlanta was decidedly within the Confederate camp (both geographically and philosophically).

The remaining Unionists in Atlanta (whose numbers in 1861 have been estimated by one historian at about one hundred families) faced increased pressures to conform or leave town. The Committee on Public Safety organized in 1861 and the Vigilance Committee, formed the following year, focused much of their attention and energies on ferreting out suspected spies and exposing abolitionists and Union sympathizers. In 1862, George W. Lee, appointed as provost marshal, instituted a wave of arrests and trials of suspected abolitionists. As a result, many Unionists either left the city, went underground, or, at the very least, kept an extremely low profile. Still, despite the dangers, a few loyal supporters continued to aid the Union cause as best they could. Some Unionist women, for example, organized missions to aid northern soldiers in Atlanta prisons and hospitals, often smuggling supplies to them. Two other Union sympathizers, William Markham and Lewis Schofield, who operated the Atlanta Rolling Mill that produced armor plate for Confederate ships, conspired to keep production levels at a pace that was high enough to keep their factory from being seized but low enough to delay Confederate boat construction.

These small individual and collective efforts did little, however, to stem Atlanta's growing importance to and alignment with the Confederacy, as the city quickly became both a major wartime producer and an important regional transportation and distribution center. Many existing industries in the city were soon converted to wartime production, and newly established factories provided much-needed Confederate munitions and supplies. In 1861, for example, the Western & Atlantic's machine shops devoted four of their forges to the rifling of gun barrels, and the shops of the Georgia Railroad were used to produce two breech-loading cannons (weighing between six and eight hundred pounds). Similarily, the Atlanta Rolling Mill (one of only two factories in the Confederacy capable of making railroad track) added to its manufacturing line the production of naval armor plate.

Newly established war production industries included the Atlanta Sword Factory that manufactured swords for the Confederate cavalry and artillery and the Spiller and Burr pistol factory (a privately owned and run operation). The biggest ordnance producer in the city, however, was the Confederate government arsenal, whose work amounted to more than forty-one million percussion caps for muskets, nearly five million percussion caps for pistols, and more than nine million rounds of small arms ammunition in the period from 1862 to 1864. The arsenal also produced thousands of saddles, bridles, cartridge boxes, canteens, and other military items and employed over five thousand Atlanta men and women. (Almost half of the workers in the arsenal's small arms laboratory were women.) A second large war-related industry and producer in Atlanta was the Quartermaster's Depot, which operated a shoe factory, a tannery, and a clothing depot that employed over three thousand seamstresses, making one hundred and thirty thousand uniforms per year at the height of production. All of these wartime industries were assisted and supported by Atlanta's railroads, which not only brought essential raw materials to the city, but also transported finished war goods throughout the Confederacy.

In 1862, with the fall of western and middle Tennessee to Union forces, Atlanta added to its wartime responsibilities by operating as a treatment center for the increasing number of Confederate and Union soldiers wounded and in need of aid. The military commandeered schools and churches and converted them for use as temporary hospitals to care for and house the injured. (At one point, there were twenty-six separate hospitals in operation.) Atlanta also served as a temporary holding area for Union prisoners and as a recruiting and training center for the Confederacy after its military switched from a policy of voluntary enlistment to one of conscription.

As the war continued, the city experienced severe growing pains, shortages, and dramatic social changes. The population of Atlanta, which in 1860 was less than ten thousand, surged during these years to approximately twenty-two thousand. Inflation and prices also skyrocketed. Although smuggling and blockade running continued throughout much of the war, goods that had formerly been purchased in the North or imported from Europe became increasingly difficult to procure, especially as the federal blockade of southern ports became more efficient. Products quickly disappeared from Atlanta store shelves, and rampant inflation exacerbated the situation by making scarce supplies even more expensive. Between 1861 and 1863, for example, the wholesale price for flour rose from $6.25 to $110.00 per barrel, while sugar went from a little over $.08 a pound to $3.75 per pound. Lard, another prime ingredient in cooking and baking, grew from $.12 to $3.00 per pound, while ham increased from $.11 to $5.00 per pound. Such economic hardships only contributed to civil unrest. Frustrated by high prices and scarce supplies, a group of hungry war widows rioted in 1863 and began looting stores along Whitehall Street. By 1865, goods in the eastern portion of the Confederacy cost ninety-two times what they had only four years earlier. The Confederate government responded by printing more paper money, but these bills retained little purchase power and were undercut even further by counterfeit dollars and "shinplasters"—notes issued by insurance companies and other businesses to be used as script.

The growing scarcity of raw materials and labor threatened both Atlanta's industrial production and its social order. The enlistment and conscription of white males into the Confederate military drained the city of much-needed manpower. (In Fulton County alone, over twenty-six hundred men enlisted or were drafted into service during the Civil War.) Enslaved African Americans were brought in from the surrounding countryside and from all over the state to support war production in and build defenses for the city. Many of these imported laborers received insufficient housing and clothing, while those with steady occupation went largely unsupervised—leading to growing concerns among white Atlantans about slave insurrections and the possibility of violence. Increasingly, white women took up the vacant positions in the city's factories. This movement of women into industrial and factory work was a new phenomenon for the city and the region. In another first for the city, women began to organize themselves into relief groups and societies. Mrs. W. F. Westmoreland, for example, founded the Ladies Soldier Relief Society, while Mrs. Isaac Winship directed the Atlanta Hospital Association, which joined forces with the St. Philips Hospital Society to offer assistance to families, wounded soldiers, and war widows.

The tremendous wartime population increase, coupled with a growing influx of slaves and other newcomers into the city, taxed Atlanta's ability to maintain social order. The small and poorly-funded local police force was often outnumbered and overwhelmed by criminal elements. But, when the city was declared a military post in 1862, martial law brought effective restraint to the citizens of Atlanta. Residents then needed a pass to move about the city, and their bags and packages had to be inspected by the city marshal. In addition, stricter regulations fell on both enslaved and free African Americans. The following year, Major G. W. Lee issued an order outlawing the sale of alcohol—considered a cause of the civil unrest—in saloons or other public places. Despite these restrictions, crime and charges of disorderly conduct continued, and the city struggled to provide protection, municipal services, and relief for the poor.

THE WAR DRAWS CLOSER

Atlanta's importance to the Confederacy as a production and transportation center also made it a major strategic target for the Union Army. The city was the hub of an important Confederate manufacturing complex (that included Macon, Columbus, and Augusta, Georgia, and Selma, Alabama.) If Atlanta fell, the Confederacy would not only lose approximately one-half of its military production capabilities, but the loss of Atlanta's rail lines would also severely curtail the Confederacy's ability to supply its troops and continue the war effort.

The potential capture of Atlanta also had important national political ramifications. In 1864 President Lincoln's reelection was far from certain. With his administration in trouble, the northern public tiring of the war effort, and anti-draft riots breaking out in New York and some Midwestern states, the viability of his political career seemed challenged. The public sentiment for a peace settlement with the South was growing, as was support for former Union General George B. McClellan and other announced "peace" candidates. If Atlanta fell, Lincoln's political and military victory seemed assured; if Atlanta held, Lincoln risked political failure and the possible emergence of the South and the Confederacy as an independent and sovereign nation.

In 1864 General William Tecumseh Sherman took command of the Union forces in the western theater and prepared for a campaign against Atlanta, where his primary objectives were to seize the railroads and bring the city under Union control. The Atlanta Campaign began on May 9, 1864, with the first engagement between Sherman's troops and the Confederate forces of General Joseph E. Johnston, at Dalton, Georgia (south of Chattanooga). Additional battles took place

Carte de visite of Union Major General William Tecumseh Sherman (1820–1891).

This is the left side of a three-part panorama taken from the dome of the Atlanta Female Institute. The cupola-topped building at upper left is the Atlanta Medical College, and the two-story building at center is the Calico House.

that same month between the two forces at Resaca (May 14–15), Calhoun (May 16), Adairsville (May 17), and Cassville and Kingston (May 18–19) as Johnston's outnumbered troops withdrew further southward, blunting but not halting Sherman's march toward the city. On May 25, Confederate forces repulsed the Federal troops along the Dallas/New Hope Church defensive line, but both sides sustained large numbers of wounded and killed. The cannon fire from the battle could be heard in Atlanta, thirty-two miles away.

The next series of major battles waged for almost a month, as Sherman tried to dislodge the Confederates from defensive lines around Kennesaw Mountain, the strongest natural defensive position in north Georgia. After losing three thousand men in a frontal attack,

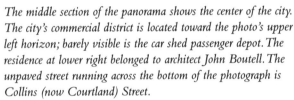

The middle section of the panorama shows the center of the city. The city's commercial district is located toward the photo's upper left horizon; barely visible is the car shed passenger depot. The residence at lower right belonged to architect John Boutell. The unpaved street running across the bottom of the photograph is Collins (now Courtland) Street.

In the third section of the panorama, the street running from the lower left corner into the distance is Ellis, crossing Ivy Street (now Peachtree Center Avenue) in the middle and cresting at the ridge, marking Peachtree Street. Note the open fields providing space for farming and livestock.

a frustrated Sherman finally succeeded in circumventing Johnston's flank. The Confederates were once again forced to withdraw southward. On July 9, Union forces reached the Chattahoochee River, and Johnston's troops took position in defensive fortifications that had been designed by engineer Lemuel P. Grant (for whom Grant park is named) and built by slaves from area plantations and farms. Atlanta's twelve-mile-long defensive works were virtually impregnable against direct attack. Unfortunately for Confederate forces, battle conditions and Sherman's strategic maneuverings would soon draw Confederate forces beyond the safety and security of these positions.

The following day, Sherman's forces began crossing the Chattahoochee, causing Confederate President Jefferson Davis to call

Carte de visite of Confederate General Joseph Eggleston Johnston (1807–1891).

for a region-wide day of fasting and prayer. Davis, concerned that Johnston had retreated nearly eighty miles without seriously damaging Sherman's army, and worried that he could not or would not defend Atlanta, decided to relieve the general of his command. On July 17, General Johnston received a wire from Confederate Secretary of War James Seddon informing him that he was being relieved of his command and would be replaced by General John Bell Hood, a military figure known for his aggressiveness (and, some would say, his recklessness). Atlantans prepared for the onslaught they felt certain would follow.

Within the city, all was chaos. By late July, much of the population of Atlanta had already departed the city. The Confederate authorities had already begun months earlier moving supplies and materials to Macon, Augusta, and Columbus. Increasingly they were joined in this exodus by refugees from the earlier fighting in north Georgia and wartime citizens of Atlanta, who began fleeing the city fearful of the violence and destruction to come. For those remaining, preparations continued for the defense of Atlanta. Mayor James Montgomery Calhoun ordered every male, irrespective of age or infirmity, to assist with these efforts, and outside the city, Confederate encampments sprang up everywhere.

Sherman's plans for the attack and defeat of Atlanta focused on capturing and controlling the four main rail lines that entered and supplied the city—the Western and Atlantic Railroad from the north, the Georgia Railroad from the east, the Macon and Western Railroad from the south, and the Atlanta and West Point Railroad from the west. Under this plan, Major General George H. Thomas's Army of the Cumberland would occupy the ridge between Nancy and Peachtree creeks in Buckhead and move forward toward Atlanta on the north side, while Major General John M. Schofield's Army of the Ohio would take Decatur east of Atlanta, and Major General James B. McPherson's Army of the Tenessee would destroy the Georgia Railroad line between Decatur and Stone Mountain. Sherman hoped the resulting battles would last no more than several days. Instead, the battles for Atlanta persisted for almost a month and a half and resulted in thousands of Union and Confederate casualties.

With his army already backed up to the very gates of Atlanta, Confederate John Bell Hood had few options other than attack. The first battle for Atlanta took place on July 20 along Peachtree Creek, north of the city. General Hood's forces advanced, caught a portion of Thomas's army by surprise, but ultimately failed to drive them from the field. On July 22, Hood again moved boldly to flank McPherson's

Notice the ruins of the buildings along the railroad. The Macon and Western rail line here begins its great bend as it turns south from its northwesterly route out of Atlanta. The curved building at right center is the Macon and Western locomotive house on Hunter Street (now Martin Luther King Jr. Drive). Harris Street, where the young diarist Carrie Berry lived, is to the west.

This 1864 photograph shows the Western and Atlantic bridge over the Chattahoochee River, near its confluence with Peachtree Creek. Confederate troops destroyed the superstructure but Union forces built a temporary wooden bridge to allow troops and provisions to cross the river.

Carte de visite of Confederate Lieutenant General John Bell Hood (1831–1879).

James Montgomery Calhoun (1811–1875) served as mayor of Atlanta 1862–1866.

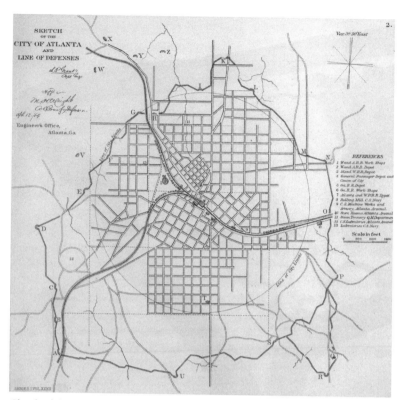

Sketch of the City of Atlanta and its line of defenses. Lemuel P. Grant, chief engineer of the military department of Georgia, designed and built these defensive fortifications starting in 1863. Colonel Grant developed a perimeter defense line consisting of seventeen redoubts connected by a sequence of rifle trenches. Eventually Grant completed more than ten miles of defense works averaging one mile from the city center.

troops east of Atlanta. General McPherson was killed in the ensuing fighting, but the Confederate attack again failed and Hood suffered fifty-five hundred casualties to Sherman's thirty-six hundred. Six days later, on July 28, another bloody engagement—the Battle of Ezra Church—erupted, this time on the west side, where Sherman was moving to cut both the Macon and Western and the Atlanta and West Point railroad lines that supplied Hood's troops. In three hours of fierce fighting, Hood lost three thousand men (against Sherman's loss of only six hundred), but did manage to keep Sherman from seizing and completely controlling either of the railroad lines.

The ruins of the Atlanta Rolling Mill overlook the site of the destruction of Hood's ordnance train. Founded in 1858, the rolling mill produced railroad iron and later manufactured cannon, iron rails, and plating for naval ironclads. Situated along the Georgia Railroad, southeast of downtown, the rolling mill is now the site of part of Oakland Cemetery and the former Fulton Bag and Cotton Mill.

Planter and slave trader Ephraim G. Ponder (1822–1887) moved to Atlanta in 1857 where he built a grand home on a high knoll north of the city. The house was topped by an observation deck, providing a splendid view from its hilltop prominence. Ironically, the vantage view that influenced the Ponders to build their house on the site also motivated Confederate engineers to construct defense works along the approach to the house. The house served as a perfect sharpshooter's position for Southern forces and subsequently a perfect target for Federal artillery in the woods near present-day Eighth Street.

On the northern perimeter of Atlanta's defenses, near Fort Hood, chevaux-de-frise protect a cannon redoubt overlooking the Ephraim G. Ponder House. A palisade runs beyond the main house and its stripped-bare outbuildings, which provided the lumber for the fortifications.

Solomon Luckie (birthdate unknown), a free African American, ran a barbershop and bathing salon at the Atlanta Hotel. On August 9, 1864, while out walking at the corner of Whitehall and Alabama streets, Luckie was wounded by an exploding shell. He died later that same day.

Nancy Cunningham Luckie (1820–1910), Solomon Luckie's wife.

Stymied in his efforts to capture and cut the rail lines to the south and west of Atlanta, Sherman embarked on a new approach, which was characterized by a prolonged shelling of the city and its residents and numerous probes and skirmishes initiated by Union troops to find weak points in Hood's defense of the railroads. Beginning on August 9, 1864, Atlanta was subjected to a withering fire of shells that targeted the buildings of the Atlanta arsenal and other industries and manufactures, church steeples, and other prominent landmarks. The remaining twenty-five hundred or so residents (many of whom were Union sympathizers) huddled for protection in basements or in "bomb proofs"—makeshift shelters dug into the ground and covered with logs and dirt. A poignant record of these experiences is contained in the journal of ten-year-old Carrie Berry, who took refuge during the bombardment in a bomb proof and in the cellar of her uncle's home (which was later struck by cannon fire). When the shelling finally ended on August 25, an estimated twenty civilians had been killed in the bombardment. The siege, however, had failed in its ultimate objective—to force Hood's army and the city to surrender.

After Sherman's guns suddenly fell silent on August 26, 1864, both Hood and the remaining Atlanta citizenry were at a loss as to what had happened to the Union troops. Many secessionists hoped that Major General Joseph Wheeler's Confederate cavalry had succeeded in cutting Sherman's supply lines and that the Union army was now in retreat. In reality, Sherman had withdrawn from the area and was making a wide flanking movement to the west in preparation for attacking and seizing the Confederate's remaining rail lines south and west of the city. On August 28, part of Sherman's army reached and seized the Atlanta and West Point Railroad at both Fairburn and Red Oak. Other Union troops positioned themselves on the Macon and Western Railroad at Rough and Ready (now Mountain View) about three miles east of East Point. The final battle for control of Atlanta's railroads took place at Jonesboro from August 31 to September 1 and resulted in another Union victory.

With his final railroad supply line cut and in enemy hands and facing the possible starvation of his army, Hood made preparations to evacuate Atlanta. On September 1, their withdrawal began, following the destruction of city ammunition dumps and five locomotives and eighty-one boxcars—twenty-eight of which were loaded with gunpowder, shells, rifles, and cartridges. The tremendous explosions and fires that resulted from this destruction convinced many Atlantans that the Union occupation of the city was already underway.

By the following day, there were only a few thousand people were left in the city (mostly Union sympathizers and those too poor

Carrie Berry (b. 1854), daughter of Maxwell and Harriet Berry, lived on Harris Street and maintained a diary during the Siege of Atlanta.

(Top left) *The Chas. E. Grenville Flour Mill. The hole in the dirt mound in front of the mill is an entrance to a bombproof.*

(Bottom left) *Those who could, built bombproof shelters or "pits" in hills or in gardens to escape the shelling from the artillery of the Union troops besieging the city.*

Residents refuged from Atlanta under General Sherman's Special Order No. 67 with only the limited amount of property permitted them.

A federal supply convoy wends its way up Peachtree Street past the Georgia Railroad & Banking Company Building and turns left onto Marietta Street at what is now Five Points.

The ruins of the Georgia Railroad roundhouse as the city burns, November 15, 1864. From Harper's Weekly, *1865.*

This photograph of the ruins of the car shed graphically illustrates the destruction of Atlanta's rail lines and railroad facilities by federal troops. Although the rebuilding of the rail facilities was rapid, it was not until 1871 that the Union Passenger Depot was built to replace a temporary structure on this site.

to travel) as Atlanta awaited the arrival of Sherman's troops. Concerned that no further harm befall the city, Mayor Calhoun assembled a carefully selected group of Atlantans (including some Union sympathizers and one free African American, Robert Webster), to officially surrender the city to federal forces. On September 2, the party rode out on horseback along Marietta Road, where they encountered an advance party of Union troops. Advised that General Sherman was still in the Jonesboro area, the committee offered a note of surrender instead to the General William T. Ward, the closest ranking Federal officer.

On September 5, 1864, General Sherman arrived in Atlanta and ordered the remaining civilian families and individuals to leave the city. The evacuees, mostly women and children, were escorted to Rough and Ready for departure. An estimated four hundred and forty-six families headed south. Many others headed north, some never to

The four daughters of Edward E. and Elizabeth Clarke Rawson: Mary, Carrie, Laura, and Eunice. Mary kept a diary during much of September, 1864, recording the battles and subsequent evacuation of Atlanta.

The Western and Atlantic freight warehouse overlooks Union soldiers destroying the railroad.

Whitehall Street at Alabama Street, the center of the antebellum business district. Sherman's plans called for all these buildings along Whitehall to be destroyed.

return. A small number of families—perhaps fifty—were given permission by Sherman to remain in the city. Most of these citizens who stayed appear to have been Union sympathizers or individuals who performed critical tasks or services. All who remained behind, however, were warned by Sherman that Atlanta would now become a Union fortress and that it could be a hazardous place to stay.

For two months following the evacuation, Sherman occupied the city as he rested and resupplied his troops. Then on November 16, 1864 (following the re-election of Abraham Lincoln as president), Sherman set off for Savannah on his famous March to the Sea. His avowed intention in this march was to "make Georgia howl" and to "march through Georgia, smashing things to the sea." Before departing, however, Sherman and his men left their mark on Atlanta as well. Fire and violent soldiers demolished the city's railroad depots, the roundhouse, the machine shops, and all other railroad support buildings. Public buildings, selected commercial enterprises, industries (including the Winship Foundry and the Atlanta Gas Light Company that were operated by Union sympathizers), military installations, and blacksmith shops were also targeted. Sherman's instructions called for engineers to level the buildings before they were torched, but eager and careless soldiers set fire to many structures before the engineers arrived. As a result, many Atlanta homes and businesses not marked for destruction were also consumed in the fires that swept the city on November 15, 1864.

Sherman's defeat and capture of Atlanta in 1864 had far-ranging repercussions. It secured Lincoln's presidential election victory in the fall of that year. It also ultimately doomed the Confederacy and its fading hopes for victory and independence. Finally, it left Atlanta burnt, barren, and bankrupt. With only $1.65 left in the city treasury and its railroads—the economic lifeblood of Atlanta—in ruins, it remained to be seen whether the famed Atlanta Spirit could overcome these conditions to restore the city to its former status and propel it toward new goals and new heights.

CHAPTER II

A New South City: 1865–1900

Atlanta's downtown was surrounded by busy train yards such as these in the late 1880s.

1886

I want to say to General Sherman, that from the ashes left us in 1864 we have raised a brave and beautiful city; somehow or other we have caught the sunshine in the brick and mortar of our homes and have builded therein not one ignoble prejudice or memory.

—Henry Grady,
Atlanta Constitution editor and
New South spokesman, 1886

AS THE CIVIL WAR DREW TO A CLOSE and Atlanta residents began returning to the city, they encountered a desolate and depressing landscape. Much of Atlanta lay in ruin, with almost every building, warehouse, and public facility in the business district destroyed. All the railroad buildings and support structures—and even the rail lines themselves—also had been demolished. "All that remained to attest to the former existence of great mills and factories," one visitor to the city wrote in early 1865, "were a few battered brick walls, and an occasional chimney looking grim and gaunt."

Despite this widespread destruction, the city quickly rebuilt, and its population soared. By 1870 there were already double the number of people in the city that had been there ten years earlier, and by 1900, Atlanta was the largest city in the state (with a population of ninety thousand) and the fourth-largest in the Southeast (behind only New Orleans, Nashville, and Richmond, Virginia). Swelling these numbers were recently arrived entrepreneurs from the North and immigrants from Europe (primarily German and Irish), but the vast majority of newcomers to the city in the second half of the nineteenth century were southerners, black and white, who flocked to Atlanta in search of employment and other opportunities. In the process they created new communities, new institutions, and new problems for the city.

A good deal of the impetus behind Atlanta's remarkable rebirth was the same industry that had created the city in 1837, shaped its early development and geography, and dominated its economy: the railroads. Two years after the Civil War ended, all of the railroads serving Atlanta and their connecting lines were once again in operation, and a railroad boom was underway that would soon connect the city to the far corners of the region and nation. Atlanta's strategic location and its railroad connections contributed to a period and rate of physical, population, and economic growth that outstripped all other interior and old port cities of the South.

Also contributing to this tremendous growth was the "Atlanta Spirit"—an aggressive, opportunistic search for new business opportunities, new sources of support (including northern investment and involvement), and new regional relationships. This approach assisted Atlanta in its drive to grow and succeed, but it also earned the ire of many other southern towns and cities that came to view Atlanta as a "damyankee" town.

The political reconstruction of the South (1866–1876) brought other dramatic changes to Atlanta, among them the rise of the Republican party, African-American participation and representation in local politics, and two periods of military occupation. Many of these changes were short-lived, however, as the military presence in the South ended following the 1876 presidential election and segregation and disfranchisement of African Americans in Atlanta and the region took firmer hold.

A far different reorientation of the South was preached in the 1880s by regional spokesmen and leaders such as Henry Grady, editor of the *Atlanta Constitution,* who advocated the development of a "New South" with a more diversified economy less dependent upon staple-crop agriculture, heightened industrialization and urbanization, sectional reconciliation with the North, and harmonious race relations (based not upon racial equality, but upon the status quo of white supremacy and racial segregation). Through the efforts of Grady and others, Atlanta soon became both the recognized capital and the premiere example of a redirected and re-energized New South.

In 1895, the city invited the nation and the world to view the progress and the potential of Atlanta and the New South when it launched the Cotton States and International Exposition. Atlanta had much to point to with pride at the turn of the century: thriving industry, a strong and diversified economy, a growing population, a new technical institute (the Georgia Institute of Technology), and an emerging center of African-American colleges and universities. Hidden beneath this bright promise and success, however, were some equally significant problems and issues, including inadequate municipal services, an overtaxed and underfunded public school system, and rising political and racial tensions, that would confront Atlanta not only in the latter decades of the 1800s, but also in the century to come.

BUILDING ANEW

Physical and Economic Reconstruction

The rebuilding task facing Atlanta at the end of the war was a daunting one indeed. According to Confederate General W. P. Howard who visited the city in 1864, an estimated four thousand to five thousand buildings—including homes, factories, public buildings, stores, and even some churches—had been demolished or destroyed by fire, leaving only about four hundred structures untouched. The rail lines had also been torn up to render them useless to the Confederacy. And to make matters even more difficult, there were very few local—and almost no state—funds available to begin the rebuilding. The city treasury, as noted earlier, had a balance of only $1.65 in Confederate currency at the end of the war.

In surveying these conditions, however, the *Atlanta Daily Intelligencer* called not for pity, but for action.

> Let no one despond as to the future of our city! ... What Atlanta now first needs is energetic good government. This, combined with devoted loyalty and enterprise on the part of her citizens, and she will soon rise from her ashes.... [Her] citizens must put their own shoulders to the wheel, and push hard.... Efforts like these will soon restore her to her former greatness.

Atlanta's postwar settlers appear to have answered the challenge. "Everyone that can," O. S. Hammond wrote in February 1865, "is returning as fast as transportation and the roads will permit."

Among the first of these returnees were the merchants, who began immediately, sometimes with their own hands, to rebuild their businesses. Before 1865 was over, one hundred and fifty stores were already back in operation, and the city's trade, according to one estimate, was already thirty percent higher than it had been in the years preceding the Civil War. By 1866, Atlanta was doing an estimated $4.5 million in business, and the following year, a contemporary observer noted that the city had more than two hundred and fifty commercial buildings.

Contributing in part to this rebuilding effort were the city's first

Atlanta switch engines still burned wood in the mid-1880s. Here a freight locomotive with tender and crew in the Atlanta yards.

postwar banks—Atlanta National and Georgia National. Currency and coin were in such short supply following the end of the Civil War that the city at first began issuing twenty thousand dollars worth of bonds in small denominations, ranging from twenty-five cents to ten dollars, which could be used in lieu of cash. This was not an ideal solution, however, and on September 14, 1865, Atlanta National Bank—the first national bank in the Southeast—was founded. The new bank was established by General Alfred Austell, a wealthy plantation owner and a brigadier general in the Georgia state militia, who had moved to Atlanta in 1857 and purchased the Bank of Fulton the following year. Atlanta National opened for business in Austell's home on December 19 with capital stock of approximately one hundred thousand dollars. Within five years, the bank's stock had tripled. A second bank, Georgia National, was established in the city in 1866.

The biggest boost to Atlanta's postwar economic and physical rebirth, however, was provided not by the banks, but through the railroads. Railroads and their associated support industries (foundries, machine shops, metalworks, etc.) remained the city's biggest employers and the most significant contributors to the local economy throughout the last half of the nineteenth century. Atlanta's rail lines also dramatically influenced the positioning of businesses, the layout of streets, and the avenues of growth and expansion. Businesses continued to position themselves as closely as possible to the railroads, and streets initially radiated off these lines, following not a regular grid pattern (which would later be imposed on city streets), but instead taking right angle paths off the curving lines of the tracks. (This explains, in part, the strange twists and turns that some downtown Atlanta streets still follow today.) The railroads effectively divided the city north and south and created a smoky, busy, and, at times, dangerous gulch at its center.

By early 1867, all of the railroads and connecting lines serving Atlanta that had been destroyed during the Civil War were once again back in operation. A railroad boom soon followed in the 1870s that would last for the next two decades. Railroads throughout the region increased the tonnage they carried, the distance they covered, and the destinations they linked to, and most of these new lines soon connected in one way or another to Atlanta. As a result, Atlanta was able to establish strong rail links to cities such as New Orleans; Birmingham, Alabama; and Richmond, Virginia. The city failed in three attempts to build its own locally-controlled rail lines—the Atlanta and Richmond, the Atlanta and Charlotte, and the Georgia Western (later the Georgia Pacific). (All three lines were eventually built, but were controlled by outside interests.) Nevertheless, Atlanta soon emerged as a transporta-

The heart of Atlanta was a smoky gulch. Trains ran at street level until the 1920s when the streets were raised.

The Western and Atlantic depot and roundhouse.

tion center of the Southeast and a regional center as well of business and commerce.

Although the city suffered somewhat as a result of discriminatory freight rates (which made Atlanta merchandise more expensive to ship than northern merchandise), Atlanta merchants were nonetheless able to take advantage of the intense competition rising between freight associations and rail lines to establish the quickest routes for shipping western foodstuffs and cotton to the Atlantic seaboard. As a result of this competition, Atlanta became a hub city for the growing rail empires, such as the Louisville & Nashville; the Southern and Central (later the Seaboard Airline); the East Tennessee; Virginia & Georgia; and the Richmond & West Point. Goods brought to the city by wagon and railroad feeder lines were also added to the rail shipments passing through Atlanta, and city merchants profited handsomely from this exchange. By 1872, shipments of western bacon, lard, corn, oats, and flour to Atlanta on the Western & Atlantic Railroad alone were four hundred to five hundred percent greater than they had been before the Civil War, and the city had firmly established itself as the primary loading point for thousands of bales of cotton brought daily to the city by wagon. Atlanta also became the regional home of the Southern and Central Railroad and the headquarters for the Southeastern Freight Association and the Southeastern Passenger Association.

Union Station, as seen from the Broad Street Bridge, c. 1898.

The second Kimball House Hotel was built in 1885 after the first burned in 1883.

Another inducement for western merchants (who were actively courted by city merchants and their representatives) to trade in Atlanta was the completion of the region's largest and most elegant hotel—the Kimball House—in 1871. The hotel, which was located adjacent to the railroad passenger terminal, was six stories high and contained over three hundred rooms furnished with rich carpets, gold ornaments, and solid-walnut furniture. Other hotel amenities included fountains, glass chandeliers, a French chef, three steam-powered elevators, and a laundry (also operated by steam) where clothes could be washed, dried, and ironed in fifteen minutes.

Accompanying all this remarkable economic and physical growth in the early years following the Civil War was a seemingly ceaseless whirl of noise and activity that was commented on by visitors and residents alike. "Atlanta is a devil of a place," one visitor wrote in 1866. "The men rush about like mad, and keep up such a bustle, worry and chatter, that it runs me crazy." Another observer, northern newspaper correspondent Sidney Andrews, noted, "From all this ruin and devastation a new city is springing up with marvelous rapidity. The narrow and irregular and numerous streets are alive from morning until night with drays and carts and hand-barrows and wagons—with hauling teams and shouting men . . . with a never-ending throng of pushing

The second Union Station was built in 1871.

and crowding and scrambling and eager and excited and enterprising men, all bent on building and trading and swift fortune-making." Both of these observers would no doubt have agreed with the assessment of a local resident in 1881 that "a nervous energy permeates all classes of people and all departments of trade, and the spirit of enterprise never sleeps."

The energy and frenetic pace that characterized Atlanta in the postwar period also invited increasing comparisons of the city to northern and western urban centers and a growing suspicion (especially among rival southern cities) that Atlanta was not as allied as it should be to the values and traditions of the South. "Chicago in her busiest days could scarcely show such a sight," noted Sidney Andrews of post–Civil War Atlanta. "The four railroads entering here groan with the freight and passenger traffic and yet are unable to meet the demand of the nervous and palpitating city." A correspondent for a Toledo, Ohio, newspaper similarly observed that "excepting that the map and the climate tell me that I am in the heart of Dixie, I would believe this to be a bustling, thriving city of the North or West."

Other observers, particularly those from southern cities, were less kind in their conclusions. "There is little that is distinctively Southern in Atlanta," wrote Edward King in 1875. "It is the antithesis

Atlanta City Hall, c. 1870s. The building was the site for both the city government and the Fulton County Courthouse.

of Savannah." A Macon, Georgia, newspaperman, similarly noted that while his city was dominated by "Southern men with Southern principles and instincts," Atlanta was filled with "itinerant adventurers who come today, swindle somebody . . . and are off tomorrow."

In part, this perception of Atlanta as a "damyankee" or non-southern city was tied to Atlanta's economic orientation and leadership. Even before the Civil War, Atlanta had relatively few ties to the plantation South. The city had fewer slaves and planters in its midst than most other large cities of the South, and almost half of Atlanta's business leaders had been born outside the region. In the period after the Civil War, some of these distinctions continued. Over a quarter of Atlanta's business and economic leaders in the period from 1865 to 1880, for example, according to one historian, had birthplaces outside the region. (In comparison, the vast majority of the city's residents—over ninety percent—had been born in the South.) Similarly, in the early postwar years, as in antebellum times, the most influential leaders in the city continued to come from the ranks of merchants and bankers and not from the planter class. In the decades that followed, Atlanta manufacturers and industrialists would join this group in larger numbers, reflecting both the changing economic orientation of the city and its emergence as the capital of the so-called New South.

Political Reconstruction

Atlanta's growing reputation in the South as a "damyankee" town also stemmed from the efforts of city leaders to bring about quick reconciliation with the North and encourage outside investment in the city. In the process of achieving those goals, city leaders and many of its wealthiest citizens honored and fêted representatives of the military force that occupied the city (both during and after the Civil War) and promised cooperation and support to the Radical Republican leadership in Congress and their efforts to reshape the social and political structure of the city and region.

In 1867, Atlanta was once again occupied by a military force, following the passage of three bills in Congress that laid out a plan for the political reconstruction of the South. Under these acts (which were vetoed by President Andrew Johnson but subsequently overridden by Congress), the region was divided into five military districts—each under the control and guidance of a military commander. Each commander was given the responsibility of registering legal voters of the ten former Confederate states (including African-American males who had been granted U.S. citizenship and given the right to vote under the Fourteenth Amendment). To be excluded in this registration were any white males who had previously taken an oath to support the Constitution and had later aided the Confederacy (i.e., former southern members of Congress and other military and political officials). In addition, the military commanders of these districts were instructed to make provisions for the election of delegates to state conventions that would draw up new constitutions that included and protected black voting rights.

Atlanta became the headquarters of the Third Military District, which included Georgia, Alabama, and Florida. The new military commander of this district was Major General John Pope, a native of Illinois, a graduate of West Point, and a Union commander during the Civil War. General Pope arrived in Atlanta by train on March 31, 1867, and was received and welcomed at the depot by a committee of citizens and escorted to the National Hotel, where additional Atlantans paid their respects. After he returned from an April trip to Birmingham, Alabama, Pope was again given an honorary dinner at the National, and a great number of toasts were offered in his honor, including one by the chairman of the reception committee who stated, "Our Pope—may he be as infallible as the law has made him powerful." A similarly warm reception was accorded Major General George Gordon Meade when he replaced Pope as commander of the district in 1868.

Perhaps the most amazing indication of the desire of the city's businessmen to placate the North and attract its capital and investment, however, was the creation in 1867 of a Lincoln Monument Association of Atlanta. This organization (with the support of six city councilmen) proposed the construction of a monument to the assassinated president consisting of a gigantic stone tower 145 feet tall, carved out of Georgia marble. The proposed monument was never built, and the city council later rescinded its initial offer of ten acres of municipal land for the project. However, the mere fact that such a proposal could be seriously considered in a southern city only two years after the Civil War had ended suggests just how different Atlanta's postwar orientation was from its sister cities and towns in the region.

The political reconstruction of Atlanta and the South also presented the city with an opportunity to secure one of its prewar ambitions—to become the state capital of Georgia. In 1867, after hotel owners in Milledgeville threatened not to rent rooms to African-American delegates to the state constitutional convention, Atlanta seized upon this opportunity to promote both its qualifications and its willingness to accommodate both the convention and the reorganized state government. City business and political leaders pointed out Atlanta's strategic railroad connections, its large number of hotels and

The cornerstone of the state capitol was laid in 1885. Construction on the site began in 1884 with the demolition of the old city hall and courthouse.

Atlanta became the capital of Georgia after the Civil War when legislators wanted to take advantage of the railroad. The Kimball Opera House functioned as the state capitol from 1869 to 1889.

other accommodations, and sweetened the pot by promising to provide, free of cost, lodging for the General Assembly, a residence for the governor, state offices, room for the state library, and quarters for the Georgia Supreme Court if the capital was relocated to Atlanta. In addition, the city offered land for a state capitol building.

Atlanta's bid proved sufficiently tempting, and after serving as the site for the 1867 constitutional convention, the city was designated in the 1868 state constitution as the new Georgia capital. In 1877 a state referendum formally approved the selection, and six years later the state appropriated $1 million for a new capitol building. Atlanta contributed $55,626 (the estimated worth of the old state capitol at Milledgeville) towards the building fund and also donated five acres of land (where City Hall had been) for the building site.

While the new capitol was being constructed, the state legislature continued to meet in the Kimball Opera House, which the city had purchased from Hannibal Ingalls Kimball (builder of the Kimball House Hotel) specifically for that purpose. Finally, in 1889 the new capitol building—at that time the tallest building in the city—was completed. Miraculously, the building came in under budget and $118 was returned to the state treasury.

Military occupation and selection as the state's new capital were not the only important changes that occurred in Atlanta during the Reconstruction era. The city also witnessed first-hand the rise (and fall) of the Republican party and the initial participation of African

The present Georgia capitol was built on land donated by the City of Atlanta as one of the conditions promised to the state legislators in return for relocating the capital to Atlanta.

Americans in the political process, including their first representation in state and local office.

In March 1868, the Georgia Republican party nominated as their candidate for governor Rufus B. Bullock. Born in New York, Bullock had moved to Augusta, Georgia, in 1859 and served during the Civil War as a Confederate army officer in the Quartermaster Corps. He was selected as a delegate to the 1867 state constitutional convention in Atlanta and voted in favor of the new constitution, which included, among other things, a property rights act for women, government inducements for business and industry, and recognition of the right of African-American men to vote. The Democrats countered with General John B. Gordon for governor. The subsequent votes on both the governor's race and the new constitution were relatively close. Bullock won the election 83,527 to 76,356 over Gordon, and the new state constitution was approved 88,172 to 70,200. In the new state legislature, Republicans held a clear but narrow majority, while in the senate the two parties were about equal.

Participating in this political and election process for the first time were thousands of new black voters, and their impact was soon felt. Thirty-seven African Americans, for example, were selected as delegates to the 1867 state constitutional convention in Atlanta, and twenty-nine black state representatives and three black senators were victorious in the 1868 elections. On the local level, two African-American candidates for office—tailor William Finch and carpenter George Graham—were elected to the Atlanta City Council in 1870. Finch, a very capable politician who won the support of Atlanta's mayor, was able to bring about the construction of new sidewalks and improve sewer and sanitation conditions in some of Atlanta's black neighborhoods. Finch and other Republicans on the council also pushed to reform the police department—making the officers wear uniforms and abolishing the notorious $1 per head fee paid for each arrest (a practice that many claimed led to the arrest of black citizens on the slightest pretext). Finally, William Finch was also successful in incorporating two schools owned and operated by the American Missionary Association for black children into the city's emerging public school system.

The political success and impact of both the Republican party and black officeholders in the state and Atlanta, however, was short-lived. In September 1868, all of the African-American state representatives and senators were expelled from office by the legislature, which argued that possession of the right to vote did not imply the right to hold office. In response, military rule was again re-instituted in Georgia, and the state was required to ratify the Fifteenth Amendment (which stipulated that the right to vote should not be denied to anyone on the basis of "race, color, or previous condition of servitude") before being readmitted into the Union.

In January 1870, the expelled black legislators finally had their seats restored, but in elections that took place later that year, the Democrats regained control of both houses. The Democratic majority then launched an investigation of Governor Bullock, charging him with corruption and malfeasance. The governor did not remain to defend himself, but instead left the state in 1871 before his term in office had expired. He was arrested five years later in New York and returned to Atlanta for trial. When the trial finally took place two years later, several of Bullock's chief accusers reversed their testimony, and he was acquitted of all charges after only two hours of deliberation.

One of Governor Bullock's main allies during his term in office was Hannibal Ingalls Kimball, builder of the elegant Kimball House Hotel and the Kimball Opera House. Kimball played a key role in the movement to transfer the state capital to Atlanta and maintained close relationships with the Republican leadership in the state. It also appears he profited handsomely from these connections. In a series of what can perhaps best be described as shady deals, Kimball received money from state bonds for three railroads he presided over but that were never built, leased his opera house to the city and later sold it to the state, and profited from the lease of the state-owned Western & Atlantic railroad to a private syndicate of which he was a member. Like his friend Bullock, Kimball fled the state in 1871, but returned three years later at the invitation of city leaders to manage a cotton factory campaign. Upon his return, Kimball challenged his detractors to indict him, but none did, and he went on to play a prominent role in Atlanta's later efforts to advertise its merits and promise as a New South city.

With the resignation of Governor Bullock in 1871, Benjamin F. Conley, a fellow Republican and president of the state senate, assumed the governorship. The Democrats responded by enacting a law, over Conley's veto, calling for a special election in December 1871 to fill the remaining portion of Bullock's term of office. James M. Smith, speaker of the House, was the Democrat's nominee, and, as it turned out, the only candidate. When Smith took office on January 15, 1872, the Democrats controlled both houses and the governorship, and the state, in the parlance of the day, was "redeemed" from Republican rule. With this change, the participation of African Americans in the political process effectively ended. In Atlanta, neither William Finch

Henry Allen Rucker served as collector of internal revenue for Georgia from 1897 to 1911.

nor George Graham were reelected to office, and subsequent changes in voting procedures effectively kept African Americans off the council and out of local office for the next century.

The political changes taking place in Atlanta and Georgia were replicated throughout the South during the 1870s. On the national level, contested irregularities in the 1876 presidential election brought about a compromise that gave the Republicans the presidency, but effectively ended the Reconstruction experiment and the military presence in the South. The nation, while celebrating its centennial anniversary, effectively turned its back on the same people it had fought a war to release from slavery, and the white South was left to establish its own brand of racial harmony, increasingly kept in check by violence (or the threat of violence) and blatant racial discrimination.

One interesting and notable exception to the diminishing political power and influence of African Americans in Atlanta during the late nineteenth century was the remarkable career of Henry Allen Rucker. Rucker was born a slave in Washington, Georgia, in 1852. Following the Civil War, he and his family settled in Atlanta, where Rucker attended Storrs School—one of the first American Missionary Association schools in the city for African Americans—and later enrolled in Atlanta University. He also established a barber shop on Decatur Street.

In 1880, during his sophomore year, Rucker left Atlanta University and began his active involvement in state Republican party politics. For the next decade, he served in a number of federal government positions, including route agent, gauger, deputy collector, and clerk. Finally, in 1897 Rucker was appointed by Republican President William McKinley as Georgia's collector of internal revenue—a position he would hold despite increasing racial tensions until 1911. Rucker held this position four times longer than the white man who preceded him, and he used his political power and influence to effectively control Republican party patronage within the state. He also managed during this same time period to invest in a number of local business projects, including the Georgia Real Estate Loan and Trust Company and the city's first office building for African Americans.

Despite Rucker's influence within the Republican party, he could not slow or halt the decline of African-American influence and participation in city and state politics. In 1892 the local Democratic party adopted the "white primary," which excluded African Americans from participating in the Democratic primary elections and thus kept them from exercising any influence in the selection of candidates for that party. Since Democrats were by this time the dominant party in the city and region, black Atlantans were in essence disenfranchised. In 1897 the white primary was extended statewide. Registered black voters remained few in number and their participation in the voting process primarily limited to bond referendums. (In the century that followed, Atlanta's African-American voters leveraged this limited franchise to good effect by withholding support for city bond referendums until city hall agreed to build its first black public high school.)

BLACK ATLANTA

Despite diminished political rights and increasing racial segregation and discrimination, African Americans in Atlanta made notable progress in the last half of the nineteenth century in establishing institutions, agencies, and businesses that could help meet the pressing educational, economic, religious, and social needs of their communities. In the process, a foundation was laid for the successes and resources that would earn Atlanta the appellation "Black Mecca" in the following century. Also accompanying these changes, however, was the establishment of a rigidly segregated and separate "black Atlanta."

The appeal of the city to African Americans was evident even in the early years following the Civil War. Black southerners flocked to the city in large numbers in search of educational and employment opportunities. In 1870, the African-American population in Atlanta already numbered close to ten thousand (a five-fold increase from ten years earlier), and constituted forty-six percent of the city's total population. By 1890, the black population of the city had grown to over twenty-eight thousand.

Early Educational Institutions

Both Atlanta University and Clark University (which today are joined as one school) had their origins in the post-Civil War period when northern missionaries established small schools to educate freed slaves. Atlanta University, which began its classes in a railroad boxcar in 1865, received its charter from the state two years later. With funds from the Freedman's Bureau, the trustees of Atlanta University were able to purchase approximately sixty acres on one of the city's highest ridges—popularly known as "Diamond Hill"—on the west side of the city. (The university's first classes were composed entirely of grammar and high school students.) On Atlanta's south side, Reverend Frederic Ayer (who along with Edmund Ware had petitioned the state to charter Atlanta University) formed another school—the Summer Hill School for black children. The school would later became known as Clark University, and in 1883 issued its first baccalaureate degree. (Clark moved to the west side, adjacent to Atlanta University, in 1941.)

Other black colleges soon followed on the heels of Atlanta and Clark universities—including Morehouse College for men, which began as the Augusta Institute in 1867 and moved to Atlanta in 1879, where it was renamed the Atlanta Baptist Seminary. The school first held its classes at Friendship Baptist Church, and a year later moved to a new building on the corner of West Hunter and Elliot streets, where it was renamed Morehouse College in 1913.

Next to arrive in Atlanta was the Atlanta Baptist Female Seminary, founded in 1881 by two New England women who petitioned and received financial support from John D. Rockefeller. The school, which held its first classes in the basement of Friendship Baptist Church, was later named Spelman Seminary in honor of Rockefeller's mother. In the same year that Spelman College was founded, yet another African-American college, Morris Brown, began operations in the basement of Big Bethel AME Church on the east side of town (in the Old Fourth Ward). Originally located at Boulevard and Houston Street near Auburn Avenue, Morris Brown College eventually moved to the west side in 1932.

All of these schools (which later, along with the Interdenominational Seminary, would constitute the Atlanta University

Center) provided valuable education and training for Atlanta's African-American community in the late nineteenth century. They also helped anchor black residential development in Atlanta and provided valuable growing room for the segregated black neighborhoods that were emerging and growing in the city's center.

By 1890, the majority of Atlantans lived in either all-white or all-black neighborhoods, and most African-American communities were confined to the least desirable areas of the city—in low-lying areas prone to flooding and poor drainage or adjacent to railroads, cemeteries, city dumps, slaughterhouses, tanneries, etc. These locations not only tended to separate black settlements from surrounding white neighborhoods, but also contributed in some cases to very high black mortality rates.

The largest black enclaves in the city arose on the west side at Jenningstown, where first Atlanta University and later Morehouse and Spelman were established; on the south side in Summer Hill near Clark University; and on the east side in Shermantown (or the Old Fourth Ward), where Morris Brown was first located. A growing concentration of African-American housing also emerged in Mechanicsville near the rail lines and railroad shops in the southwest quadrant of the city. Other smaller black communities were scattered throughout the city, and in some areas, whites and blacks continued to live in close proximity. Nonetheless, the emerging pattern in the late nineteenth century was one of separation and increasing racial division as areas of black settlement became more concentrated and well defined. The result, as described by W. E. B. Du Bois, was that Atlanta's black population by the turn of the century "stretched like a great dumbbell across the city, with one great center in the east and a smaller one in the west, connected by a narrow belt."

Black Churches

Black colleges and universities were not the only institutions providing assistance and training to Atlanta's African Americans and anchoring black residential development in the last half of the nineteenth century. The city's black churches also contributed in both these areas. As noted before, churches like Friendship Baptist and Big Bethel AME housed the first classes of Morehouse, Spelman, and Morris Brown. Religious denominations and area churches were also connected to the rise of other area elementary and college-level schools. But church influence in the black community was not restricted to education. These religious institutions also organized

Portrait of an African-American child nurse with her charge.

programs to meet the pressing social and economic needs of their communities. The First Congregational Church of Atlanta, for example, under the direction of Reverend Henry Hugh Proctor sponsored a home for black working women, business and cooking schools, a kindergarten, and an employment bureau. The church also organized the first National Medical Association and the city's first black Boy Scout troop. Ministers of the city's other largest and oldest black churches—Friendship Baptist (1862), Big Bethel AME (1865), First Congregational (1867), Wheat Street Baptist (1870), and Ebenezer Baptist (1886)—also led efforts to improve living conditions in black neighborhoods and served on the boards of black colleges, businesses, and social-service institutions (such as the Carrie Steele Orphanage and the city's many African-American fraternal orders).

African-American Labor and Business

One of the most pressing needs facing Atlanta's black communities, despite the impact, influence, and active involvement of the city's African-American colleges and churches, was in the area of employment. After the Civil War, work opportunities for African Americans were largely confined to unskilled labor, domestic service, or to jobs that whites did not want. Rural blacks migrating to the city tended to swell the ranks of unskilled workers, and even those freedmen who worked as craftsmen or artisans before the war were often denied opportunity to use those skills by prevailing white prejudice and an increasingly specialized urban job market. As a result, the vast majority of the city's unskilled labor positions (over seventy-six percent in 1870 and almost ninety percent in 1890) were filled by African Americans.

The economic insecurity facing black Atlantans during this period was further reflected in the relative scarcity of African Americans who owned property and the number of black women employed in personal and domestic service. In 1870, only 311 black men and 27 black women (about three percent of the adult African-American population) were property owners. Ten years later, the number of black property owners had almost doubled but still lagged far behind the total for whites. Because of the low average earning power of black males, black women also worked in much larger numbers than their white counterparts. The vast majority of African-American working women (ninety-two percent in 1890) were confined to low paying, domestic service positions.

On the few occasions in the nineteenth century when black workers in Atlanta attempted to organize to negotiate for more pay, better working conditions, or increased job security, their efforts were

largely unsuccessful. In 1881, for example, an estimated three thousand of Atlanta's black washerwomen joined forces to strike for higher wages and the establishment of a city-wide charge of one dollar per dozen pounds of wash. The city government and enraged white employers responded to these demands with arrests, fines, and threats of economic reprisals and incarceration. Under the weight of this economic pressure and government and public hostility, the strike eventually collapsed. Nine years later, in 1899, protests by African-American firemen at the Georgia Pacific Railroad also proved unsuccessful, as the striking workers were quickly replaced by white applicants for their jobs.

Despite the considerable obstacles facing them, some black Atlantans did succeed during this period in establishing thriving businesses and accumulating wealth and property. David T. Howard, for example, was the first black undertaker to graduate from the Clark School of Embalming in Georgia and opened his own mortuary in 1882. By the turn of the century, he owned a small country estate eight miles from Atlanta with groves of fruit trees, several well-stocked lakes, game birds, and Jersey cattle. He also continued to assist the less fortunate of Atlanta's black communities and sent several students through college so that they might, as he phrased it, "help our race forward to better things."

Other successful Atlanta black businessmen included grocers James Tate, Willis Murphy, and Floyd Crumbley (each of whom owned property estimated at seven thousand dollars or more in 1890); coal and wood dealer Jacob McKinley, who left an estate of

Alonzo F. Herndon (1858–1927), founder of the Atlanta Life Insurance Company and Herndon's Barbers Inc., arrived in Atlanta in 1882 and soon became a prominent citizen.

over forty thousand dollars; and hotel owner and grocer Moses Calhoun, who was designated by one of the city's newspapers in 1886 as the "wealthiest colored man in Atlanta."

Most of these businessmen provided services to a black clientele ignored or underserved by the city's white businesses. Another vehicle for black economic success, however, involved one of the few areas in late-nineteenth-century life in which black businessmen catered to a white audience—barbering. Until the end of the century, black businessmen had a near monopoly in barbering in most southern cities, and Atlanta was no exception. Some of the most enterprising and fortunate of these black barbers parlayed that business into accumulations of considerable wealth. By 1890, for example, Moses H. Bentley of Atlanta employed eighteen men in his shop, the oldest and largest in the city. He also owned a confectionery and a restaurant. Bentley was an active participant in community affairs, serving as a senior captain of the State Colored Military Company, president of the Social Etiquette Club of Colored People, and chairman of the Republican County Executive Committee. The most prominent and successful barber, however, was Alonzo F. Herndon. Born a slave in Social Circle, Georgia, Herndon came to Atlanta in 1882, where he found employment as a journeyman barber. Four years later, at the age of twenty-eight, he opened his own shop in the Markham House (a large, elegant hotel). That barbershop was eventually destroyed by fire (as was a subsequent location on Marietta Street that employed thirteen barbers and four porters), but by the turn of the century, Herndon was making approximately eight thousand dollars a year from barbering alone. He was also acquiring real estate that surpassed in value all of the black colleges in the city, save Atlanta University. In the next century, Herndon's wealth and holdings would increase even more as he established another elegant barbershop on Peachtree Street, built a mansion next to Atlanta University on the city's west side, launched what would become the Atlanta Life Insurance Company, and involved himself in a number of businesses headquartered on Auburn Avenue—the emerging black central business district of Atlanta.

The Rise of Jim Crow

Despite the wealth and level of education that some of Atlanta's African-American entrepreneurs achieved, segregation and racial discrimination insured that they did not enjoy the political or economic clout of their white counterparts. Increasingly, as the nineteenth century drew to a close, Jim Crow found its way into almost all areas of Atlanta public life, including parks, cemeteries, hospitals, sporting events, and public transportation. In 1881, a black citizen of Atlanta unsuccessfully brought suit against the city for being ejected from City Hall Park because of his race. Six years later, African Americans were denied entrance to Ponce de Leon Springs, and in 1891, a city statute excluded African Americans from Inman Park. In other instances, however, blacks and whites shared the grounds at Piedmont and Grant parks, albeit in segregated spaces. When a new zoo opened in Grant Park, for example, (consisting of eight cages occupying the center of the zoo building) there were separate aisles on each side of the cages—one for whites and one for blacks—with separate entrances and exits so that the two groups did not mix. Jim Crow was also extended to restaurants, sporting events, hotels, hospitals, orphanages, poorhouses, prisons, government buildings, and public transportation. All of the passenger trains arriving in or passing through Atlanta and other areas of the South carried separate cars for their black and white riders (or confined black passengers to the smoking cars). In the case of Atlanta's streetcars, African Americans boarded and sat at the rear while white passengers entered from the front and occupied the forward seats.

Even in death, separation of the races continued, as African Americans were buried in segregated sections of public cemeteries or in separate cemeteries established exclusively for blacks. Oakland Cemetery had a separate hillside for African-American interment that was described in 1884 by an *Atlanta Constitution* reporter as "a dreary spot, devoid of shrubbery" with gravesites packed so close together "that it is about impossible to step among them without stepping on [one]." Beginning in 1878, African-American leaders began urging the city to purchase a separate site for a black cemetery. Instead, the city threw its support to a private, white-owned company that wanted to build a new cemetery—Westview. To garner city council support, the Westview company promised the city that it would inter both white and black paupers and that it would establish a separate black section on its grounds. Many African Americans, however, were not interested in replicating their earlier treatment and experience at Oakland Cemetery, so a new black burial organization was founded called South View Cemetery that petitioned the city for the right to bury African-American paupers. Westview directors opposed the idea, but eventually (after four years) the city granted South View's request.

The imposition of Jim Crow into all areas of public life increased racial tensions in Atlanta, but resulted in surprisingly little violence. While the Ku Klux Klan was present in the city after the Civil War, it was not nearly as active nor as formidable a force in the city as in the countryside. "Come . . . whatever your political and religious credo," an Atlanta booster proclaimed in 1870, "and have no fear of G.A.R.'s, K.K.K.'s or anything else." Newspaper editors and other boosters often went so far as to deny that the organization was even present in the city, and local black citizens testifying in 1871 before a congressional committee investigating Klan activity in the South supported these claims and pointed out that many African Americans had come to Atlanta from rural districts specifically to escape Klan violence and intimidation. (The Klan would, however, become more visible and influential in Atlanta in the next century, following the rebirth of the organization on nearby Stone Mountain in 1915.)

While the Klan was not a formidable force in post-Civil War Atlanta, racial violence did nonetheless occur in the city. On September 9, 1867, for example, nine white soldiers from Fort McPherson roamed through Shermantown, vandalizing homes and stores and beating African Americans (including Festus Flipper, the father of the first black graduate from West Point). About two hundred Shermantown residents responded by arming themselves to prevent further attacks. Similar skirmishes between black citizens and federal troops also took place in other Atlanta neighborhoods in the late 1860s—most of them, fortunately, without loss of life.

Another area of rising racial tension was the increasingly hostile relationship between white policemen and African Americans. On numerous occasions during the latter decades of the nineteenth century, episodes of violence broke out as black Atlantans resisted arrest or attempted to rescue African-American prisoners from police captivity. In 1868, for example, an attempt to gain the release of an African American taken into custody by police resulted in a riot in which a policeman was injured, a black man was killed, and two others were wounded. In the 1880s these incidents increased in frequency and level of violence as police and protestors engaged in periodic battle. Fortunately, loss of life was rare in these occasions, but the possibility of a much bigger and more deadly racial conflict loomed on the horizon. "It is but the beginning," one white newspaper editor concluded, "of that war between the races . . . which will develop . . . whenever and wherever attempts are made to force social equality." In 1906, these predictions would come to pass when a violent race riot erupted in the city, resulting in loss of life, rampant destruction of property, and a serious blow to Atlanta's reputation as a racially progressive city and a center of black success and pride.

With the decline of the Republican party, the sweep to power and control of state office by the Democrats, the end of military rule in the South, and the gradual disfranchisement and increasing segregation of African Americans, a new vision of the South arose—one that differed in many important respects from the earlier Republican plan for reconstruction of the region. Proponents of this "New South" called for reconciliation with the North, industrial growth, a more diversified regional economy (less dependent upon staple crop agriculture), and continuation of the social status quo (with reduced political rights for African Americans). The New South vision had many advocates throughout the region, but perhaps the best known and most articulate of these spokesmen was Atlanta newspaper editor Henry Woodfin Grady.

Henry Grady was born in 1850 in Clarke County, Georgia, the son of a prosperous Athens merchant. In 1876, Grady became a reporter for the *Atlanta Constitution;* four years later, he was managing editor of the paper and one of its principal owners. Under Grady's direction, the *Constitution* (which had been founded in 1868) grew tremendously in circulation and influence and, in fact, at one point had the widest geographic distribution of any newspaper in the nation.

Although Grady did not coin the term "New South," he committed his energies and finances wholeheartedly to the cause, promoting such disparate projects as the South's first baseball league (for health and entertainment); the new Georgia Institute of Technology (to serve the state's growing industrial needs); agricultural experiments (to help Georgia's farmers); and grand public expositions (such as the 1881 International Cotton Exposition [sponsored, in part, by General William T. Sherman] and the Piedmont Exposition of 1887 to advertise and promote the region's resources and untapped potential). Other local projects sponsored and endorsed by Grady included the establishment of the Piedmont Chautauqua (or self-improvement club), the founding of a new Atlanta hospital (renamed Grady Memorial Hospital after his death), and the creation of the city's first cotton factory.

Grady's greatest talent, however, may have been his ability to articulate to northern white audiences the broad goals and pressing needs of a New South. In a famous speech to the New England Society of New York City in 1886, for example, Grady not only praised the resiliency of Atlanta following the Civil War (see the epigraph to this chapter), but also painted a vision of a new breed of hard-working southern leaders who bore no animosity towards the North and who wanted only to build a new kind of life for them-

The Atlanta Constitution Building, 1890. The newspaper had the widest geographic distribution of any in the country at the time.

Grady Memorial Hospital with a horse-drawn ambulance, 1896.

Henry Grady (1850–1889), managing editor of the Atlanta Constitution from 1880 until his death, promoted the idea of the "New South" based on reconciliation with the north, industrial growth, and diversification of the regional economy—but advocated the status quo on racial issues. Evan P. Howell (1839–1905) was president and editor-in-chief of the paper from 1887 to 1897.

selves and their region. The need for the South to industrialize and to diversify its economy was another common theme in Grady's speeches to both northern and southern audiences. So too was his continuing belief in white supremacy and the need to deny African Americans the vote. In a speech in Dallas in 1888, Grady put it most bluntly, proclaiming that "the supremacy of the white race of the South must be maintained forever, and the domination of the negro race resisted at all points and at all hazards—because the white race is the superior race." In his last public speech, given in Boston shortly before his death (at age thirty-eight) in 1889, Grady again revisited this theme, declaring that African Americans were not yet ready and able to exercise the vote and begging the North's patience and understanding.

The formula that Henry Grady and other New South spokesmen laid out for the region's rebirth and growth found widespread acceptance among white audiences, both northern and southern. It was also largely adopted and practiced by Atlanta, the self-proclaimed capital of the New South. During the latter decades of the nineteenth century, the city experienced dramatic growth in industry, commerce, and population. Atlanta also witnessed the emergence of new colleges and universities, expanded roles and social outlets for women, and the first of the city's new streetcar suburbs. In 1895, the grandest of the

President Grover Cleveland, the first sitting president to visit Atlanta, seen on Marietta Street at Forsyth Street.

city's big nineteenth-century fairs—the Cotton States and International Exposition—would celebrate many of these changes to Atlanta and the region and forecast an even brighter future for the city and the New South. Lurking beneath this bright promise, however, were some troubling problems, including inadequate municipal services, underfunded public schools, and rising racial and class tensions, that were already making their presence felt and would follow the city into the next century.

Industry and Labor

An increase in southern industries and factories was one of the primary elements of the New South vision. Grady, for example, called for a "diversified industry" that would meet the "complex need of a new complex age." Beginning in the 1870s, Atlanta's business leaders made great efforts to increase this industrial presence and to train and attract the necessary workforce. The Mechanic's Institute, for example, was established in 1874 to promote the "knowledge of the skills of workingmen's trades," and three separate associations were also formed to solicit and promote industrial development. By 1880 Atlanta had 196 different manufacturing firms and almost four thousand workers (some thirteen times the number of factories and twelve times the number of workers found in the city twenty years earlier).

The biggest area of industrial growth for Atlanta was in cotton textile mills. Cotton, the staple crop of southern agriculture, played an important economic role in the city in several ways. As noted earlier, cotton was brought by the wagonloads to Atlanta to be shipped via railroads to other destinations. Increasingly, Atlanta's cotton brokers bypassed the region's seaport cities and instead transported their product directly to northern markets. By 1880 the city was receiving over 107,000 bales of cotton (an almost six-fold increase from thirteen years earlier) and was the South's fourth-largest interior port in terms of cotton received and shipped. Nine years later, cotton receipts totaled 270,000 bales and Atlanta was handling and shipping more cotton than most of the large seaport cities of the South, including Charleston.

The establishment of cotton warehouses, cotton presses, and seed oil mills in Atlanta in the late 1870s and 1880s, coupled with the city's transportation connections and thriving cotton brokers, meant that the city had the facilities necessary to gin, bale, and process cotton and cotton seeds and ship these items in all directions. The emergence of cotton textile mills added other new products—such as thread, yarn, and bags—for Atlanta's merchants to market, sell, and distribute.

The first cotton mill to arise in the city during this period was the Atlanta Cotton Factory, which was established in 1879 with New South promoter and entrepreneur Hannibal Kimball as its president. Once again, controversy surrounded Kimball's involvement in this project. He was caught by his own board, for example, with five carloads of company wood and coal (which he was apparently using to heat his house) and was charged with subscribing sixty thousand dollars worth of company stock for which he paid only twelve hundred dollars. Despite these setbacks, the Atlanta Cotton Factory opened to great fanfare on July 1, 1879, with Georgia Governor Alfred H. Colquitt, Atlanta Mayor William L. Calhoun, and former governors Joseph E. Brown and Benjamin Conley in attendance.

The next big textile factories to establish operations in Atlanta were the Exposition Cotton Mills and the Fulton Bag and Cotton Mill, both of which had their origins in 1881. The Exposition Mills was a by-product of the International Cotton Exposition of 1881 (whose executive committee was chaired by Kimball). When the exposition ended, the main exhibit hall was converted into a textile mill, which began operations the following year with more than five hundred employees. During the remainder of the decade, Exposition Cotton Mills spun more than fifty million yards of yarn.

The biggest and most successful textile mill from this period, however, was the Fulton Bag and Cotton Mill, founded by German Jewish immigrant Jacob Elsas who first settled in Cincinnati, Ohio, after coming to the United States, but moved to Atlanta following the Civil War. Elsas began his career in the city as a dry goods retailer, but branched out into manufacturing paper bags before founding the Fulton Cotton Spinning Company in 1881. In 1890 the company was renamed Fulton Bag and Cotton Mills, and at its peak, the mill operated one hundred thousand spindles and employed thousands of workers. The surrounding mill village—Cabbagetown—was home to three thousand residents, most of whom worked at the mill or ran small retail shops that served the community.

Cotton mills, while among Atlanta's largest manufacturing concerns, were not the only industries present in the city. Building construction, metals fabrication, paper goods manufacturing, fertilizer production, and lumber processing, for example, were also represented, and many of Atlanta's prominent business and political leaders singled out industrial growth as a key to the city's continued development and prosperity. Jonathan Norcross, a former mayor of Atlanta, for example, warned in 1874 that "this city must not only enlarge as a commercial center, but must from the nature of things, at no distant day, become a great manufacturing centre."

The Fulton Bag and Cotton Mills was the anchor of the Cabbagetown community from 1881 to 1977.

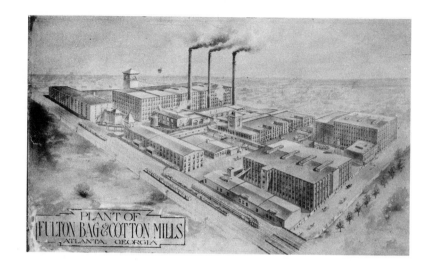

To realize this dream, local manufacturing associations were formed to attract new industries to the city. The Atlanta Agricultural and Industrial Association (founded in 1872), the German Manufacturing Association (1875), and the Atlanta Manufacturers' Association (1872) collected statistics on local industry, courted new manufacturers, and pressured the city council to remove taxes on goods manufactured in the city. Other organizations were formed to attract the necessary labor for these factories, including the German Immigration Society (founded in 1868), the Immigration Association of the State of Georgia (which established its headquarters in the city in 1871), and the Negro Anti-Emigration Club (which was formed in 1876 to dissuade black laborers from joining the so-called "exodusters" migrating to the Southwest).

With a growing abundance of labor, excellent railroad connections, and access to cotton, coal, and iron, Atlanta industries expanded in number and size. In 1880 the city had almost two hundred manufacturing concerns and ranked seventy-ninth in the nation in terms of the value of industrial products (which was higher than any other southern cities except New Orleans, Nashville, and Richmond, Virginia). Ten years later, the number of industries in Atlanta had more than doubled with twice as many workers as in 1880 and four times the amount of accumulated capital.

The rise of industry in Atlanta also brought increasing numbers of women into the workforce. By far the largest number of paid workers were African-American women engaged in domestic service. (Over two-thirds of the estimated nine thousand women in the workforce in 1890, for example, were African Americans employed as domestics—house-keepers, laundresses, cooks, etc.) Also present in the workforce, however, were thousands of white women employed by the textile mills and hundreds of white and black dressmakers, milliners, and seamstresses.

Commerce

Commerce was another important element of Atlanta's increasingly diversified economy, and in the last two decades of the nineteenth century, the city was able to firmly establish itself as a commercial center for the state and the region. During the 1880s, Atlanta's commerce tripled in volume, and by 1890 had an estimated value (exclusive of locally-manufactured goods) of approximately $115 million. Atlanta retailers, dealing in all kinds of goods, regularly traded within a two-hundred-mile radius of the city, and wholesale businesses (including dry goods, hardware, and groceries) numbered close to one hundred. Many of these enterprises grew quite large, and some (such as the cotton brokerage house of Samuel M. Inman & Company) expanded to establish branches in other cities.

As commercial growth continued and accelerated, so too did commercial construction in the downtown area. City blocks of new brick buildings arose to house the growing number of hardware, grocery, and dry goods stores, and mixed among these enterprises were some of Atlanta's first department stores. One of these early department stores was a business founded by Morris Rich, a Jewish immigrant from Hungary. Rich and his two brothers established a wholesale and retail dry goods store in 1867 that later evolved into Rich's department store—one of the South's largest department store chains and a commercial institution that would play a key role the following century in the city's growth and development.

In the 1890s, the city also witnessed its first skyscrapers—the eight-story Equitable Building, which was completed in 1893, and the eleven-story English-American Building (also known as the Flatiron Building), which was constructed in 1897 and still stands at the intersection of Peachtree and Broad streets. These new buildings, which featured all of the latest conveniences of the time (including telephones and elevators), not only expanded the city's skyline, but also presaged and contributed to Atlanta's emergence in the early twentieth century as a regional office center and headquarters for many of the nation's largest corporations and businesses.

On the "other" side of town, another concentration of businesses—a separate and segregated black business district—was starting to emerge along Auburn Avenue. Most of the commercial building

Founded in 1867, Rich and Bros. Dry Goods Store evolved into one of the earliest department stores in Atlanta. The store is shown here in 1880.

The flagship Jacob's Pharmacy was located at Five Points.

along "Sweet Auburn" would take place in the following century—especially following the destructive and violent race riot of 1906. But in 1895, the first hotel for African Americans was built in this area, and six years later, Henry Rucker constructed the city's first office building for African Americans.

A number of the new businesses that arose in Atlanta during the latter decades of the nineteenth century proved to be quite successful and profitable. An R. G. Dun and Company report in 1895, for example, noted that the Atlanta wholesale and retail dry goods firm of W. A. Moore, W. W. Marsh & Company was valued at close to $1 million and thirteen other commercial ventures ranged in worth from $200,000 to $750,000. The Atlanta-based business that would achieve the greatest prominence and success, however, was not large dry goods, hardware, or even a grocery business. It was instead a locally-produced beverage—Coca-Cola.

In 1886, Dr. John Stith Pemberton, a pharmacist and developer of a number of elixers and patent medicines (including Triplex Liver Pills, Globe of Flower Cough Syrup, and French Wine of Coca-Ideal Tonic), concocted a syrup that he believed would soothe headaches and quench thirst. He named his new invention Coca-Cola after two of the main ingredients in the syrup—the coca leaf and the kola nut—and began selling the beverage in local drugstores. Pemberton's frail health and inability to effectively market and sell his new product eventually induced him to sell the rights to the product, and after a series of transfers of ownership, Asa Candler purchased all the existing shares and gained complete control of the new soft drink.

Candler was by training a druggist, but his real talents, it soon became apparent, lay in marketing and sales. He used a variety of modern advertising techniques, including rebates, premiums, targeted advertising, and giveaways to popularize his product and entice new customers. Sales of the soft drink grew quickly, and by 1900, Coca-Cola had branch factories in Dallas, Chicago, Los Angeles, and Philadelphia and bottling plants in Chattanooga, Tennessee, and several other cities. Soon the soft-drink giant began expanding its distribution into international markets. Despite its widespread production, distribution, and popularity, the specific formula for Coca-Cola remained a closely-guarded secret at the insistence of Candler—a practice that is still followed today by the modern Coca-Cola Company.

Key Elements for New South Prosperity

Atlanta's impressive industrial and commercial growth in the late nineteenth century can be attributed, in large part, to two forces that continued to play a dominant role in the city's growth and development—Atlanta boosterism and the railroads. Even before the Civil War, Atlanta's business and political leaders had attempted to draw regional and national attention to the city, its resources, and its potential. In the late nineteenth century, Atlanta business leaders and promoters used new techniques, including speeches, editorials, publications, and large fairs and expositions to advertise the unique promise and potential of their New South city. These local business leaders and their allies in city hall were members of a growing urban middle class that, like their pre-Civil War counterparts, had few ties to the Old South or the planter elite. As a result, Atlanta's New South leaders were much more inclined than some of their counterparts in other southern cities and communities to embrace new economic approaches and alliances. They also welcomed and sought out both local and outside (including northern) investment, actively promoted the city and its resources, and did all they could to create in Atlanta a hospitable environment for industrial and commercial growth.

Investment capital was a necessary ingredient for industrial and commercial development, and Atlanta's New South business leaders and promoters left no stone unturned in their search for funding. In part, this financial support came from outside the region, but in most instances, the funding for these projects was homegrown. One of the main sources for this local support was the growing number of Atlanta banks and building and loan associations. By 1890 there were eighteen banking institutions in the city with a combined capital stock of $2.5 million and net deposits of $60 million. There were also twenty-one building and loan associations with combined capital in excess of $4 million and loans

Skyscrapers appeared in Atlanta starting in 1892. Construction of the Bradford Gilbert-designed English American Building, known as the Flatiron Building, began in 1897.

The cornerstone of the Daniel Burnham- and John Wellborn Root-designed Equitable Building was lowered into place June 25, 1891, on the site of the present-day SunTrust Bank headquarters.

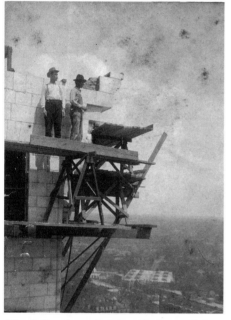

The skyline changed again with the completion of the seventeen-story Candler Building, designed by George Stewart and George Murphy, in 1906.

of over $1.25 million. These institutions invested heavily in the city's commercial and industrial projects. As lumber merchant Frank P. Rice noted in 1889, "Atlantans have built up the city themselves, and they are always ready to put their own money into any local enterprise that promises good for the community at large."

In searching for capital or in promoting the growth of the city's commercial and industrial enterprises, Atlanta's New South leaders enlisted the aid of a number of business-oriented organizations. The city's Chamber of Commerce, for example, (which grew from 137 members in 1883 to more than 600 in 1890) organized committees to deal with local issues and to advertise the city and its resources. Similarly, the Atlanta Manufacturers' Association (with 200 member companies) pressured railroad companies to lower freight rates and city council to lower taxes on local industries. Even the editors, columnists, and management of newspapers such as the *Atlanta Constitution* extolled the virtues of Atlanta—the healthful climate, the irrepressible spirit of enterprise, the relative absence of class or caste, and the city's progress and potential. Similar themes were endorsed in books and publications from Atlanta boosters such as physician J. S. Wilson (*Atlanta, As It Is*) and newspaper publisher Colonel E.Y. Clarke (*Atlanta*

A survey was completed in the 1890s for the construction of the Atlanta Car Works, the first motor works in the south.

Illustrated). Small wonder that a Massachusetts newspaper labeled Atlanta "one of the best-advertised cities in the United States."

The most dramatic and far-reaching expression of the New South vision, however, was not contained in the speeches or writings of Atlanta boosters, but in a series of grand expositions that the city hosted in the 1880s and 1890s. While similar in some ways to earlier agricultural and state fairs, these Atlanta expositions had a broader focus and purpose and featured exhibitions and activities designed to draw attention and investment to southern agriculture, commerce, industry, and labor. Privately funded, these expositions also had as their goal the promotion of Atlanta as a regional center of New South enterprise.

The first of Atlanta's grand fairs or expositions was the International Cotton Exposition of 1881, organized by Henry Grady and his partners at the *Atlanta Constitution*. Hannibal Kimball was also involved in the project and took a lead role in helping raise the necessary funds. Local businessmen, at Kimball's urging, were able to pull together enough money to purchase thirty-six thousand dollars of exposition stock, and the remainder of the funds came from outside the region (primarily from investors in New York, Boston, Cincinnati, and Philadelphia). The exposition featured over one thousand exhibits

President Grover Cleveland relaxing at Stone Mountain during his visit to the Piedmont Exposition, 1887.

from thirty-three states and seven foreign countries. Most of these displays focused on cotton cultivation or cotton textiles, but other exhibits emphasized key southern natural resources, such as timber and minerals. Attendance for this exposition was at first slow, but after a three-hundred-room hotel was constructed next to the fairgrounds and some of Atlanta's elite opened their homes to visitors, the numbers began to pick up. The centerpiece of the exposition was a state-of-the-art cotton factory, and the most celebrated event occurred when the governors of Georgia and Connecticut were provided with finished suits made from cotton that had been picked from the exposition grounds, ginned, woven, dyed, and made into garments in a single day. By the time the exposition closed, over 350,000 people had attended.

The second of Atlanta's grand expositions—the 1887 Piedmont Exposition—was smaller in size and scope than its predecessor, but again succeeded in drawing national attention to the city and in establishing Atlanta's growing reputation as the regional center of New South industry and commerce. The Piedmont Exposition lasted for two weeks and attracted thousands of visitors, mostly from the South. The focus of this exposition was southern manufacturing, with exhibits devoted to showcasing regional industry and its potential. The highlight of the event was the visit of President Grover Cleveland on October 18, 1887, at the personal invitation of Henry Grady.

As important as these New South banks, boosters, and their expositions were to Atlanta's development, the driving force behind the city's rapid economic growth in the late nineteenth century remained the railroads and the ever-expanding network of rail systems that connected to the city. These railroads brought passengers and raw materials to the city, distributed cotton and finished goods from Atlanta to destinations throughout the eastern United States, and expanded the reach and impact of the city's merchants and salesmen.

By 1890 there were eleven different railroad lines that passed through or connected to Atlanta, including three that were added in the 1880s. The East Tennessee, Virginia and Georgia—which stretched from Bristol, Virginia, to the Georgia coast at Brunswick—entered the city in 1882. The following year, Atlanta gained connections to the important coal and iron fields of Alabama through the Georgia Pacific Railroad. And in 1887, the Marietta and North Georgia Railroad completed a short run to Murphy, North Carolina.

Atlanta's vast network of railroad lines spurred both industrial and commercial growth in the city. For the city's manufacturers, the railroads brought much-needed raw materials and distributed their finished products. As testimony to this critical relationship, industrial developments in Atlanta were frequently located adjacent (or in close proximity) to the rail lines. The Atlanta Manufacturers' Association, for example, purchased a large tract of land in 1887 alongside the Central of Georgia Railroad on the outskirts of town, which they divided into 282 sites for future plants and factories (a precursor of the modern industrial park).

Railroads also spurred and supported the city's many commercial ventures. Drummers (or traveling salesmen) who traveled by rail were no longer restricted to communities within fifty miles of the city and instead expanded their sales territories to encompass regions several hundred miles outside of Atlanta. Despite discriminatory freight rates, Atlanta's merchants were also able to take advantage of local rail connections to ship products throughout the eastern United States. By 1890 the value of Atlanta's wholesale trade had increased to an estimated $80 million, and most of it was conducted via the railroads.

As the turn of the century approached, Atlanta had already firmly established itself as a state and regional marketplace, and once again railroads played a key role in this process. The addition of new rail lines brought large numbers of out-of-town buyers and shoppers to the city

The Blood Stock Exhibition at the Atlanta Exposition.

Joel Hurt (1850–1926) developed Atlanta's first planned suburb, Inman Park (beginning in 1889), and engaged Frederick Law Olmsted to work on the preliminary plans for Druid Hills (1893).

every day. These customers and shoppers often stayed in the city's hotels (most of which were located downtown, in close proximity to the railroads), and visited Atlanta's widening range of wholesale and retail establishments. Their presence and spending enriched the local coffers and gave rise to a host of new service, hospitality, and entertainment industries (such as restaurants, department stores, hotels, an amusement park, theaters, etc.).

CITY GROWTH AND EXPANSION

Atlanta's commercial, industrial, and overall economic growth in the latter half of the nineteenth century also spurred a dramatic increase in the city's population. In the twenty years from 1880 to 1900, Atlanta's population more than doubled (from 37,400 to 89,872), making it the largest city in Georgia and the fourth-largest in the Southeast (behind New Orleans, Nashville, and Richmond, Virginia). This rate of growth exceeded the national average, but did not mirror the increases in the largest cities of the North that were fueled by overseas immigration. Atlanta's population increase was less the product of immigration and more the result of the migration of rural southerners (both black and white) to the city.

As Atlanta's population increased, so too did the city's limits. In 1874 the circular boundaries of the city were expanded from a radius of one mile to 1.5 miles and in 1889 to 1.75 miles. New residential developments also accompanied this expansion, including Baltimore Block (Atlanta's only section of row houses), Peters Park (on the northwest edge of the city), and Grant Park (a subdivision and public park developed by Lemuel P. Grant—the engineer who designed the Confederate defense fortifications for the city during the Civil War). Grant donated eighty-five acres to the city to establish a public park and subdivided some of his remaining property (he owned more than six hundred acres in the city) into house lots. When Grant Park opened to the public in 1883, it contained landscaped trails, a lake, and a small menagerie of animals that later became a part of Zoo Atlanta.

Streetcar Suburbs and Trolley Wars

Transportation again played a key role in this residential expansion as new housing developments followed first the railroads and then horse-drawn trolley and electric streetcar lines. The horse- and mule-driven trolley lines (which originated in 1871) initially ran along the primary streets of the city—Peachtree, Whitehall, Marietta, and Decatur. The addition of electric streetcar lines in the 1890s connected growing suburban towns, such as East Point, Chamblee, Oakland City, Edgewood,

Atlanta's only street of row houses, Baltimore Block, was built in 1885 by Jacob J. Rosenthal. Named for the developer's hometown, the land for the fourteen original units was, in accepted Baltimore custom, leased to homeowners for ninety-nine years.

Kirkwood, and West End, to downtown Atlanta and the businesses located there. It was the streetcar as well that contributed to the development of the city's first planned suburb—Inman Park.

Inman Park was the brainchild of Joel Hurt, one of the most successful real estate developers of the nineteenth century. Hurt, a trained civil engineer, arrived in Atlanta in 1875 and founded a building and loan association. Several years later he created a streetcar company (the Atlanta and Edgewood Street Railroad Company) and a real estate and development firm (the East Atlanta Land Company) that sought to create new, planned residential communities on the city's east side.

Hurt was greatly influenced by Frederick Law Olmsted (the dean of American landscape architecture) and the Olmsted-designed Riverside community outside of Chicago. Like Riverside, Hurt's plans for Inman Park featured curvilinear streets that followed the natural terrain of the landscape, open spaces, parks, and water (in this case, a lake). Between 1885 and 1889, Hurt surveyed, laid out streets, graded lots, and planted more than seven hundred trees in the 190-acre tract of land about two miles east of downtown Atlanta that would become Inman Park. He also began construction of a streetcar line that ran between the suburban community and the Equitable Building (an eight-story skyscraper that Hurt built on Edgewood Avenue in downtown Atlanta).

Belgian blocks are piled on the sides of the street as streetcar track is laid, 1901.

Whitehall Street, shown here looking south from Hunter Street, was the hub of town and the center of retail business in 1876.

Consolidated Streetcar No. 17 was one of the first electric streetcars in Atlanta. The Equitable Building is seen in the background.

Horse-drawn trolleys provided a means for Atlantans to travel into previously undeveloped areas. This trolley was headed for Ponce de Leon Springs in 1874.

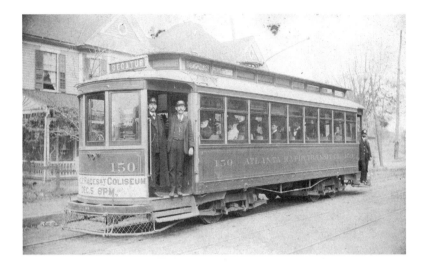

The Atlanta Rapid Transit Company's Decatur Street line served the growing suburban population, 1901.

The creation of streetcar lines allowed Atlanta to grow beyond downtown.

Hurt's next big real estate venture was Druid Hills, another (and larger) residential community further east. For this project, Hurt hired Frederick Law Olmsted himself, who drew out a preliminary plan for the development. Hurt then began platting and grading lots for the new community, which, like Inman Park, would be connected to the city via a streetcar line. Before any lots could be sold or homes constructed, however, Hurt was forced by financial difficulties to sell his interest in the project to a local syndicate composed of Coca-Cola magnate Asa Candler, Georgia Railway and Power Company president Preston Arkwright, and realtors Forrest and George Adair for about half a million dollars. Construction of the community finally began early the following century.

Part of the difficulties facing Hurt stemmed from an escalating and costly battle over the city's emerging electric streetcar system. Hurt and his Atlanta Railway and Power Company were aligned on one side of this struggle against Henry M. Atkinson and his Atlanta Rapid Transit Company. Each side had a great deal invested in this new form of public transportation, including streetcars, electric light, and steam interests. As the companies negotiated and competed for new streetcar lines, their battles spilled over into the newspapers, city council (where they petitioned for new franchises), and the courts (where they each brought suit against the other). The matter was finally resolved when a Boston syndicate (secretly representing Atkinson) bought out all of Hurt's holdings. In 1902 all of the electric and street railway facilities were finally consolidated under the Georgia Railway and Electric Company.

The students of Boy's High School in front of Atlanta City Hall, 1884. The school was renamed Henry W. Grady High School in 1947.

Located in the Kimball House Hotel was the Prather Home School for Girls.

BIG CITY OFFERINGS/ BIG CITY PROBLEMS

As Atlanta grew and matured in the late nineteenth century, it began to lose some of its rough, frontier atmosphere and appearance and started to display some of the hallmarks of a true urban center, including public schools, colleges, and universities; increased cultural offerings; and more varied forms of public entertainment and public service. Local boosters' claims of Atlanta being the "New York" or the "Chicago of the South" were, of course, greatly exaggerated, (Atlanta had but a tenth of the population of either of these two great cities of the North and Midwest and still trailed several other older cities of the South), but Atlanta was growing quickly and thriving and, in the process, experiencing not only big city offerings and opportunities, but big city problems as well.

Public Education

In 1872 Atlanta created its first public school system with eight elementary schools and two high schools (one for white girls and one for white boys). There were no provisions made for a high school for African Americans (until Booker T. Washington High was built in 1924), but the city did establish three black grammar schools.

Private home kindergartens, like the Settlement Home Kindergarten, were started throughout the city.

Local charities, such as the Atlanta Children's Home, were also the site of private kindergartens.

In the 1880s and 1890s, public kindergartens also began to appear throughout the city. The first of these were organized and held in the private homes of women of wealth and influence, but in 1888 the Washington Seminary for girls opened a kindergarten on its premises. Other school- and organization-sponsored kindergartens soon followed, including the Atlanta Kindergarten School (which was formed at the Atlanta Normal Training School, now Georgia State University) and the Sheltering Arms Day Nursery Association (which originated at a mission on Marietta Street). In 1896, the Atlanta Free Kindergarten Association was formed and set up a dozen kindergartens around the city. In keeping with the segregated nature of education, a separate black kindergarten association—the Gate City Free Kindergarten Association—was organized through the efforts of Gertrude Ware at Atlanta University and formed kindergartens for African-American children in black communities in the Old Fourth Ward, in south Atlanta, and on the west side near Atlanta University.

None of these kindergarten efforts were assisted or funded by the city or the Atlanta Board of Education, whose total expenditures for its schools were among the lowest in the nation for similarly-sized

The Houston Street Kindergarten, with only African-American teachers, was the first segregated public school in Atlanta.

cities. As a result there were not enough schools, teachers, or textbooks to meet the growing needs of Atlanta's school-aged children. Only 2,800 pupils out of a possible 9,400 students, for example, were enrolled in the city's public schools when they first opened, and even that restricted number strained the school board's resources and budget. To meet the budget crisis, the board shortened the school year and even tried charging for tuition and books. In 1887 the schools also went into double session, with individual classes often containing seventy or more students. Black elementary schools were in even worse shape during this period with far fewer supplies and support and with teachers who earned far less than their white counterparts.

In the area of higher education, the picture was much brighter. As noted earlier, a strong concentration of black colleges and universities was already emerging on the city's south, east, and west sides that would eventually come together to become the Atlanta University Center. In white Atlanta, the first post-Civil War college to emerge was Oglethorpe College, which opened its doors in 1870. Next to come was the Georgia Institute of Technology, which opened with 130 students and ten faculty members in 1888 and a single course offering in mechanical engineering. By the following decade, however, dorms were being built on the Tech campus and the school also was offering degrees in electrical and civil engineering.

The main campus of Atlanta University, 1890.

Since Atlanta University was founded in 1865 and Spelman in 1881, Atlanta has been a center for higher education for African-American men and women.

Marking the completion of the two main buildings at the Georgia Institute of Technology in 1889.

Agnes Scott College, the first college for white women in Atlanta.

The ushers for the opening of the DeGive Opera House, 1870.

The first college educational opportunities for white women in Atlanta occurred in nearby Decatur, Georgia, at Agnes Scott College. Founded by George Washington Scott, a wealthy businessman (who donated one hundred thousand dollars to the project), and Reverend Frank H. Gaines, pastor of the Decatur Presbyterian Church, the school opened in 1889. Named in honor of George Scott's mother, Agnes Scott College offered a curriculum that was competitive with most colleges in the country (male or female). In fact, it was the first school in the metropolitan Atlanta area to be accredited by the Southern Association of Colleges and Secondary Schools.

New Social and Cultural Outlets

At the same time that Atlanta's educational options were expanding, so too were its social and cultural offerings. The first full opera came to the city in 1866, when Ghioni's and Sussini's Grand Italian Opera Company appeared for three nights at the six-hundred-seat Bell Johnson Opera Hall, complete with seventy-five artists, including the orchestra. Another new opera house, the sixteen-hundred-seat Davis Hall, opened the following year, but burned to the ground three years later.

In 1870, the elegant, twelve-hundred-seat DeGive Opera House (built by Belgian consul Laurent DeGive) opened to rave reviews. Only three years later, the building was renovated and enlarged, with raked and cushioned seating for two thousand patrons, frescoed walls and ceilings, a magnificent drop curtain (complete with a copy of The Golden Horn by Jacob). For the remainder of the century, the DeGive Opera House hosted a diverse mixture of performances and presentations, including opera, instrumental and choral concerts, lectures, and even the city's first can-can show (in 1875).

Additional cultural offerings and performances (including minstrel and variety shows) were presented at other city theaters, such as the Cole Opera House, the Varieties Theaters (on Pryor and Peachtree streets), the five-hundred-seat Concordia Hall (with ties to Atlanta's German population), and Hibernian Hall (which featured many Irish-oriented plays, musical concerts, orations, etc).

One local musician who played a key role in bringing classical music to Atlanta during this period was Alfredo Barili, who was born in Florence, Italy, and moved to the New South capital in 1880. Barili, a talented pianist, composer, conductor, and teacher, premiered major keyboard works by Beethoven, Mendelssohn, and Chopin in the city and organized the first Atlanta Music Festival in 1883. He also founded his own music school, established one of Atlanta's first choral groups, and brought a number of well-known musicians and singers to perform in the city, including his aunt, acclaimed soprano Adelina Patti.

Other venues where Atlantans could gather for amusement and recreation included the fairgrounds at Oglethorpe (which featured a lake and a race course), the landscaped grounds surrounding City Hall, Oakland and Westview cemeteries (which also functioned as public parks), and the lake, trails, and fledgling zoo at Grant Park. Another very popular public spot was Ponce de Leon Springs (located where City Hall East now stands). Opening in the 1870s, Ponce de Leon Springs operated as a spa and a park, with amenities that included a lake, two springs, a bathhouse, trails, bridges, and grounds where people could gather for barbecues, picnics, and Sunday outings. The springs would also later become the site where one of the city's most popular professional sports was played—baseball.

Organized baseball first arrived in Atlanta in 1866 when Captain Tom Burnett and the Atlanta Baseball Club took on a rival local team—the Gate City Nine. The game was played on May 12, 1866, in a makeshift field near Oakland Cemetery, and although there were no stands, concessions, or tickets, a crowd nevertheless gathered to watch. The contest lasted four-and-a-half hours and ended with the Gate City Nine winning 127–29. (Twenty-five runs were scored in the first inning alone.) The Gate City Nine went on to record thirty-six wins and one loss (to an Athens, Georgia, team) that season.

Nineteen years later, Atlanta fielded its first professional baseball team when the Southern League was organized by Henry Grady. The league featured teams from Atlanta, Augusta, Columbus, and Macon in Georgia, and additional teams from Birmingham, Alabama; and Chattanooga, Tennessee. The Atlanta team won the league championship in 1885, 1886, and 1895, before the league disbanded in 1898.

In 1902 a new Atlanta baseball team was organized—the Atlanta Crackers—that would eventually play all their home games at Ponce de Leon Ball Park, the original site of Ponce de Leon Springs.

Social clubs and organizations also began to appear in Atlanta during this period, including the Capital City Club (1883) for businessmen and the Piedmont Driving Club (1887), the city's most prestigious social club. Women played a key role in organizing clubs, and, in fact, were responsible for founding the country's second-oldest chapter of the Daughters of the American Revolution (1890) and one of the first chapters of the United Daughters of the Confederacy (1895). The Atlanta Woman's Club (the largest member group of the Georgia Federation of Women's Clubs) was founded in the mid-1890s, as was its

Ponce de Leon Springs was considered a fashionable destination for Sunday gatherings.

Established in 1850, the eighty-eight-acre Oakland Cemetery was often a place for afternoon outings and picnics.

Henry W. Grady, (far right), became president of the Southern Baseball League.

black counterpart, the Atlanta Federation of Negro Women's Clubs. In keeping with the demands of Jim Crow, women's organizations in Atlanta remained strictly segregated, but sororities, literary societies, chautauquas, and kindergartens arose on both sides of the color line.

Increasingly, many of these women's organizations and clubs began to branch out into social and progressive reform movements that addressed a range of issues, including school improvement, prison reform (for female inmates), equal education for women, age of consent laws, and alcohol abuse and temperance. Some women in Atlanta also began to push for equal suffrage (or the vote for women). In 1894 the Atlanta Equal Suffrage Association was formed. Like many other white southern women's associations, the Atlanta organization sought public support for their cause by emphasizing, in part, that equal suffrage for white women could work to counter and neutralize the votes and voting rights of African-American men.

Black women leaders, on the other hand, in Atlanta and elsewhere in the South, recognized that equal suffrage had the potential to not only add black women to the voting rolls, but also to work towards changing the role of African-American women in southern society by giving them the chance to address important racial and political issues. As a result, increasing numbers of women on both sides of the color line supported giving women the vote. But despite similarities in mission, make-up, and background, black and white women's clubs and organizations in Atlanta remained separate and, for the most part, non-affiliated.

A ladies' luncheon at the Piedmont Driving Club. Women played an important role in Atlanta's social clubs.

Women's suffrage float in Civic Parade, 1913.

Growing Pains: Municipal Services

Public education was not the only area in which the city faced mounting needs and inadequate resources. Other basic municipal services, including water, sewers, sanitation, lighting, paved streets, and welfare assistance, also were in short supply and unevenly distributed.

An Atlanta board of water commissioners was appointed in 1870 to address the city's growing water needs. The commission's main priorities, however, were not to provide safe, clean water to the city's residents, but instead to establish a more efficient system of water delivery and to keep fire insurance rates low for Atlanta's factories and industries. In 1875 the city built its first water plant, but when this water service was quickly outstripped by Atlanta's growing population, the city council approved in 1885 the drilling of an additional artesian well near the intersection of Peachtree and Marietta streets in downtown Atlanta. This well managed to supply the city with two hundred thousand gallons of water a day, but even this amount soon became inadequate. By 1890 there were over forty miles of water pipes laid in Atlanta—most of these located in the central city area or along Peachtree and Pryor streets, where the city's elite lived. Even those that were served by the water lines, however, had reasons to be concerned about the water's quality. The main streams that fed the water reservoir, for example, were subject to pollution from homes and industries along their banks. As a result, municipal authorities began searching for a purer and more plentiful source of water.

The artesian well at Five Points was an experiment by the Water Department to deliver water to the downtown business district.

Atlanta Water Works employees in front of the Water Works office, 1887.

In 1893, the downtown artesian well was capped, and the city switched to a water delivery system (with a large, new waterworks on Hemphill Avenue) that drew from the Chattahoochee River. Despite these improvements, more than two-thirds of Atlanta's population at the turn of the century still lacked access to city water.

Atlanta's sewer system faced similar problems in terms of quality of service and delivery. In 1888, the city's sanitation commission hired noted sanitary engineer Rudolf Herring to examine Atlanta's existing sewers and make recommendations. Unfortunately, Herring's recommendations failed to address key issues and actually compounded existing problems. The discharge of sewer lines onto grounds beyond the city limits, for example, contaminated pasture land, while the emptying of sewers into Atlanta streams and waterways within the city polluted those waters as well.

By 1890 there were almost thirty-five miles of sewer lines in Atlanta, but large areas of the city remained unserved. In addition, health problems in some of Atlanta's minority neighborhoods were actually worsened by the city's fledgling attempts to control sewage. The city's largest sewer, for example, emptied onto the grounds of the Hebrew Orphans' Home, south of the capitol, and other lines discharged raw sewage into streams running through Atlanta's black neighborhoods, polluting their major drinking supply. As a result, typhoid deaths in the city, especially for African Americans, remained among the highest in the nation until Atlanta's first sewage treatment plant was built in 1911.

The volunteer Hook and Ladder Company
No. 1 in front of the first Kimball House Hotel,
c. 1880s.

(Above) *Much of the construction of the waterlines at Marietta
Street and North Avenue was done by African-American labor.*

(Left) *Telegraph lines were laid in Atlanta in the 1880s. By 1889
Atlanta relayed the third largest volume of telegraph messages of
any American city.*

Sanitation and the removal of solid waste also remained a problem for the city. Waste was typically picked up by scavengers, private parties, and fertilizer manufactures until 1874, when the newly-formed sanitation commission hired draymen to remove dead animals from the streets and to pick up "night soil" from private privies and deposit in the city dump, which at that time was still located within the city limits. By 1885, another dumping ground was finally established outside the city, but in the interim, many Atlanta citizens continued to dump their garbage and waste in the nearest vacant lot. In 1894, Atlanta's first crematorium was constructed to dispose of dead animals and carcasses, and human waste (but not garbage) began to be collected more systematically throughout the city.

The conversion of street lights in Atlanta from gas to electric began in 1887. Three years later there were already 167 of the larger "arc lights" and 436 of the smaller "series lights" illuminating the city's streets. As with piped water, these lights were largely confined to the business areas of the central city or to the main thoroughfares leading to the wealthier residences. Outlying or in-town, impoverished communities remained unlit.

Street maintenance and paving remained the largest single component of the city's budget during these years, and progress was clearly made between 1880 and 1890 in paving some of Atlanta's central thoroughfares. By 1890, almost thirty-five miles of road within the city had been paved. This represented only about fifteen percent of Atlanta's roads, however, and like many other municipal services, it too was largely confined to the central business district.

Public relief and welfare services were not simply underrepresented in the city budget, they received no city funding at all during the latter half of the nineteenth century. As a result, private charities, benevolent societies, and welfare assistance associations arose to meet this need—most of them directed towards a special racial, ethnic, religious, or gender group. In 1858, for example, the Hibernian Benevolent Society was organized to care for needy Irish families and communities. Other contemporary organizations, such as the Saint Andrew's Benevolent Society, the German Turnverein, and the Concordia Association (which served German Jews) were founded for similar purposes. African-American counterparts included the Sisters of Honor and the Brothers of Aid. The Salvation Army—an international relief agency—arrived in the city in 1890 and was followed by other prominent white charities that were founded by women, including the Home for the Friendless, the Women's Christian Association Mission School, and the Sheltering Arms

Nursery. A separate orphanage to serve African Americans was founded by Carrie Steele Logan in 1890.

VISIONS OF THE COMING CENTURY: THE COTTON STATES AND INTERNATIONAL EXPOSITION

Although it lagged behind some other large cities in the levels and effectiveness of its municipal services, Atlanta at the turn of the century was clearly a city on the rise—a southern urban center of prosperity and promise. In 1895 Atlanta attempted to draw attention to this success and potential when it hosted the biggest and most widely-attended southern exposition of the times—the Cotton States and International Exposition.

The 1895 Cotton States Exposition was both an imitation of and a response to the 1893 Columbian Exposition held in Chicago. Displeased at how the South had been presented at Chicago, wealthy citizens and boosters of Atlanta met to propose and plan an event that they hoped would present a more positive image of the region and stimulate much-needed economic activity following the national economic depression of 1893. In May of the following year, representatives of Atlanta met with the House Committee on Appropriations in Washington in hopes of landing two hundred thousand dollars in federal funding for the proposed exposition. Accompanying the delegation from Atlanta was Booker T. Washington, an African-American educator from the Tuskegee Normal and Industrial Institute in Alabama, who spoke in favor of the exposition and emphasized the importance of southern blacks achieving economic and political progress through thrift, hard work, industrial and technical education and training, and the acquisition of property. Booker's message soothed Congressional concerns, and the requested funds were granted, with one important stipulation—the exposition had to include an exhibition hall that would celebrate the achievements and potential of black southerners in the post–Civil War period.

The resulting Cotton States and International Exposition featured thirteen main buildings and some six thousand exhibits focused on key New South resources, such as minerals, agriculture, forestry, manufacturing, and railroads. Included among the main buildings of the Exposition was the requested Negro Building—a 270-foot-long wood-frame and concrete hall and the first of its kind at a world's fair. Designed, built, and managed by African Americans, the exposition's Negro Building featured the first major exhibit on southern black achievement in the nation's history. Black visitors were allowed access,

The Liberty Bell was displayed at the 1895 Cotton States and International Exposition.

not only to this building, but to all of the public venues (although they were excluded from many private exhibitions and were denied the opportunity to purchase food and beverages anywhere except the Negro Building).

Also present on the exposition grounds was a building devoted to the "New Woman," who, according to Emma Mims, president of the Board of Women Managers, was "neither the antagonist nor the rival of man, but his co-worker and helpmeet." The Woman's Building was designed by Elise Mercur of Pittsburgh, Pennsylvania, and included an assembly room for daily conferences of women's organizations, a library, a hall of women's inventions, a model school, a day nursery and kindergarten, exhibits, paintings, and a model kitchen. Several of Atlanta's women's organizations date their origins to the conferences held at the Woman's Building, including local chapters of the National Association of Colored Women, the National Council of Jewish Women, and the Atlanta Federation of Woman's Clubs.

The 1895 exposition was a great success for Atlanta. It drew almost thirteen thousand visitors a day and over eight hundred thousand people before it was over. Its activities and offerings were followed closely in the regional and national press and even received mention in many international newspapers. The signature event of

Piedmont Park, site of the 1895 Cotton States and International Exposition.

Entertainment could be found at the Trocadero Theater at the exposition.

the exposition, however, happened on the very first day, when Booker T. Washington addressed the crowds assembled.

Many whites on the organizing committee were concerned about the possible public reaction to a black man addressing a racially-mixed southern audience. Their fears, however, proved unwarranted. Following an introduction by former Georgia Governor Rufus Bullock who termed Washington "a representative of Negro enterprise and Negro civilization," the educator from Tuskegee delivered a message that paralleled many of the points he had made one year earlier to the Congressional Appropriations Committee.

In this speech, Washington advised whites and blacks in the South to "cast down your buckets where you are . . . by making friends in every manly way of the people of all races by whom we are surrounded." He went on to assure concerned southern whites that "the wisest among my race understand that the agitation of questions of social equality is the extremest folly" and counseled African Americans instead to learn a skill, tend their garden, and save their money. In an oft-quoted passage alluding to the need to put off agitation for social and political rights in return for increased access to economic opportunities, Washington declared that "in all things purely social we can be as separate as the fingers, yet one as the hand in all things essential to mutual progress."

Washington's speech was music to the ears of assembled whites, who believed that racial harmony was now at hand. The *New York*

World, for example, reported that "a Negro Moses stood before a great audience of white people and delivered an oration that marks a new epoch in the history of the South....The whole city is thrilling tonight with a realization of the extraordinary significance of these two unprecedented events. Nothing has happened since Henry Grady's immortal speech before the New England Society in New York that indicates so profoundly the spirit of the New South, except, perhaps, the opening of the Exposition itself."

Local African-American leaders, such as John Hope and W. E. B. Du Bois of Atlanta University were less gracious. Du Bois, who at first congratulated Washington on his speech, later labeled it "the Atlanta Compromise" and decried the legitimacy it conferred upon the Jim Crow restrictions and discrimination then engulfing the city and region. In the year following Booker T. Washington's speech, the concept of separate but equal would gain further legal sanction through the U.S. Supreme Court's landmark ruling in *Plessy* v. *Ferguson.*

Atlanta and its white leaders and city boosters were understandably proud of the 1895 Cotton States and International Exposition, the exposure it received, and the city's ascendant place in the New South order. The shiny veneer of the New South promise, however, hid many dramatic tensions and social undercurrents—growing pains, racial unrest, and uncomfortable adjustments to a new urban environment—that would surface early in the next century.

CHAPTER III

Forward Atlanta: 1900–1940

The original Equitable Building was demolished in 1972. Some of its Corinthian columns can be seen today in front of the SunTrust Building and on the banks of the Chattahoochee River, in east Cobb County along Columns Drive.

Atlanta is the ideal point for your factory branch. . . . Here you find economies in labor, power, taxes, and many other basic items. And from here your men and your shipments may be most efficiently routed over the rich Southern territory.

—Excerpt from a
Forward Atlanta ad, ca.1928

THE DRAMATIC GROWTH THAT CHARACTERIZED ATLANTA in the late 1800s accelerated during the opening decades of the twentieth century. The city's population, which stood at eighty-nine thousand in 1900, tripled during the next thirty years, and its boundaries were expanded through the annexation of new territories and communities. Beyond the city limits, new suburban developments arose, made possible by the presence of the streetcar and later the automobile. Even Atlanta's skyline began to expand vertically with the addition of the city's earliest "skyscrapers"—the Equitable Building, the Flatiron Building, the Empire Building, and the Candler Building. A building boom in downtown Atlanta added new structures to the urban landscape, including department stores (such as Muse's and Davidson-Paxon); large, elegant hotels (such as the Piedmont, the Georgian Terrace, the Ansley, and the Winecoff); and new government buildings (a city auditorium, a post office, and federal courthouse, a new Fulton County courthouse, and a new million-dollar city hall). At the same time that Atlanta's population, boundaries, and skyline were expanding, the city also managed to extend its regional significance by taking advantage of new developments in transportation and commerce. The emergence of an early trucking industry and the construction of new roads and highways, for example, augmented Atlanta's existing rail connections, established the city as a distribution center for the entire Southeast, and helped fuel business and commercial growth. When a failing cotton market and a Florida land boom (and eventual bust) in the 1920s threatened to negatively affect this growth, the city's boosters, led by the

Downtown business district.

Chamber of Commerce, responded with a massive advertising campaign called "Forward Atlanta" that drew national business attention to the city's important rail and trucking connections, growing (and largely non-union) labor force, prospering local economy, and pleasant climate. The Forward Atlanta campaign proved to be a considerable success and drew hundreds of new businesses and thousands of new employees to the city.

But Atlanta's rapid growth in the early twentieth century had unwelcome repercussions as well. The city's increasing population strained municipal and welfare services and the greater competition for living space and working wages exposed and possibly inflamed mounting social, political, and racial tensions. Periodic episodes of violence and protest erupted. Unruly incidents of note included a race riot, a notorious lynching, multiple labor strikes, and the reemergence of the Ku Klux Klan. Adding to the pressures associated with growth and changes in the local economy and workforce were efforts to segregate the city and its institutions along racial lines. As Jim Crow, a widespread system of racial segregation and discrimination, took firm hold in the city and region in the early twentieth century, Atlanta became, in effect, two separate cities—one white, one black. Whites and African Americans resided in different neighborhoods; attended separate parks, schools, churches, and places of entertainment; and in situations or public areas where both races were present—i.e., sporting events, concerts, movies, streetcars and buses, government and public buildings, etc.—occupied strictly segregated spaces. These tightening codes and customs that discouraged racial mixing encouraged the growth of separate institutions for blacks and whites in Atlanta, including the development of a thriving black business and entertainment district along Auburn Avenue.

Despite these divisions and disturbances, Atlanta continued to prosper during the first three decades of the twentieth century. A national economic depression in the 1930s eventually slowed the pace of urban growth and development, as Atlanta experienced high unemployment, business and bank failures, and widespread hunger and poverty. The city was ill-equipped to handle these emergencies, but "New Deal" federal government agencies and programs stepped into the breach, funding public works projects in the city that resulted in the construction of new buildings, the repair of the city's failing infrastructure (including its sewer system), and the employment of thousands of Atlantans, both black and white. By the end of the decade, Atlanta was beginning to exhibit promising signs of recovery and was poised to enter yet another era of rapid growth and development.

THE ATLANTA SPIRIT

Atlanta's explosive growth in the early twentieth century was regarded by most city boosters as a positive development, one that should be promoted and encouraged. Louie Newton, editor of the *City Builder* magazine, for example, lauded what he termed the "Atlanta Spirit"—the pervasive belief that whatever was good for business was good for Atlanta and that what was good for Atlanta was good for all of its citizens. Thus, in the name of business and progress, the city's early twentieth-century boosters encouraged not only commercial growth, but also the development of a myriad of cultural, artistic, and sports activities and institutions that they hoped would transform Atlanta into an urban center of regional and national prominence. In the process of promoting and implementing these changes, Atlanta was remade and its economic, cultural, and physical structure dramatically altered.

THE GROWTH OF COMMERCE

Atlanta's early-twentieth-century growth and expansion followed, in part, from the development of a new economic orientation for the city. In the nineteenth century, the city's vital railroad connections had spurred its development into a rail and distribution center for the Southeast. The railroad industry's impact on and dominance of the local economy during this period was reflected not only in the number of railroad-related industries found in Atlanta, but also in the physical positioning of the city around the railways. The center or heart of Atlanta lay at the convergence of its railroad lines, and Atlanta's primary businesses situated themselves along or near its tracks. The turn of the century, however, witnessed a gradual realignment of the city's economy and its relationship to the railroads. The rail transportation industry remained the city's largest employer until the 1920s, but commercial growth increasingly stimulated Atlanta's economic and physical expansion. The emergence in the early twentieth century of a new business corridor that stretched northward along Peachtree Street away from Five Points (and the railway hub that had earlier marked the economic and physical center of Atlanta) and the construction (beginning in the 1920s) of a series of viaducts that elevated the city above the tracks symbolically signaled the end of the railroad's dominance of the local economy and the rise of a more diversified economic order.

FORWARD ATLANTA

Atlanta's business and civic leaders were well aware of the economic changes taking place in the city during the first decades of the twen-

The Sears-Roebuck distribution center on Ponce de Leon Avenue nears completion, 1926.

Atlanta Chamber of Commerce, 1920.

Businessman and politician Ivan Allen Sr., (1876–1968).

tieth century, and city hall and the chamber of commerce joined together to vigorously promote the growth of commerce. The most ambitious and successful of these promotional efforts began in 1925 when W. R. C. Smith and Ivan Allen Sr., of the Atlanta Chamber of Commerce launched an aggressive national advertising campaign entitled "Forward Atlanta" that was designed to lure new businesses to the city. The campaign proved to be a phenomenal success. Some 762 new businesses moved to Atlanta between 1925 and 1929, bringing tens of thousands of jobs and adding an estimated $34 million in annual payrolls to the city's economy. Included among the businesses that made Atlanta their regional headquarters during this period were such corporate giants as the Davison-Paxon department store (later merged with Macy's); Sears-Roebuck, which built its southeastern retail and mail-order headquarters on Ponce de Leon Avenue; and General Motors, which established a manufacturing plant at Lakewood in 1928.

The success of the Forward Atlanta campaign reshaped the city's economy and put it in better shape to weather the gathering storms of an imminent national economic depression. The program also completed Atlanta's transformation into a city of commerce. By 1930 Atlanta was only the twenty-ninth largest city in the United States, but it ranked second in terms of available office space. Additionally, early-twentieth-century Atlanta contained a widening array of commercial structures concentrated in the Fairlie-Poplar area of downtown and a large number of theaters and hotels in the entertainment district known as the "Great White Way."

SWEET AUBURN

To the east of Fairlie-Poplar and the "Great White Way" lay Auburn Avenue, a business and entertainment district reserved for Atlanta's nonwhite residents. As late as the turn of the century, many African-American entrepreneurs in Atlanta were still locating their businesses next door to those of white businessmen, and some even provided services to an exclusively white clientele. Alonzo F. Herndon, a former slave and the founder of Atlanta Life Insurance Company, for example, owned a successful barbershop located on Peachtree Street whose clients were white and included some of the wealthiest and most powerful business and civic leaders in the city. With the rise, however, of Jim Crow segregation and the violence and destruction occasioned by the 1906 race riot (discussed later in this chapter), black-owned and - operated businesses in Atlanta increasingly restricted their services to the African-American community and their addresses to Auburn Avenue.

Atlanta's entertainment district, known as the "Great White Way."

The construction of new buildings along Auburn Avenue during the early part of the twentieth century provided much-needed office space for the increasing number and diversity of black professionals, businesses, and trade and service organizations that were moving to the city. The Odd Fellows Building, completed in 1915, housed a drugstore, an auditorium, offices for black professionals and entrepreneurs, and a rooftop garden where dances and receptions were held. Other important office buildings and multiuse structures constructed on Auburn Avenue during this period include the Rucker Building (built in 1904 by Henry A. Rucker, the first African-American collector of internal revenue in Georgia) and the Herndon Building (built in 1924 by Alonzo Herndon). By 1920 there were already 72 black-owned businesses and twenty black professionals located on the avenue; ten years later that number had climbed to 121 businesses and thirty-nine professionals. Included in this mix were insurance companies such as Standard Life Insurance and Atlanta Life Insurance Company (one of the largest black-owned companies in the nation); stores; banks and lending institutions, such as Citizens Trust Bank and Mutual Federal; entertainment centers; hotels; restaurants; beauty schools; funeral homes; and newspapers, including the *Atlanta Independent* and later the *Atlanta Daily World*. Many of the city's largest and best-known black churches, like Big Bethel A.M.E., Wheat Street Baptist, and Ebenezer Baptist (where Martin Luther King Jr., his father, and his grandfather served as pastors) also stationed themselves along the avenue.

Businessman and politician Henry Allen Rucker (1852–1924).

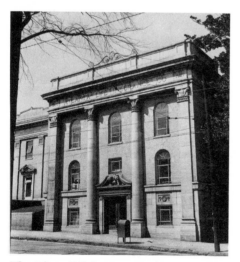

The Atlanta Life Insurance Building on Auburn Avenue.

"Sweet Auburn" (as John Wesley Dobbs, grandmaster of the Prince Hall Masons, dubbed the street in the 1930s) provided Atlanta's African-American community with many of the services, jobs, and funds denied them elsewhere in the city as a result of racial discrimination and segregation. And as Sweet Auburn continued to grow and prosper during the first half of the twentieth century, it made gains in its regional stature and influence. "Auburn [Avenue] is not just a street," the *Atlanta Independent* observed in 1926. "It is an institution with influence and power not only among Georgians but American Negroes everywhere. It is the heart of Negro big business, a result of Negro cooperation and evidence of Negro possibility."

In 1932 African-American business leaders established their own separate chamber of commerce to promote black commercial growth and development within the city. Ironically, although the Atlanta Chamber of Commerce and the Negro Chamber of Commerce never merged during this period, both remained members of the same national chamber of commerce. Thus while black and white business leaders in Atlanta operated in different sectors of the city and engaged in separate promotional efforts, both groups contributed to the growth of a more diversified local economy and the transformation of Atlanta during the early twentieth century from a regional transportation hub into a center of commerce.

ARTS AND ENTERTAINMENT

Fine Arts

Commercial growth and expansion were not the only goals of the city's early-twentieth-century boosters. In their push to make Atlanta a city on a par with other national urban centers, Atlanta's civic and business leaders also stressed the need to develop a wide range of cultural, artistic, and recreational organizations and activities. The effort was not a new one. Atlanta had hosted opera singers, musicals, plays, and symphonies during the nineteenth century and even constructed elegant settings in which to view these performances (such as the sixteen-hundred-seat Davis Hall, built in 1866, and the DeGive Opera House, constructed in 1870). In the early twentieth century these attempts continued and resulted in a local performance by the Metropolitan Opera Company of New York in 1901 and again in 1905. Unfortunately, few people attended either of the shows.

By 1909, however, a critical moment for cultural development had arrived. Civic leaders and music lovers were anxious to show off the city's new auditorium-armory (which had cost $250,000 to con-

The Atlanta Symphony Orchestra at the Howard Theater with conductor Enrico Leide, 1924.

struct) and to announce Atlanta's arrival as a center of culture and refinement in the South. Accordingly, the city organized a "Great Southern Music Festival," which brought the Dresden Philharmonic Orchestra and Metropolitan Opera star Geraldine Ferrar to Atlanta to perform. The success of this endeavor prompted local sponsorship of the Met; and beginning in 1910, the opera company began traveling to Atlanta for an annual spring performance—an arrangement that would last, with occasional interruptions, until 1986. (An early highlight of this annual series was the performance in 1910 of world-famous tenor Enrico Caruso as Radames in *Aida*.)

Other local organizations, like the Atlanta Music Club (established in 1916), enticed additional nationally-known musical entertainers and symphonies to the city during this period and promoted as well the development of Atlanta's own symphony orchestra. Also emerging during the first decades of the twentieth century were a number of civic and cultural organizations, including the Atlanta Art Association (chartered in 1905), to which Harriett (Mrs. Joseph) High later gave her home (and her name) for an art museum; the Atlanta Writers Club (organized in 1914); and the Atlanta Historical Society (founded in 1926).

Popular Music

In popular culture too, Atlanta held a respectable position. During the 1920s, the city became a recording center for blues and country music. Musicians from across the South traveled to Atlanta to perform and record. Blues singers such as Blind Willie McTell, Buddy Moss, and Barbecue Bob Hicks not only played in area clubs, taverns, and homes, but also recorded songs in local studios set up by Columbia

Walter McElreath (1867–1951), one of the founders of the Atlanta Historical Society.

and Decca Records. Country musicians also found an important haven in Atlanta during this period. Companies such as Okeh and Columbia Records sent representatives to the city to capture the musical offerings of early country stars like Fiddlin' John Carson and Gid Tanner and the Skillet Lickers, who performed at local fiddling contests and square dances. Those Atlantans who were not able to see these country musicians live or to buy their records had the opportunity to listen to them on the South's first radio station, WSB, which began broadcasting in Atlanta in 1922.

Atlanta audiences could also take in concerts and performances from some of the nation's best-known musicians during this era. Vocalists such as Rudy Vallee and band leaders Tommy Dorsey and Benny Goodman included Atlanta on their concert tours. Blues singers Bessie Smith, Ethel Waters, and Ma Rainey also traveled to Atlanta to sing, most frequently at the 81 Theater on Decatur Street or the Top Hat Club on Auburn Avenue. Other well-known black musicians, including Count Basie, Duke Ellington, and Cab Calloway, initially reluctant to travel to the South because of Jim Crow restrictions, started to appear in local nightclubs, theaters, and auditoriums in the mid-1930s.

While the musical appeal of the diverse group of artists who performed and recorded in Atlanta during the 1920s and 1930s crossed racial lines, the audiences that came to hear these musicians and the sites in which they performed remained strictly segregated. Black Atlantans, for example, could not attend the performances of the Metropolitan Opera; instead they organized their own classical concerts and offerings held in area churches or on the campuses of the Atlanta University Center schools. At other times, when both white and black audiences came to hear a musical performance, racial segregation mandated a variety of inventive arrangements. Artists who performed at the Top Hat on Auburn Avenue played throughout the week to black audiences. On Saturday nights, however, the establishment was reserved for whites. On another occasion, when both black and white Atlantans came to a classical musical concert sponsored by the Commission on Interracial Cooperation, the audience had to be split down the middle, with African Americans on one side and whites on the other. However, restricting African Americans to the balcony (or "buzzard roost," as it became known) at a performance served as the most common segregation pattern for racially mixed audiences. At the Fox Theatre, for example, African Americans had to enter through a long flight of stairs on the outside of the building to reach their seats in the balcony. But when racially mixed

Social event at the Piedmont Driving Club.

audiences attended performances of black musicians and bands at the Municipal Auditorium, whites had to sit in the stands while African Americans, on the floor, could dance if they wished.

Social Dancing

As the preceding example suggests, southern racial etiquette of the times did not permit African Americans and whites to mix on the dance floor—largely because of white concerns that such associations might encourage thoughts of physical intimacy and social equality. Therefore, segregation also prevailed in the city's clubs and dance halls during this era. Black Atlantans were barred from white dance halls and attended instead dances held at the rooftop garden of the Odd Fellows Building, the Top Hat Club, the Sunset Casino, or a number of other nightclubs located in the city's black communities. White Atlantans similarly patronized white establishments.

With the growth of elite private social clubs such as the Piedmont Driving Club, the Capital City Club, and the Brookhaven, Druid Hills, and East Lake country clubs, the Atlanta dance scene became even further segregated by class and religious background. Membership in these clubs was restricted to the wealthiest and most influential of Atlanta's elite white society and remained closed not only to African Americans but to Jews as well. Atlanta's Jewish community responded to this slight by establishing its own private social clubs—the Standard, the Mayfair, and the Progressive.

Carole Lombard and Clark Gable are introduced by Mayor William B. Hartsfield (served 1937–1940 and 1942–1962) at the world premiere of Gone With the Wind, *1939.*

Moving Pictures

Moving pictures, which had first appeared in Atlanta during the 1895 Cotton States and International Exposition, became an increasingly popular diversion in the early twentieth century. In the first six months of 1907, for example, twenty-one storefront theaters, known as "electric theaters" or "nickelodeons" opened in Atlanta. The vast majority of these establishments went out of business before the year was out, but the popularity of movies as a form of public entertainment was already established. By 1914 estimates of daily attendance of white Atlantans stood between twenty-five thousand and thirty thousand. No comparable figures are available for African-American theatergoers, but black movie theaters, such as the 81, Strand, Royal, Ashby, Lincoln, Harlem, and Carver theaters, (all of which were owned by Tom Bailey, a white businessman) were present in the city at this time. In addition, the largest movie houses in Atlanta also admitted African-American viewers to their films, though they were frequently required to use separate entrances and confine themselves to the balcony. By the 1920s new and elegant movie theaters, such as the Howard Theater (built in 1920), the Fox Theatre (opened to the public in 1929), and the Loew's Grand (originally the DeGive Opera House), were part of the city's entertainment landscape.

A number of major film events also occurred in the city during this era, including the 1915 showing of D.W. Griffith's *Birth of a Nation*, which was viewed by over a fourth of Atlanta's white population. In 1929 another important milestone occurred with the opening of the Fox Theatre. The "Fabulous Fox," an architectural landmark of the era, was conceived, designed, and constructed through the efforts of the Yaarab Temple of Atlanta (a Shriner organization) and featured storefront space, a banquet hall and ballroom, and kitchen facilities. The crowning achievement of the complex was the auditorium, or theater, with its combined Egyptian and Middle Eastern decorative motifs, tented balconies, simulated "starlit" sky, remarkable acoustics, and 3,610-pipe Möller organ, which could be hydraulically raised to stage level or lowered out of sight.

Although the Yaarab Temple ran into financial difficulties before the theater was completed, a leasing agreement worked out between the Yaarab Temple and Fox Theatres Corporation of New York allowed the theater to open to the public on Christmas Day 1929— only two months after the stock market crash that signaled the beginning of the Great Depression. The depression was nowhere in evidence on opening day, however, as crowds lined up around the block, despite the cold, drizzling rain, to buy tickets (priced between fifteen and seventy-five cents) for the afternoon's entertainment. Included in the opening day's presentation were a community sing-along featuring the "Mighty" Möeller organ; a performance by the Fox Grand Orchestra, under the directorship of Enrico Leide; a program of dancing girls (Fanchon and Marco's "Sunkist Beauties"); a showing of *Steamboat Willie*, a proto-Micky Mouse cartoon; Fox Movietone News; and the feature film *Salute*, a West Point romance starring George O'Brien, Helen Chandler, and Stepin Fetchit.

As exciting as this opening event was, an even grander moment in Atlanta's motion picture history occurred ten years later with the release of the movie *Gone With the Wind*. The movie, based upon the highly successful novel of the same name by Atlanta native Margaret Mitchell, created great public interest from its inception. In 1936, the year of the book's release, the novel sold more than a million copies in the first six months and garnered the Pulitzer Prize the following year. Encouraged by the book's success, film producer David O. Selznick paid $50,000— then a record—for the movie rights to the novel. Public expectations and excitement surrounding this film project grew to enormous levels.

While the film was being produced, rumors circulated that the premiere might occur in New York City, but Atlanta, home of the book's author and site of many of the novel's scenes, eventually received its rightful honor to host the event. On December 14, 1939 the festivities began with a Peachtree Street parade and ended later that evening with a series of parties, including a *Gone With the Wind* ball at the Municipal Auditorium sponsored by the city's Junior League. Performing at the ball were the Ebenezer Baptist Church choir (which included a youthful Martin Luther King Jr.) and the orchestras of Kay Kyser and Enrico Leide. The NBC radio network broadcast portions of the evening's performances nationally.

The movie's world premiere the following evening focused even more national and international attention on Atlanta. More than two thousand notables, including the book's author, the stars of the film and other Hollywood celebrities, various local politicians and civic leaders, and the governors of five southern states attended the event, held at the Loew's Grand on Peachtree Street. The theater's original façade was altered to resemble a Greek Revival plantation house, and a huge medallion, featuring the likenesses of Rhett Butler (played in the movie by Clark Gable) and Scarlett O'Hara (Vivien Leigh), hung above the pediment. Movietone News and Pathé film crews, as well as representatives from newspapers, magazines, and radio stations all over the country, came to Atlanta that night to capture the moment for their audiences back home.

In keeping with the Jim Crow practices of the times, the high-profile events surrounding the *Gone With the Wind* premiere also included strict segregation. Many black Atlantans stood among the estimated 300,000 people lining Peachtree for the motorcade and parade of movie stars, but they could not attend the movie's premiere at the Loew's. Instead, the city's African-American moviegoers had to wait several months for the "colored" premiere of the film at the Bailey's Royal Theater in late April 1940. In the other signature events associated with film's opening, African Americans attended only as performers or workers. The Junior League ball, a white-only event, for example, featured the sixty-voice Ebenezer Baptist Church choir under the direction of Reverend Martin Luther King Sr. Just one month earlier, Reverend King had led more than one thousand African Americans on a voter registration drive and had publicly stated his opposition to the discriminations and restrictions of Jim Crow. On this evening, however, both Reverend King and the choir were dressed as slaves (including ten-year-old Martin Luther King Jr., who sang with the choir). The following week the Atlanta Baptist Ministers Union censured Reverend King for participating in this segregated event.

Elsewhere during these two days of movie activity, the customs and restrictions of Jim Crow continued to make their presence felt—from the exclusion of Vivien Leigh's and Irene Selznick's African-American maids from the Georgian Terrace, where the stars were staying, to the decision by producer David O. Selznick not to invite the film's major black actors—Hattie McDaniel, Butterfly McQueen, Eddie Anderson, and Oscar Polk—to participate in the film's premiere. Selznick worried that white southerners might resent the inclusion of McDaniel and the film's other black actors in the activities. His fears, however, appear to have been misplaced. Most southern whites found little to object to, for instance, in McDaniel's portrayal of Mammy, and although both she and the film received harsh criticism from the National Association for the Advancement of Colored People for the film's depiction of African Americans, other individuals and groups (including the Atlanta Ladies Memorial Association) were quick to praise the authenticity of McDaniel's performance. At the Academy Awards later that year, McDaniel became the first African-American actor to win an Oscar when she triumphed in the best supporting actress category.

Gone With the Wind soon proved to be as phenomenal a success as a film as it had been a book. The movie grossed $14 million in its first year of distribution and won ten Academy Awards in 1939, including best picture, best actress (Leigh), and best supporting actress (McDaniel). In the years following its release, *Gone With the Wind* continued to be an enormously popular film, both in America and abroad. By 1989, the fiftieth anniversary of the film's debut, ticket sales, foreign rights, rentals, and sales of the movie worldwide already totaled more than $840 million. In the process, the fictional characters, story, and images from *Gone With the Wind* became firmly associated in the public's mind with the city of Atlanta.

SPORTS

Organized sports, yet another hallmark of a growing urban metropolis, became an increasingly popular diversion for Atlantans in the early twentieth century. At the top of the list, in terms of popularity and local fan support, was the "national pastime"—baseball. Organized baseball made its first appearance in Atlanta in 1866, when Captain Tom Burnett formed the Atlanta Baseball Club and faced off against a rival local team called the Gate City Nine. Burnett's team lost this initial contest 127–29 and he soon disbanded his club, but the Gate City Nine went on to finish their inaugural season with thirty-six wins and one loss (to the Dixie Club of Athens).

Professional baseball arrived in Atlanta nineteen years later in 1885, when the Southern League formed with Henry Grady as its president. The league, which existed until 1900, featured teams from Atlanta, Augusta, Columbus, and Macon, Georgia; Birmingham, Alabama; and Chattanooga, Tennessee. Atlanta's baseball franchise won the Southern League championship in 1885, 1886, and 1895.

A new era of professional baseball began in Atlanta in 1901 with the creation of the Southern Association. This new league proved over the years to be one of the most stable in all of minor league baseball, with six of its charter teams remaining in the organization for fifty years or more. One of these long-lived teams was the Atlanta Crackers. Organized by New Orleans businessman, Charles Abner Powell, in 1902, the Crackers joined the new league that same year. (Also included in the league were the Birmingham Barons, the Chattanooga Lookouts, the Little Rock Travelers, the Memphis Chicks, the Mobile Bears, the Nashville Vols, and the New Orleans Pelicans.) Over the next four decades, the Crackers won nine league pennants and in 1938 became the first team in the league to achieve a "Grand Slam"—winning not only the league title, but also the All-Star game, the Shaughnessy play-offs (featuring the league's four best teams), and the Dixie Series

Shown in 1925 are Georgia sports legends left to right *Bobby Jones (1902–1971) and Ty Cobb (1886–1961).*

Ponce de Leon Ball Park, c. 1955.

Atlanta Crackers outfielder Wilbur Goode at bat, 1925.

(which pitted the Southern Association Shaughnessy winners against the Shaughnessy champions of the Texas League). In the process, the Atlanta Crackers built a large and loyal following among both Atlanta's white and black baseball fans and gained financial support from sources such as Coca-Cola Company president Robert Woodruff, who bought the team in 1933.

Good teams require good facilities, and beginning in 1907, the Atlanta Crackers played their home games in what was considered one of the finest ballparks in the league—Ponce de Leon Ball Park. Set on the site of an amusement park on Ponce de Leon Avenue, the ballpark featured a somewhat eccentric layout, with a fully grown magnolia tree and an embankment both situated in fair territory. In 1923, when the park's wooden stands burned down, R. J. Spiller, the ballpark's owner, replaced them with concrete stands capable of seating fourteen thousand. The park also had standing room for an additional six thousand fans. Spiller tried to christen the new structure with his own name, but fans and players over the years continued to refer to the field and the stadium as Ponce de Leon Park, or Poncey.

Baseball during this era in Atlanta, as elsewhere, remained racially segregated. No black baseball players broke the color line until Jackie Robinson joined the Brooklyn Dodgers in 1947. Two years later, Robinson appeared in an exhibition game at Ponce de Leon

Park between the Crackers and the Dodgers—the first time in Atlanta's history that blacks and whites competed together in an organized sport. (It would be another thirteen years, however, before an integrated Atlanta baseball team and integrated seating were introduced at Poncey).

In the absence of integrated teams and facilities, professional black athletes in early-twentieth-century Atlanta joined all-black baseball teams such as the Atlanta Deppens. This team had toured the South before the turn of the century, playing other black baseball teams from New Orleans, Birmingham, Macon, and Chattanooga. The Atlanta Cubs, a semiprofessional team composed primarily of African-American college students from the Atlanta University schools, later succeeded the Deppens. Many of the local fans referred to the Cubs as the "Black Crackers," and by 1920 the nickname had become so popular that the Cubs officially changed their name to the Atlanta Black Crackers. Some of the Black Crackers' home games were played at Ponce de Leon Park (when the white Crackers were out of town), but most of the time they played on fields located at local black schools such as Morris Brown College and Morehouse College.

In the 1920s the Black Crackers joined the newly formed Negro Southern League. Although teams in the league varied from year to year, they usually included the Atlanta Black Crackers, the Birmingham Black Barons, the Jacksonville Red Caps, the Memphis Red Sox, the Montgomery Grey Socks, the Nashville Elite Giants, and the New Orleans Crescent Stars. The Negro Southern League franchises were, for the most part, not as financially sound as those in the white Southern Association, and the lack of funds was readily evident. The visiting and home teams, for example, each had to furnish two balls per game, and games often had to be stopped for ball retrieval. Money from gate receipts went not only to the home team but also to the visiting team, as reimbursement for travel expenses. Moreover, since the teams could carry only twelve players, the athletes had to play more than one position, and membership on teams changed constantly.

In 1937 the financial problems of the Black Crackers eased somewhat when the team was bought by John and Billie Harden, owners of a gas station on Auburn Avenue. The Hardens not only provided their players with a more secure income (the average monthly salary for a player in the Negro Southern League was only $250), but acquired a bus and new uniforms for the team as well. The following year, the Black Crackers joined the Negro American League and won the league pennant and Negro National Championship.

Despite the team's success, the Atlanta Black Crackers did not remain in the Negro American League beyond the 1938 season and instead affiliated once again with the Negro Southern League. The Southern League's days were numbered, however. Jackie Robinson's integration of the Dodgers the following decade opened baseball's major leagues to the region's best black players, and the Southern League was soon forced to disband. The Atlanta Black Crackers played their last season in 1949.

Football also proved to be an increasingly popular spectator sport in early-twentieth-century Atlanta. Like baseball, football had made its first appearance in the city before the turn of the century. In fact, the state's first intercollegiate football game (between the University of Georgia and Auburn University) took place on February 20, 1892, at Piedmont Park. Auburn won the game 10–0, and despite the fact that none of the participants wore a helmet, no injuries occured. Five years later, however, a critical injury suffered in a University of Georgia football game nearly brought about the collapse of the intercollegiate sport in the state and region. In a game against the University of Virginia, Georgia fullback Richard Von Gammon sustained a blow to the head and died of a brain concussion. His death triggered a regional outcry against the sport. The tide of popular opinion soon turned, though, when the victim's mother wrote a letter to the University of Georgia Trustees stating her belief that her son would have wanted the sport to continue.

The Georgia Institute of Technology's famous football rivalry with the University of Georgia also began in the late nineteenth century. The first game between these two Georgia schools happened on the afternoon of November 4, 1893, in Athens and was won by Tech, 22–6. One of the stars of that game and the captain of the Tech team was Leonard Wood, a part-time student as well as the surgeon general at Fort McPherson. Five years after this inaugural game between Georgia and Georgia Tech, Wood saw action during the Spanish-American War as a commander in Teddy Roosevelt's Rough Riders and, following the war, served as governor-general of both Cuba and the Philippines. Eventually he became chief of staff of the army. In 1920 General Wood was also one of the leading Republican candidates for president before delegates turned instead to Warren G. Harding as a compromise candidate.

Atlanta's interest in football and in Tech football in particular increased during the next few decades as the Ramblin' Wreck grew into a regional and national football powerhouse. Under the leadership of Coach John Heisman, who had earlier coached at Auburn and Clemson universities, Tech piled up an impressive record from 1904 to

Atlanta University football team, 1922.

1919 of 101 wins, 28 losses, and 6 ties. Included in this record were a stretch of 33 consecutive wins from 1915 to 1917 and a national championship in 1917. Heisman not only produced a winning football program at Tech, he also helped revolutionize the game. It was Coach Heisman, for example, who introduced the shift (known as the "Heisman shift"); the center snap (previously the ball had been rolled with the feet); the "hike" or "hut" vocal signal for starting play; the numbers on jerseys; and the scoreboard listings of downs and yardage. He also lobbied for the adoption of the forward pass, which was finally legalized in 1906. (The Heisman trophy, given annually to the nation's best collegiate football player by the Downtown Athletic Club of New York, is named in his honor.)

Football proved equally popular on Atlanta's black college campuses. Morehouse College organized its first football team in 1900, and within a few years played against teams from Atlanta University, Fisk, Talladega, Tuskegee, and Hampton. During these early years of football, Morehouse went through a period of five undefeated seasons and was generally regarded as one of the best African-American football teams in the region. Clark College established its first football team only one year after Morehouse, but success on the gridiron generally eluded Clark until the 1920s. Then, under the guidance of Coach Samuel B. Taylor, Clark's "Black Battalion of Death" became a

The golf course at the Capitol City Club, 1919.

power to be reckoned with in the Southern Inter-Collegiate Athletic Conference. In 1928 Clark defeated the seemingly invincible Golden Tigers from Tuskegee, who had won forty-seven consecutive games to that point, and Taylor's team eventually became co-champions of its conference. Morris Brown came relatively late to organized football, forming its first team in 1911, but soon established an intense rivalry with Atlanta University (that lasted until 1929 when Atlanta University ceased offering an undergraduate curriculum) and with cross-campus opponent Clark College. A similar rivalry developed between Morehouse and Atlanta University. As a result, football games between these Atlanta University Center schools soon came to be eagerly anticipated annual events.

Golf also proved to be an increasingly popular sport in Atlanta during this period. The Piedmont Driving Club constructed the city's first course in 1896, a modest seven-hole challenge. The professional assigned to oversee the course gave no lessons, and devoted most of his energies to supervising the caddies and repairing members' golf clubs. Ten years later, another seven-hole course was constructed at the East Lake Country Club by the Atlanta Athletic Club, and in 1912, two more private golf and social clubs appeared in the exclusive residential communities of Ansley Park and Druid Hills. But the city's private golf courses were not the only places where the game could be played. By the end of the 1920s Atlanta operated five public golf courses: Piedmont Park, Candler Park, James L. Key, Bobby Jones, and John A. White.

Atlanta was also home to a number of well-known golfing champions, including Perry Adair, who won the southern championship trophy in 1921, and Alexa Sterling, who captured the national women's amateur title in 1917, 1919, and 1920. The greatest golf hero in Atlanta during this period, however, was Robert Tyre Jones Jr.

Jones was born in Atlanta on March 17, 1902. In 1908 his family moved to a home near the thirteenth green of the East Lake golf course, where young Bobby Jones took up the game that would soon bring him worldwide fame. Three years later, at the age of nine, Jones won East Lake's Junior Championship. In 1916 Jones battled friend and fellow East Lake golfer Perry Adair in the newly organized Georgia State Amateur Championship and won the competition on the last green. That same year, Jones competed in his first United States Amateur Championship and reached the quarter finals before being eliminated—becoming the youngest player in the tournament's history to advance that far.

For the next five years, Bobby Jones won only two tournaments while he finished high school and received a degree from Georgia Tech. But in the period from 1923 to 1929, he dominated both British and American golf, winning the U.S. Open in 1923, 1926, and 1929; the United States Amateur in 1924, 1925, 1927, and 1928; and the British Open in 1926 and 1927. At the same time he was winning these tournaments, Jones also managed to complete a second bachelor of science degree at Harvard University, get married to a woman named Mary Malone, enter law school at Emory University, gain admittance to the Georgia bar, and join an Atlanta law firm.

As successful as these remarkable years were, they were more than eclipsed by Jone's achievements in 1930, when he had what is arguably the best year in U.S. golf history. During that year, Jones won the Savannah Open and the Southeastern Open, and he captained the U.S. Walker golf team to victory in England. He also triumphed in the four most prestigious tournaments in golf at that time—the British Amateur, U.S. Open, British Open, and U.S. Amateur. Bobby Jones was the first golfer ever to win this "Grand Slam," and he quickly became a national and international sports hero. New York City honored him with a ticker-tape parade, and Atlanta followed with an even grander Bobby Jones Day parade down Peachtree Street. In fact, Atlanta proved so eager to honor its native son in 1930 that humorist Will Rogers remarked, "Atlanta no more than gets cleaned up from one Bobby Jones celebration till another comes along. You can easily exist in Atlanta by eating only at Jones testimonial dinners."

Bobby Jones retired from tournament golf in 1930, the year of his greatest triumph. In his fourteen-year career, he had played in only fifty-two tournaments (fewer than most professional golfers of today play in two years on the circuit) but had won twenty-three. Even in retirement, Bobby Jones remained an influential force in the game. He was president of the Atlanta Athletic Club and the Peachtree Golf

The New York Sun *pronounced that by winning the "Grand Slam" in 1930, Bobby Jones had "stormed the impregnable quadrilateral of golf."*

Horse racing at Piedmont Park.

Club, and he co-designed the Augusta National Golf Course, host site of the popular annual Masters tournament. He also produced short films on golfing fundamentals featuring well-known Hollywood actors and wrote several books on the sport.

In 1948, after being diagnosed with syringomyelia, a degenerative spinal ailment, Bobby Jones quit playing the game he loved. Yet he maintained his other career pursuits, remaining a lawyer and an executive in several local business ventures. He died in Atlanta on December 18, 1971.

PUBLIC PARKS AND AMUSEMENT

Atlantans' growing infatuation with sports in the early decades of the twentieth century was reflected in the increasing number of recreational facilities to be found in the city. At the turn of the century, two large public parks had already been established in Atlanta—Grant Park (donated to the city by Colonel Lemuel P. Grant in 1882) and Piedmont Park (site of the 1887 Piedmont Exposition and the 1895 Cotton States and International Exposition, and purchased by the city in 1904)—as well as a number of smaller neighborhood parks, such as Springvale (in Inman Park) and Mims Park (in northwest Atlanta). During the first two decades of the twentieth century, the city bought additional park space in the residential communities of West End, Ansley Park, Druid Hills, and Candler Park and put those areas under the supervision of Atlanta's park commission.

Lakewood Park, 1919.

Lakewood Park, 1941.

Ponce de Leon Park, 1906.

Washington Park, c. 1950.

Auto racing at Lakewood Race Track.

These new public parks added much-needed green space to the expanding city and also provided new recreational facilities, such as baseball fields, tennis courts, and swimming pools. Linked by streetcar lines to the rest of the city, Atlanta's public parks and golf courses became the locus for a widening range of outdoor sports activities.

The parks, however, were not open to all Atlantans. In fact, African Americans found their access to these parks increasingly restricted by Jim Crow laws, regulations, and customs even as the number of public parks and recreational options were on the rise. Black Atlantans and organizations like the Neighborhood Union (founded by Lugenia Burns Hope) pushed the city to create public parks and spaces that could be utilized by the city's African-American communities. In 1922 the city finally authorized the construction of Washington Park, the first public park for Atlanta's black citizens. Located on the west side of the city in an area developed by black businessman, realtor, and builder Heman Perry, Washington Park contained many of the same recreational facilities found in Atlanta's parks for whites, including the city's first public swimming pool for African Americans.

Another type of public park—the amusement park—also proved to be a popular recreational pursuit for Atlantans in the early twentieth century. One of the most frequently attended of these sites was Ponce de Leon Park, built on the grounds of a nineteenth-century resort and picnic area called Ponce de Leon Springs. In 1906 the Ponce de Leon Park Association spent some fifty thousand dollars converting the resort into a new amusement center complete with midway, skating rink, picnic grounds, and rides. (One year later, the park would also become home to the Atlanta Crackers baseball team.)

Another popular spot, Lakewood Park, located on the southwest side of the city, contained some 375 acres of largely undeveloped woodland and an amusement park since 1894. In 1916 it became the site for a far larger enterprise—the Southeastern Fair. New buildings were constructed within the park to house the fair's many proposed exhibits, shows, and performances, and in its inaugural year, the Southeastern Fair offered visitors art, livestock, agricultural, and farm machinery exhibits; an automobile show; a women's suffrage demonstration; and a fireworks display. Although it would later encounter some tough times during the Depression, the fair survived and continued to be a popular attraction for decades to follow before it finally ceased in 1978.

MUNICIPAL SERVICES

As Atlanta's population increased and its borders expanded during the early twentieth century, the city's municipal services strained to keep

Construction of Atlanta's water and sewer system.

up with the growth. In 1910 more than eighty miles of Atlanta's streets still lacked water mains or sewer lines; two-thirds of the streets were unpaved; sewage disposal in general was inadequate and haphazard; water pressure in the city's lines was frequently too low to fight fires; the city's main public hospital, Grady, could not keep up the increasing demands on its services; and only about one-half of Atlanta's student-age population was enrolled in the city's overcrowded and dilapidated public schools. To help remedy this situation, Atlanta residents passed a $3 million bond issue in 1910, the largest in the city's history to that date. The strain on the city's systems continued, unfortunately, and in 1919 Atlanta attempted to pass an additional bond referendum to upgrade, improve, and extend its municipal services. It took two years to pass.

The thinly spread town resources sharply affected local fire protection. The city's first professional fire department had been organized back in 1882, but the widespread use of flammable building materials, the lack of enforceable fire codes, and problems with the city's water lines handicapped fire-fighting efforts for decades thereafter. In 1917 all of these factors conspired in a horrifying conflagration that proved far more destructive than Sherman's famous leveling of the city during the Civil War.

The Great Fire of 1917 appears to have started around noon on May 21, in an area north of Decatur Street between Fort and Hilliard streets. After wreaking havoc in the surrounding black residential section near Auburn Avenue, the fires swept northeast across Boulevard Avenue and destroyed homes and structures in the white middle-class neighborhood located there. Firefighters from as far away as Birmingham,

PONCE DE LEON APTS.

GEORGAIN TERRACE HOTEL

AUBURN AV.

LYONS AV.

IRWIN ST.

JACKSON ST.

HILLIARD ST.

Aftermath of the Great Fire of 1917.

Columbus, and Chattanooga traveled to Atlanta to help with the battle, but the fire continued to spread until authorities dynamited houses along Ponce de Leon Avenue to establish an effective fire break. The flames lasted ten hours and caused extensive damage to public and private property. Over three hundred acres (fifty blocks) of the city had been leveled by the fire. Within that area, the ashes and rubble from around two thousand buildings lay scattered about while ten thousand people, suddenly without homes, took shelter where they could. The total damage from the fire to public and private property was estimated at $5.5 million.

The city's social welfare programs also proved insufficient to meet the population's growing needs. Atlanta did cover some of the expenses for the indigent at Grady Hospital and cooperated with the state in the operation of the Battle Hill Tuberculosis Hospital and the Confederate Veterans Home. But there were relatively few official city agencies dedicated to assisting the poor and even fewer whose caseload included African Americans. In fact, it was 1908 before the city established its first social service agencies and programs for black Atlantans. In the absence of city assistance, African-American community needs were met (as they had been during the nineteenth century) primarily through the actions of individuals or the programs of a growing array of black self-help, fraternal, and religious organizations. Prominent among these were individuals such as Carrie Steele Logan, who founded the city's first black orphanage in 1889; self-help agencies like the Neighborhood Union, which established health centers, boys' and girls' clubs, and vocational classes for children and lobbied for improved public facilities for African Americans; and fraternal organizations like the Odd Fellows, the Prince Hall Masons, and the Good Samaritans, who raised thousands of dollars for the poor and infirm of the city.

The black churches of Atlanta also helped organize programs to meet the pressing social and economic needs of their communities. The First Congregational Church of Atlanta, under the leadership of Reverend Henry Hugh Proctor, for example, sponsored a home for African-American working women, business and cooking schools, a kindergarten, and an employment bureau. Similar community services and programs were provided by some of the city's other prominent black churches, such as Big Bethel A.M.E. Church and Ebenezer and Wheat Street Baptist churches.

While impoverished white Atlantans may have had more access to city programs and agencies than their black counterparts, Atlanta did not act especially generously to either group. The most active agent for social service was not a city agency at all, but the Community Chest,

The Hebrew Orphans' Home operated from 1889 to 1930.

The Oakland Cemetery gravestone of philanthropist Carrie Steele Logan (1829–1900) is inscribed "The Mother of Orphans. She hath done what she could."

which combined the programs of thirty-nine different local charities. But even the Community Chest's efforts proved insufficient with the Depression looming and demands on the organization increasing. In 1929 more than 197,000 private individuals and families received aid from the Chest. The organization's attempts to raise $480,000 for relief failed, however, and in 1930 Atlanta ranked last among similarly sized cities in terms of its per capita expenditures for welfare programs.

EDUCATION

Public Schools

Public education was another area in which the needs and demands of Atlanta's growing population quickly outstripped the existing facilities. In 1910 only about one-half of the city's student-age population attended school. The absence of a compulsory attendance law, coupled with weak and poorly enforced child-labor regulations, meant that many impoverished children did not go to school, instead assisting their families by working in area mills and factories. The fact that Atlanta did not provide free textbooks to its pupils until the 1920s also discouraged school attendance among the poor. Even those students who did attend the city's public schools frequently had to endure overcrowded, dilapidated, unsanitary structures with budgets as meager as their facilities.

The widespread overcrowding that occurred in Atlanta's public school system during the first decade of the twentieth century meant that most schools utilized double sessions (each lasting part of a day) to accommodate the demand. In 1914, after intense pressure from white, middle-class parents, the city finally eliminated the double sessions and restricted class size to forty-five students in the white public schools. Nevertheless, problems associated with overcrowding, insufficient funding and supplies, and outdated facilities continued to surface during the 1920s and 1930s.

Each of these problems was even more acute in the city's black public schools. Since its establishment in 1872, the Atlanta Board of Education had placed a low value on the education of African Americans. In 1913 the board proposed eliminating the seventh and eight grades altogether in the city's black schools, arguing that such a level of education was unnecessary for students most likely to find future employment as manual laborers. Although this proposal never succeeded, the first public high school for African Americans anywhere in the city was Booker T. Washington High School (which initially also included seventh and eighth grades) which opened on the west side in

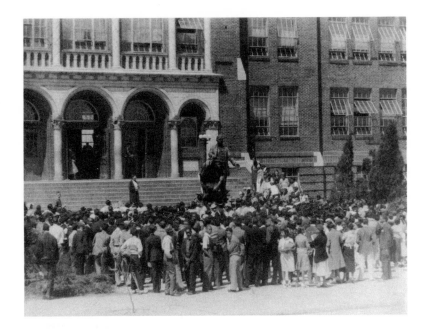

Students in front of Booker T. Washington High School.

1924. Not surprisingly, given the board's orientation, expenditures for the city's black schools remained much lower than the monies allocated for white schools. As late as 1940, for example, the average amount spent on Atlanta's African-American students reached only one-third of the average amount allocated for white students. Black teachers also continued to be paid less than their white counterparts, and the city's black public schools were more likely than white schools to be without kindergartens, auditoriums, gymnasiums, and cafeterias.

That the African-American community in Atlanta was able to secure a public high school for its children at all was primarily due to the organizational skills and growing political strength of the city's black leadership. Since 1892 local Democratic officials had made use of a "white primary" law to effectively restrict voting in primary elections to white males. This ordinance, utilized throughout the South to limit the voting power of African Americans, minimized black influence within the Democratic Party—by far the most dominant and powerful political party in the region. But while African Americans in Atlanta had no voice in primary elections, they could still vote in special elections, such as school bond referendums. In 1902 and again in 1909 the black community supported proposed bond issues in the hope that some of the money would be applied to their schools. The bond issues passed, but the school board refused to allocate additional funds for black schools as requested. In 1917 local NAACP leaders came before the board, asking for improved facilities, but again they were rebuffed. Finally, in 1919, distrustful of city hall and school board promises, black Atlantans used their vote to help defeat two proposed school bond measures. Two years later, when a $4 million school bond referendum again came up for a vote, African American leaders promised support for the measure only if their demands for a new public high school were met. The strategy worked and the city built Booker T. Washington High School in order to pass the bond.

Just how desperately a black public high school was needed and how much it was appreciated by the Atlanta African-American community was quickly evident once Washington High School opened its doors. As the only black secondary school in the metropolitan area, Washington High drew students not just from Atlanta but also from the surrounding communities of East Point, College Park, Decatur, and Marietta. Moreover, since there had been no earlier opportunity for African-American students to progress past elementary school (except through tuition-based classes at Atlanta University), some of the first students at Washington were well beyond the normal age range for its classes. Thus several eighteen- and nineteen-year-olds enrolled in the school's seventh- and eighth-grade classes, and some students in upper-level grades were the same age as their teachers.

Race was not the only factor that served to segregate Atlanta's public schools in the early twentieth century. Many of the city's public schools were also divided by gender and curriculum. Boy's High School and Girl's High School, both founded in 1872, were the flagships of the Atlanta school system and featured a rigorous curriculum of classics, mathematics, and languages. Tech High, founded in 1909 for boys, took a more vocationally oriented position, although it featured college prep courses as well. Commercial High School, established six years later, gave an education similar to Tech's. It was also the city's first coeducational high school. When Booker T. Washington High finally opened in 1924, it incorporated all of the features of Atlanta's four white high schools, providing both academic and vocational training in a coeducational setting. Students at Washington High not only took courses in biology, chemistry, physics, math (algebra, trigonometry, and calculus), English composition, history, and economics, but were also offered training in such areas as tailoring, brick masonry, home nursing, cooking, and cafeteria management.

The appointment of Dr. Willis A. Sutton (former principal of Tech High) to the position of city school superintendent in 1921 and changes in the city's approach to public education brought about additional reforms in Atlanta's public schools. Sutton, who later became president of the National Education Association, encouraged and supported the introduction of new subjects, such as music (including bands, orchestras, and vocal choirs), arts, crafts, and drama into the school's curriculum. He also mitigated the widespread and frequent use of corporal punishment by teachers and administrators. The passage of a compulsory school attendance law in 1920, coupled with the distribution of free textbooks and strengthened child labor laws later in the decade, dramatically improved another problem area for Atlanta's schools. By 1940 approximately ninety percent of the city's school-age children were enrolled in school.

These progressive changes, however, could do little to ameliorate the biggest challenges to Atlanta's public school system in the 1920s and 1930s—continued overcrowding and shrinking financial resources. At Washington High, for example, temporary wooden structures housed an overflow student population and double sessions were reintroduced in order to accommodate growing student demand in the 1930s. The tremendous increase in students at Washington and other schools in Atlanta put additional strain on an already financially distressed system. Despite city charter amendments in 1918 and 1922 that guaranteed a fixed percentage of municipal revenues for the public school system, the Atlanta Board of Education continued to run out of funds. As the situation worsened during the Depression, teachers took a series of drastic pay cuts. Eventually, the city could not pay the teachers at all and instead issued them scrip—promissory notes that the city would pay them when it was able. Fortunately for the teachers, Rich's department store agreed to accept the scrip for cash, an action that earned the store the undying loyalty of many city employees.

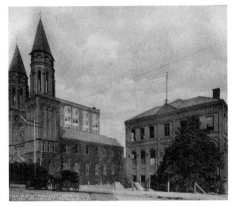

Left to right: Sacred Heart Church and Marist College on Ivy Street, currently Peachtree Center Avenue.

Private Schools

At the same time that Atlanta's public school system was experiencing growing pains, a number of private educational institutions were also emerging within the metropolitan area. In 1900, for example, the Georgia Military Academy opened in College Park with a student enrollment of forty and a faculty comprised of Colonel John C. Woodward and one assistant. Later the school was renamed Woodward Academy and a junior college department was added to its offerings. Another military day school, Marist College, founded in 1901 by the Marist Order of the Roman Catholic Church, located itself in downtown Atlanta. Eight years later, the North Avenue Presbyterian School, which several decades later would establish a college preparatory school for boys named Westminster, was opened.

Cox College and Conservatory, an all-women's university in College Park.

129

A number of other private colleges and universities also found a home in the budding metropolis. Oglethorpe University, which had once been located in downtown Atlanta but which had closed its doors in 1872 due to financial difficulties, reemerged in 1916 at a new location along Peachtree Road in the city's suburbs (where it remains today). Dr. Thornwell Jacobs, a minister and grandson of an Oglethorpe mathematics professor, succeeded in raising almost half a million dollars to fund the school's construction. He also managed to enlist the generous support of William Randolph Hearst, the nationally known newspaper magnate and owner of the *Atlanta Georgian* newspaper. Over a thirty-year period, Hearst contributed more than $400,000 to the school and helped Oglethorpe gain control of four hundred acres of land surrounding the university, including Silver Lake, which was renamed Lake Phoebe in honor of Hearst's mother.

Emory University also moved its campus to the Atlanta area. And, as in the case of Oglethorpe, a millionaire played an important role in the school's move. This time the benefactor was Asa G. Candler, owner and guiding force of the Coca-Cola Company.

In 1913 the General Conference of the Methodist Episcopal Church decided it needed a new university in the region and established an educational commission to pursue the matter. Two brothers on the commission—Warren A. Candler and Asa Candler—took the lead in seeing that the new university was located in Atlanta and that a transplanted Emory College (originally located in Oxford, Georgia) formed the basis of the university's "academic department." (Warren Candler, a Methodist bishop and chair of the commission, had earlier served as president of Emory College, and his older brother, Asa, had been selected as a trustee for the school.)

To help seal the school's move to Atlanta and its selection as the conference's new university, Asa Candler pledged $1 million to endow the school and seventy-five acres of land in the emerging subdivision of Druid Hills as the site for the university's campus. Persuaded by these generous offers, Emory moved to its new home in 1919, where schools of theology, medicine, and law were soon in operation. (The liberal arts division of the school remained for the time being in Oxford, although it would later relocate to Atlanta as well. Emory at Oxford remains a two-year liberal arts college). Bishop Warren Candler served as the first chancellor of the new university.

Eight years later another theological school relocated to the Atlanta area when the Columbia Theological Seminary established its present-day campus in Decatur. Columbia had begun its existence in Lexington, Georgia, as the Theological Seminary of the (Presbyterian)

Synod of South Carolina and Georgia, but had moved to Columbia, South Carolina, shortly after its founding. In the 1920s, a campaign was undertaken to relocate the school to a more central location in the region, and the $500,000 raised in the Atlanta area for equipment and endowment directed the seminary to the city's environs.

TENSIONS AMIDST THE GROWTH

The 1906 Race Riot

As the first decades of the twentieth century unfolded, the promise of new jobs and opportunities brought thousands of newcomers to Atlanta. But undercurrents of tension in this period of rapid growth manifested themselves in periodic outbursts of violence and hostility.

One of the earliest and most violent of these episodes was the 1906 race riot (ironically, the same year that Atlanta hosted the annual conference of the recently formed National Negro Business League). A long and bitter campaign for governor in which the victor, Hoke Smith, the one-time president and publisher of the *Atlanta Journal*, called for the disfranchisement of black citizens through a constitutional amendment fomented racial agitation. His opponent, Clark Howell, a former editor of the *Atlanta Constitution*, also publicly opposed black political "equity" but felt that the white primary system was a sufficient guard against such a "threat." One month after Smith's election, the city erupted in the worst race riot in its history. On the heels of incendiary news reports alleging black assaults on white women, angry white mobs (numbering as large as ten thousand) roamed the downtown indiscriminately attacking black citizens on the streets, in streetcars, and even in their homes and businesses. The rioting began the evening of Saturday, September 22, and lasted until the following Tuesday. The state militia had to be used to restore order under martial law.

It is difficult to determine how many Atlantans lost their lives in this riot, as the estimates of the numbers killed and wounded vary widely among contemporary accounts. The official total (which is probably far too low) was twelve dead—ten black and two white; and seventy injured—sixty black and ten white. Less uncertainty, however, surrounds the impact of this disturbance on black housing and business patterns in the city. The riot clearly hastened the city's move toward the economic exclusion and residential segregation of African Americans. Following the riot, those African Americans who remained in the city were most likely to settle in established black communities, particularly those located on the eastern fringe of downtown in the Old Fourth Ward or on the west side of the city near Atlanta University. And black

The Georgia State Militia was called out during the 1906 race riot.

businesses, some of which had once been interspersed among white commercial ventures on Peachtree Street, were now increasingly located to the east along Auburn Avenue.

Modest efforts to promote racial understanding followed in the wake of the riot, culminating in the formation of the Commission on Interracial Cooperation (CIC) in 1919. An offshoot of the CIC was the Association of Southern Women for the Prevention of Lynching (ASWPL), organized by Jessie Daniel Ames (chair of the Texas Interracial Commission) in 1930 and based in Atlanta. Neither of these interracial organizations, however, struck at or challenged the under-lying premise of Jim Crow—that blacks and whites should remain sep-arate. The ASWPL, for example, did not even include black women among its members.

As the century progressed, efforts to segregate African Americans in Atlanta continued and expanded. In 1913 Atlanta became the first city in Georgia to attempt to extend segregation to housing patterns through use of a residential segregation ordinance. Although this law was struck down by the Georgia Supreme Court two years later, the Atlanta City Council passed a similar statute in 1917 (that was also later ruled unconstitutional) and in 1922 hired an urban planner from Cleveland, Ohio, to draw up a comprehensive zoning ordinance for the city that included residential zones based upon race. This zoning plan received the support of the state legislature and was even strengthened by a 1928 amendment to the Georgia constitution that allowed residential zoning. Although Atlanta's racial zoning plan was eventually struck down by the state supreme court, this defeat did not spell the end of segregated residential districts in the city. Instead, for the next few decades, the city would maintain Jim Crow segregation through extralegal pressures and the equally effective tool of restrictive covenants—agreements between private parties or property owners that established limitations on the sale of property to particular groups—most notably African Americans and Jews.

The Leo Frank Trial and Atlanta's Jewish Community

The 1906 race riot had exposed some of the racial tensions present in early-twentieth-century Atlanta. Less than a decade later, another violent episode in the city's history—the trial and lynching of Leo Frank—brought to the surface growing class and religious antagonisms that were in turn linked to dramatic changes taking place in the city's population and labor force.

Leo Frank (1884–1916).

Industrialization and urbanization combined early in the century to swell Atlanta's population and remake its workforce. Drawn by the lure of employment in the city's factories and businesses, thousands of men and women flocked to Atlanta during the first two decades of the century, doubling the city's population in the process. As the pool of available applicants for jobs broadened, the makeup of the workforce also changed. One of the most obvious changes was the increased presence of women in the workplace. By 1920, forty-two percent of all Atlanta women aged sixteen and older had joined the workforce (a rate of female employment exceeded only in Washington, D.C., and in the Massachusetts textile cities of Fall River, Lowell, and New Bedford). Even more significant was the number of white women entering the job market during this period. In 1900 this group made up only twenty-eight percent of the total number of female wage earners in Atlanta; by 1920 they comprised forty-eight percent of the total and were present in great numbers in fields such as clerical and textile work. Atlanta's black female wage earners, on the other hand, found fewer and fewer opportunities for work in the city's factories and businesses, and instead found themselves increasingly confined to laundry and domestic work.

The opportunities for employment and business growth in turn-of-the-century Atlanta also drew newcomers from abroad, including an increasing number of Jewish immigrants from Eastern Europe. Jews had been present in Atlanta since its beginnings and had

Lynching of Leo Frank, Marietta, 1916.

played an important role in the city's business, civic, and political life. Jewish residents, for example, were responsible for establishing such important local businesses as Rich's department store and the Fulton Bag and Cotton Mill and had played a leading role in developing the city's public school system, establishing Grady Hospital and the Piedmont Sanitorium (later Piedmont Hospital), and bringing the grand opera to Atlanta. Despite their small numbers (less than three percent of the total population in 1910), Atlanta Jews had also played a prominent role in the city's politics. About a dozen Jewish leaders held political office in Atlanta in the period from 1874 to 1911. The most prominent of these politicians, Aaron Haas, served as councilman, alderman, and mayor pro tem (the city's first in 1875).

At the turn of the century the composition of the Jewish community in Atlanta began to change. Traditionally, most of the Jewish residents in Atlanta had emigrated from Western Europe—particularly Germany. In 1880, 600 of the 612 Jews in the city were German. During the next decade, however, an increasing number of Jewish immigrants arrived from Russia and other Eastern European locales. By 1896 there were already 317 Russian Jews in the city, most of them living and working around Decatur Street. Beginning in 1911 a third group of Jews immigrated to Atlanta. Most of these new residents were Sephardic Jews from Turkey and the Greek Isle of Rhodes. This influx of new settlers from Eastern Europe and the old Ottoman Empire not only increased the number of Jews in Atlanta, but also dramatically altered the makeup of the Jewish community. By 1910 the German Jewish population in the city stood at fourteen hundred; the number of Jewish residents from Eastern Europe totaled twenty-four hundred (one-third of Atlanta's entire foreign-born population).

The differences between Atlanta's traditional Jewish community and the new immigrants were reflected in a myriad of ways. Most of the German Jews were members of the Reform branch of Judaism and emphasized the importance of assimilation into the larger Atlanta community, even conducting their synagogue services in English. The newly arrived Eastern European Jews, on the other hand, tended to be Orthodox in their religious beliefs, with customs and languages that were alien to many Atlantans. Finally, the Sephardic Jews brought with them customs, speech, and religious practices that differed from both the German and the Eastern European communities. Social barriers erected between the groups further underscored the various religious divisions within the Jewish community. The prestigious Standard Club, for example, established by the German Jews in 1904, refused membership to either the city's Eastern European or Sephardic

Jews. The older German community also tended to resent the unwillingness or inability of the new Jewish immigrant groups to assimilate and feared that their "distinctiveness" might jeopardize the position and influence of the more established Jewish community.

Despite the several distinctive groups within the city's Jewish community, many non-Jewish Atlantans tended to view the Jewish population as a monolithic whole and some even blamed the Jews, a few of whom owned or managed some of the city's largest mills and factories, for the various "evils" of industrialization (including the employment of vulnerable white southern women). As nativist and anti-Semitic opinions gained prominence in the early twentieth century, this bigotry found expression in a number of venues—editorials, cartoons, vaudeville acts, and even movies playing in Atlanta. But none of those events could compare in intensity or importance to the actions of the public during the trial of Leo Frank.

In July 1913 Leo Frank, a prominent member of the German Jewish community and a National Pencil Company superintendent, was arrested and charged with assaulting and murdering a thirteen-year-old, white female employee named Mary Phagan.

In a highly charged atmosphere marked by sensationalistic press coverage and virulent anti-Semitism, the court found Frank guilty and sentenced him to death. (Ironically, the prosecution's chief witness against Leo Frank was James Conley, a black custodian in the factory, and Frank's trial was the first occurrence in Georgia in which the testimony of a black man was used to convict a white man.) As national Jewish organizations rushed to Frank's defense, the case quickly became a national and international *cause célèbre*. Frank's lawyers continued to appeal the conviction, citing the mob atmosphere during the trial, but in April 1915 the U.S. Supreme Court denied a plea to reverse the decision, and upheld Frank's sentence. His lawyers had also appealed to Governor John M. Slaton, however, to commute Frank's sentence, and on June 21, 1915 (two days before his term ended), Governor Slaton changed Frank's sentence to life imprisonment.

Local reaction to the commutation was quick and, in many instances, hostile. Tom Watson, editor of *The Jeffersonian* and a future U.S. senator from Georgia, declared in his newspaper that the governor had sold out to the Jews and urged Atlantans to lynch Frank and "get the governor." Some apparently took Watson's advice to heart, and two companies of the National Guard as well as county police had to be called out to protect the governor's Buckhead mansion. In the process, twenty-six men carrying pistols and dynamite were arrested. Slaton escaped injury (by leaving the country for an extended European vacation), but Leo Frank was less fortunate. On the evening of August 16, twenty-five armed men who called themselves the Knights of Mary Phagan broke into his jail cell at Milledgeville, took him to Marietta, and lynched him at Frey's Gin, near the neighborhood where Mary Phagan had lived.

The Resurgence of the Ku Klux Klan

The impact of the Leo Frank trial and lynching was felt on the local, regional, and national level. The publicity surrounding the case, for example, helped establish the fame and reputations of some individuals who were only peripherally associated with the trial, including Tom Watson and country musician Fiddlin' John Carson, whose song "The Ballad of Mary Phagan" soon grew into a regional classic. The case also brought about changes at the factory where Mary Phagan and Leo Frank had worked. Following the trial, Sigmund Montag, owner of the National Pencil Company, shifted to a predominately male, African-American workforce (which, in turn, gave way to an increasingly black female workforce during World War I). Finally, the case directly contributed to the growth of two disparate but significant national organizations—the Anti-Defamation League of B'nai B'rith and a revived and reinvigorated Ku Klux Klan.

On Thanksgiving Day 1915 (some four months after Leo Frank's murder), thirty-four men gathered atop Stone Mountain to bring back to life the Reconstruction-era vigilante organization known as the Ku Klux Klan. A few weeks later, the group made use of the Atlanta showing of D. W. Griffith's classic film *Birth of a Nation* to both publicize their cause and increase their local membership. Draped in sheets and mounted on horseback, the founding members of the recreated KKK paraded down Peachtree Street on December 6, 1915, firing guns into the air and exhorting their white brethren to help "save, reform, and protect" the South. How much Griffith's film, which glorified the exploits of the earlier Ku Klux Klan and vilified black southerners' attempts to gain political and social equality, contributed to the contemporary organization's growth is difficult to gauge. But it is clear that the film struck a resonant chord among white audiences in Atlanta. The Atlanta Theater, where the film ran, held the movie over for an unprecedented second and third week, and local journalists estimated that nineteen thousand Atlantans saw the film during the first week alone (with up to one thousand people being turned away at each matinee showing) and that thirty-five thousand—about one-fourth of the city's white population—had seen the film by the end of the second week.

Even more dramatic than the large numbers of white Atlantans who saw the film was the reaction of these viewers to Griffith's story. Atlanta film critics described scenes in which audience members (and the critics themselves) cheered, clapped, and jumped to their feet in either approval or indignation. One showing of the film, attended by more than a hundred Confederate veterans, even elicited authentic rebel yells from the audience.

Led by William J. Simmons, a former preacher and organizer for a national fraternal order called the Woodmen of the World, the revived Ku Klux Klan quickly grew and spread its nativist message of opposition to Judaism, Catholicism, and racial equality. The KKK also operated in many localities as a vigilante enforcer of local morality, selectively punishing drunkards, adulterers, and wife beaters in addition to terrorizing African Americans. By 1924 the Klan had expanded far beyond its southern base with "Klaverns," or branches, in almost every northern state and a reported national membership of six million.

Locally, the Klan was a very prominent force during the 1920s and 1930s. Atlanta served as the headquarters or "Imperial City" of the Invisible Empire for almost a decade after the Klan's inception, and in 1921 the Klan purchased an elegant home at the corner of Peachtree Road and East Wesley Road that served as its "Imperial Palace." By 1923 membership in the city's Nathan Bedford Forrest Klan No. 1 stood at over fifteen thousand and included notable Atlanta businessmen, educators, members of the clergy, judges, policemen, and politicians. Although the Klan's influence waned somewhat in the late 1920s, the tensions and economic uncertainties of the Depression kept the organization alive, and it remained a powerful extralegal force in the city, dedicated to maintaining and enforcing Jim Crow restrictions and practices.

Ku Klux Klan rally.

THE NEW WOMAN

Despite the efforts of organizations like the Ku Klux Klan to promote and maintain a nineteenth-century southern racial and social order, the traditional roles and status of southern women were clearly changing in the early twentieth century. The entrance of more Atlanta women into the workforce and women's involvement in temperance, education, and prison reform movements accompanied calls for political equality and voting rights for women. These demands for equal suffrage, it should be noted, had both a classist and a racist cast to them. The women's organizations and suffrage societies that lobbied most actively for the vote consisted primarily of white, urban women of the middle and upper classes. In the city's separate black women's

Ardent prohibitionist Mary Harris Armour was nicknamed the "Georgia Cyclone."

Parading in 1913 were advocates of woman suffrage. The Atlanta group's effort succeeded when the city granted women the right to vote in local elections even before universal suffrage was granted by the Nineteenth Amendment to the U.S. Constitution.

organizations there was little support of or interest in the suffrage question. To be sure, some individual leaders (like Lugenia Burns Hope) were suffrage sympathizers, but many other African-American women appear to have viewed the equal suffrage campaign as a white woman's issue. And even those local black women who did support the movement realized that their power as voters would be limited by the same Jim Crow laws and discriminatory restrictions that served to disfranchise black males.

The equal suffrage movement in Atlanta had its beginnings in the late nineteenth century. In 1894 a woman suffrage league formed, and the following year the National American Woman Suffrage Association, led by Susan B. Anthony, held its annual meeting in Atlanta. In 1902 a formal request was made to the Atlanta City Council to grant women the right to vote; the council rejected the request. The issue did not die, however, and instead gained both local and national momentum. In 1913 two more woman suffrage organizations appeared in the city—the Georgia Equal Suffrage League and the Georgia Men's League for Woman Suffrage. Success for the suffragists finally arrived in May 1919 when the Democratic Executive Committee of Atlanta voted 24–1 to give women the vote in municipal elections. The following month, an amendment to the U.S. Constitution granting women the franchise was sent to the state for approval. The Georgia legislature voted against the proposal (and did not officially ratify the amendment until 1970), but the Nineteenth Amendment to the U.S. Constitution became law anyway, taking effect on August 20, 1920.

LABOR STRIKES

Urbanization, industrialization, and the growth of a permanent working class did more than just intensify class and religious antagonisms within the city. These forces also raised important questions regarding the rights of workers, the responsibilities of employers, and the duties of unions in labor/management negotiations. These and related issues increasingly became matters of public debate as a series of labor strikes broke out in Atlanta's textile, streetcar, and automobile manufacturing industries during the first four decades of the twentieth century.

In Atlanta, as elsewhere in the industrialized South, textile mills became the locus of much labor unrest. Walkouts and work stoppages occurred in mills throughout the region as labor attempted to secure better pay and working conditions. Despite the assistance of national labor unions and the sympathetic writings of journalists, who focused their attention on the large number of women and children employed

The Fulton Bag and Cotton Mill, founded in 1889, employed many Cabbagetown men, women, and even children (until the Fair Labor Standards Act was passed in 1938 banning child labor).

in the industry, these strikes were largely unsuccessful. Atlanta had few laws to guide or control negotiations, and employers (particularly in urban areas) could frequently draw from a ready pool of unemployed labor to replace striking workers. The 1914 strike at Atlanta's Fulton Bag and Cotton Mill, the city's largest textile mill, was in many ways characteristic of this trend.

Fulton Bag and Cotton formed in 1889 under the ownership of Jacob Elsas, who built houses for his employees in an area first known as "The Factory Lot" and later as "Cabbagetown." By 1914 the mill had branch offices throughout the country and employed some thirteen hundred people in its Atlanta factory—thirty-five percent of whom were women and twelve percent of whom were boys and girls under sixteen years of age.

The first stirrings of labor unrest at the mill occurred in October 1913 when several hundred weavers and loom fixers staged a work stoppage to protest both the firing of a loom fixer and the management's decision to require an even longer period of notice prior to quitting. According to the contracts employees signed, the company was not responsible for work-related injuries and could discharge workers at any time. Employees, on the other hand, were financially responsible for damage to machinery, could be fined for minor infractions, and were required to give notice before they quit or risk forfeiting a week's wages.

In May 1914 workers at Fulton Bag and Cotton Mill again walked

(Right and below) *Workers were detained by the Georgia National Guard at Fort McPherson during the textile strike of 1934.*

off their jobs, this time to protest Elsa's firing of union employees. Initially, the strikers demanded only the reinstatement of the discharged workers, but as the strike continued, their requests multiplied to include calls for higher wages, shorter hours, an end to child labor, and termination of the dreaded labor contracts.

The United Textile Workers Union of America (UTW), which had formed Local No. 886 at the mill in the wake of the 1913 work stoppage, sent organizers to the city (as did the American Federation of Labor) and set up tents to house those evicted from their jobs and their factory-owned homes. Journalists and local organizations like the Men and Religion Forward Movement focused public attention on the plight of women and child laborers and demanded of mill employers a "living wage" that would enable a man to support his wife and children and keep them out of the factories. Despite this attention and support, the strike eventually collapsed, and in May 1915, the UTW closed its camps and admitted defeat.

In 1934 another, much larger textile strike met with a similar end when workers in the mills of Atlanta and throughout the region took part in a nationwide strike to protest violations of the National Industrial Recovery Act. Thus, while New Deal legislation brought about the national recognition of unions and gave workers the right to organize, poor working conditions, low wages, and a decidedly hostile anti-union climate continued to predominate in most mills in Atlanta and elsewhere throughout the South.

There were areas of union strength in Atlanta, particularly in the transportation industries, where workers were a bit more successful during the early twentieth century in gaining better working conditions and recognition of their unions. In 1916 hundreds of Atlanta streetcar workers walked off their jobs, launching one of the most tumultuous strikes in the city's history. In the ensuing labor dispute, which was marked by violence (including a wave of dynamiting), the workers did not achieve their immediate demands, but they did gain widening public support and even influenced local elections. Two years later, another, more successful strike of streetcar operatives occurred. After National War Labor Board hearings on the strike in 1919, the local streetcar company signed a contract with Local No. 732, reinstated some of the union men who had been fired, and agreed to improve working conditions. Two years later the Amalgamated Association of Street and Electric Employees of America held its international convention in Atlanta depicting the importance of the earlier labor victories.

As significant as these two streetcar strikes were, it was a work stoppage in a local General Motors plant in 1936 that had the most far-reaching impact. On November 18, 1936, workers at the Lakewood General Motors and Fisher body plants shut down the assembly lines while demanding different pay scales, better working hours, overtime pay, and negotiations between management and the United Automobile Workers Union (Local No. 34). Following the assembly line shutdown, workers in the plant stayed in the building, occupying the factory overnight and into the next morning. The workers finally exited after receiving assurances from management that the factory would not resume operations until the labor issues could be resolved. This historic occasion marked the first sit-down strike in the automobile industry and launched a series of General Motors plant closings and strikes across the nation, culminating in the famous Flint, Michigan, sit-down strike in 1937. The local strike at the Lakewood plant lasted a little more than three months and ended when management finally agreed to recognize the local union. Changes in pay and working conditions followed shortly thereafter.

TRANSPORTATION

The Railroad

The same transportation industries that experienced strikes and labor unrest in the early twentieth century also worked to transform the spatial and residential layout of Atlanta. The railroads were the reason for Atlanta's founding and spurred the growth of the city both before and after the Civil War. Even as late as the 1920s, they remained the city's foremost employer, pumping an estimated $100 million a year into the local economy. The railroads also transported products and people to and from Atlanta, securing the city's position and reputation as a major regional transportation center. Rail lines such as Seaboard Air-Line (between Birmingham and Atlanta) and the Louisville and Nashville linked up with the city during this period and increased both Atlanta's passenger and freight loads. New and impressive railroad stations were built to handle this increasing business—Terminal Station in 1905 and Union Station in 1930. By 1927 some 326 passenger trains alone passed through Atlanta each day.

Streetcar Suburbs

As important as railroads were to Atlanta's economy and growth during the first half of the twentieth century, it was the newer and emerging forms of transportation, such as electric streetcars, automobiles, and airplanes, that would have the greatest impact on the city's layout and future development. The emergence of electric streetcars in the late nineteenth and early twentieth century spurred the development of the city's earliest suburban communities. Joel Hurt, a civil engineer and realtor, played a prominent role in this development, helping to found not only the Atlanta and Edgewood Street Railroad Company in 1886 but also the East Atlanta Land Company, which laid out, promoted, and constructed Inman Park—the city's first planned suburban community. A number of the city's elite, including Asa Candler, lived in Inman Park and commuted to the city via the streetcar line that Hurt's company had constructed along Edgewood Avenue. Other streetcar lines served the emerging elite communities of Druid Hills (designed by famed landscape architect Frederick Law Olmsted) and Ansley Park. By 1913 the city's extensive streetcar system, owned and operated by Georgia Railway and Power Company (later Georgia Power), carried over fifty-seven million passengers a year and served not only upper-class suburban communities, but also working-class neighborhoods, industrial and commercial sectors, and the city's expanding parks and recreational areas. Trolley lines also played an important role in Atlanta's preparations for World War I. Camp Gordon, a U.S. army camp and processing center, was erected in 1917 on a two-thousand-acre tract of land east of Atlanta in Chamblee. Both a rail line and the Peachtree Street streetcar line reached the camp which housed 150,000 soldiers during the war. These streetcars provided a much needed system of convenient public transportation.

Union Station opened in 1930.

The Automobile

Another form of transit was already developing that would challenge and eventually supplant the streetcar as the preferred means of transportation—the automobile. It was the automobile as well that did the most to hasten the move to the suburbs and redraw Atlanta's residential "color line." By the 1930s two major population shifts existed in the metropolitan area: a movement of middle- and upper-class white Atlantans to the north side of town and a migration of black Atlantans from the east to the west side of the city.

Despite the impact of the railroad and the streetcar, Atlanta, at the turn of the century was, in many ways, still a pedestrian town. City administrators continued to pay far more attention to the construction and maintenance of sidewalks than they did to the paving of streets. In fact, before 1905 there were actually more paved sidewalks in Atlanta than paved streets, as almost seventy percent of the city's two hundred miles of streets remained unpaved. (By way of contrast, only thirty percent of New York City's streets were unpaved and just two percent of Boston's).

Atlanta was also a relatively small city in terms of geographical size, especially in comparison to the northern metropolises that the city hoped to emulate. In 1903 Atlanta's eleven-square-mile land area was about one-quarter the size of Boston's and one-thirtieth the size of New York's. (The size and shape of the city was approximately the same as Boston's in 1850.)

The growing popularity of the automobile began to change all this. The city and its environs expanded, new roads were built and

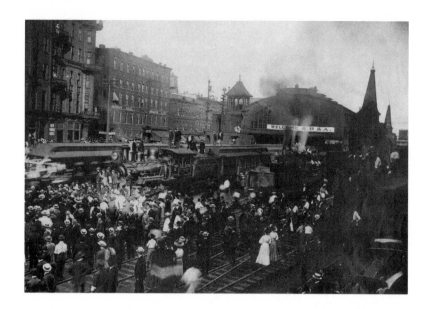

Union Depot on the occasion of the running of the "Atlanta Chamber of Commerce Special," the first regular passenger train of the Atlanta division of the Atlanta, Birmingham & Atlantic Railroad; June, 1908.

paved, the downtown became elevated via the construction of viaducts, and the elite and middle classes, seeking to escape the noise, congestion, and pollution of downtown Atlanta, increasingly began to fill in the suburban areas beyond the reach of the railroad or streetcar.

Atlanta's love affair with the automobile appears to have begun in 1901 when bicycle dealer William D. Alexander purchased three primitive 650-pound steam-driven Locomobiles that he had shipped to the city. The cars had to be assembled upon arrival and operated without headlamps, top, or horn. For the most part, they resembled carriages and were propelled by a steam engine mounted to the axle. Alexander's maiden nine-mile journey took two hours to complete, but despite the slow speed and primitive design of the vehicle, the automobile was in Atlanta to stay. Within eight years, there were thirty-five car dealerships in the city offering customers a wide range of makes, including Pierce-Arrow, Premier, Cartercar, Maxwell, Hupmobile, Silent Selden, Hudson, Stearns, Pullman, Lambert, and Ford. From 1917 to 1926 Atlantans could also purchase a Hanson Six, which was produced locally by former wholesale grocer George W. Hanson and sold for one thousand dollars.

The presence of the automobile in Atlanta added greatly to the traffic congestion and safety problems in the city. As noted earlier, a great number of trains made their way into and through Atlanta's central business district each day. These trains brought not only passengers and freight but also noise and pollution, and grade-level crossings,

Terminal Station opened in 1905.

where city streets met rail lines, proved to be increasingly dangerous and congested. As automobiles appeared and multiplied, traffic and safety problems became even more acute, and Atlanta leaders began entertaining the idea of constructing a series of viaducts to bridge the noisy and dangerous downtown railroad chasm.

In 1909 the Atlanta Aldermanic Board and the Chamber of Commerce brought up the possibility of hiding the unsightly railroad lines by constructing a long axial mall some forty feet above the tracks where shoppers and workers could stroll along a pedestrian concourse flanked by palatial buildings. A similar (but even more elaborate) scheme arrived in the city seven years later by a New York engineering firm, but neither this nor the earlier "Bleckley Plan" (designed by local architect Haralson Bleckley) ever got off the drawing board.

However, congestion increased, as did the pressure to do something about it. In 1917 Mayor Asa Candler attempted to gain the support of the various railroads and property owners for the construction of a system of viaducts over the tracks. Four years passed before the city finally approved the plan through passage of a bond referendum. Construction of Atlanta's first viaduct for nonpedestrian traffic began in late 1921, and two years later the Spring Street viaduct, which linked Spring Street on the south with Madison Avenue on the north, was complete. It would take five more years, another bond referendum, and contributions from the railroads and Georgia Power totaling about $1.25 million before the Pryor Street and Central Avenue viaducts

Looking west, Railroad Plaza and viaducts from Central to Broad streets, 1938.

The many modes of early-twentieth-century transportation in Atlanta.

would be completed with lateral viaduct connections to Hunter (now Martin Luther King Jr. Drive), Alabama, and Wall streets.

The impact of the automobile not only spurred the elevation of the city's downtown, but also influenced the dispersal of Atlanta's population into the city's suburbs. As Atlantans in the mid-1920s began to seek suburban retreats farther away from the center of the city (and from the reaches of existing street-railway tracks), the motor vehicle increasingly became the preferred means of transportation. By 1930 the electric streetcar had fallen victim to the more flexible and convenient automobile and bus, and expanded (and paved) roads began to link the suburban hinterlands with the central city and Atlanta with other cities in the state and region.

One of the most dramatic changes wrought by the appearance of the automobile was a suburban real estate boom that completely restructured Atlanta's residential patterns. Before the automobile, Atlanta's residential neighborhoods were highly centralized. Between 1910 and 1930, however, increased commercialization in the downtown area, growing population throughout the city, and a severe shortage of housing generated a demand among the middle class for decentralized residences in less congested areas outside the city limits. The result was suburban residential expansion and the construction of a ring of bungalow-style houses (one-story structures that usually featured five to eight rooms on modest lots) surrounding Atlanta in a perimeter two to five miles from downtown. Included in this ring were Home Park and Virginia-Highland to the north; Candler Park/Edgewood to the east; Sylvan Hills and West End on the south; and Washington Park to the west.

The arrival of the automobile also brought about a dramatic shift in the residential distribution of Atlanta's white elite. In 1900 Atlanta's white, upper-class families lived within a few blocks of the financial and cultural institutions in the center of the city. Between 1910 and 1930, however, these families began to move farther north. By 1930 approximately forty-seven percent of Atlantans listed in the *Social Register* lived north of Ansley Park. This northward trek also greatly contributed to the growth of the Buckhead community, which grew from a population of 2,603 in 1920 to 10,356 ten years later.

On the other side of the color line, some suburbanization also occurred, particularly on the west side, where Heman Perry (founder of the Service Realty Company and a dozen related corporations that purchased, subdivided, and sold undeveloped land; provided financing for homeowners; and constructed houses) developed the black residential community of Washington Park. Despite the success of this project, which helped establish the west side of Atlanta as an area for black residential growth and expansion following World War II, suburbanization in Atlanta during this period remained, for the most part, "lily white." As a result, racial distance and separation in Atlanta was now not only political and social, it was increasingly spatial as well.

The Airplane

The automobile was not the only new mode of transportation that had an impact on Atlanta during the first half of the twentieth century. The airplane made its appearance in the city in the 1920s, and by the end of the decade, Atlanta had an airfield, a terminal, a series of air mail and passenger routes, and an early connection with the airline industry that would serve the city well in the future. A young city councilman and future mayor of Atlanta, William B. Hartsfield, brought much of this important business to the city.

Hartsfield was elected to the Atlanta City Council in 1922 and received the chair of the council's aviation committee the following year. At that time, Candler Field, which featured a two-mile auto speedway and racetrack, served as the informal center of the city's limited aviation activities. In 1925 Asa Candler offered the city a five-year lease on the field in return for a waiver of property taxes. Hartsfield, at the urging of Mayor Walter Sims, surveyed the site and other potential airfield locations around the city (by air and by car) and convinced the city to accept Candler's proposal. While many Atlantans

Terminal at Atlanta Municipal Airport.

intially considered this expenditure a folly, Hartsfield recognized the potential value of establishing Atlanta as a regional center of aviation, and he played an instrumental role in securing the selection of Atlanta in 1928 as the southern terminal for an air mail route from New York to the Southeast and as a drop-off point for a national east-west air mail route two years later. In 1929 the city purchased Candler Field for $94,500, and within a year Pittcairn Aviation was making both mail and passenger runs out of Atlanta Municipal Airport at Candler Field.

The growing connection between Atlanta and the emerging aviation industry continued in the 1930s. In 1931 the city opened America's first air passenger terminal, and seven years later it built the nation's first air traffic control tower. Once William B. Hartsfield became mayor in 1936 (a post he would hold for twenty-four of the next twenty-six years), the city's importance as a regional air center was certain. (Atlanta's Hartsfield International Airport, today one of the busiest and largest airports in the world, fittingly bears his name.)By the eve of World War II, Atlanta was the center of an impressive network of rail and air lines. The construction of a highway link to Savannah in 1935 and Georgia's first "super-highway" running between Atlanta and Marietta in 1938 also established the city's importance as a regional trucking center. In the decades to follow, these links would expand and grow in importance as Atlanta established its preeminent position as the transportation capital of the Southeast.

THE GREAT DEPRESSION

Local Relief Programs

The growth and prosperity that characterized Atlanta during the early decades of the twentieth century was interrupted by a severe economic depression that gripped the nation in the 1930s. And like many cities in the South, Atlanta could not adequately handle the emergency. Atlanta ranked last among similarly sized cities in 1930 in its per capita expenditures for welfare, and few municipal agencies or programs existed to help the rapidly growing number of unemployed. In 1932 thousands of hunger demonstrators marched on the Fulton County Courthouse to demand food and to protest a proposed plan by the county to slash its relief appropriations by one-third. Influenced by the turnout, the county commissioners instead voted to increase the relief budget to $6,000. Despite this increase and the establishment of other local relief efforts—such as Fulton County's "self-help" program, which offered $1.25 toward groceries and a free lunch in return for work, and the Atlanta Chamber of Commerce's ill-fated "back to the farm" project, which attempted to resettle the dispossessed on abandoned farms around the city—there were not enough resources to meet the city's growing needs. By the spring of 1933, unemployment relief requests averaged over twelve thousand per month with only $10.12 allocated for the average case, and by that summer approximately sixty thousand Atlantans were already on the welfare roll.

New Deal Relief and Employment Programs

Some relief for unemployed and underemployed Atlantans during the early 1930s finally arrived with the inauguration of Franklin Delano Roosevelt as president and the institution of New Deal legislation and programs. In May 1933 the Roosevelt administration established the Federal Emergency Relief Administration (FERA), which was designed to provide both local relief and employment. Federal funds amounting to $3.3 billion became available to the city through this

First Lady Eleanor Roosevelt observes the efforts of the Works Progress Administration in Georgia.

agency, and Atlanta mayor James Key quickly began preparing agencies to receive and administer these funds for the city and Fulton County. Georgia Governor Eugene Talmadge vehemently opposed Roosevelt and his programs and resented the amount of money allocated for Atlanta. (Talmadge's supporters lived mainly in the rural counties of Georgia, and his resentment toward Atlanta's power and influence was emblematic of a continuing battle between the city and the rural politicians of the state.) Through his control of the Georgia Relief Commission, Talmadge managed to hold up relief work in Atlanta by refusing to help the city meet its part of the financial obligation. Harry Hopkins, the director of FERA, responded to the governor's resistance and interference by taking the Georgia Relief Commission completely out of Talmadge's hands and appointing Gay B. Shepperson as director of the state agency. As a result, Atlanta become one of the first cities in the nation to have a federally-operated relief program, and under Shepperson's leadership, FERA provided direct relief to the city, sponsored worker education classes at Atlanta University and elsewhere, set up public health services, and established work-relief projects.

New Deal programs and agencies that followed, such as the Civil Works Administration (CWA), the Public Works Administration (PWA), and the Works Progress Administration (WPA), pumped millions of additional dollars into Atlanta projects and employed thousands of city residents in the process. Projects undertaken by these agencies

Teaching blind students to read Braille during the New Deal.

included the building or repair of area schools, hospitals, gymnasiums (including Georgia Tech's combination auditorium and gymnasium), and other public institutions; the grading of runways at Candler Field; the organization of a forty-five-member symphony orchestra; the repair and touch-up of the Cyclorama; and the construction of a new Atlanta sewer system. The new sewer system, which included 5.4 miles of trunk sewers and five sewage disposal plants and cost $11 million to construct, made a particularly significant improvement to city life. The old sewer system was inadequate and over-burdened and had contributed, according to health officials, to a death rate from diphtheria in Atlanta that was the highest in the nation in 1935 and a typhoid rate twice the average level of the fifteen largest urban areas in the country.

Public Housing

The New Deal also spurred the construction of the nation's first public housing projects—Techwood Homes (for whites) and University Homes (for blacks). The idea for these projects had originated with Atlanta real estate developer Charles F. Palmer, who wished to rid the city of some of its slums and replace them with federally-funded public housing. Accordingly, Palmer selected a site (just south of Georgia Tech) where both blacks and whites were living in substandard housing, drew up plans and budgets for his proposed project, and began lobbying in Washington, D.C., for funding. Palmer also started a collaborative effort with John Hope, president of Atlanta University,

Rear view of dilapidated housing conditions in the shadow of the state capitol.

who was desirous of developing additional housing for black Atlantans near the university.

Not everyone saw the wisdom of Palmer's and Hope's proposal. Many local realtors and developers actively opposed the idea, and Washington dragged its feet when it came time to approve and fund the project. Others criticized public housing as being communistic and dangerous. Finally, however, Palmer got his way, and Roosevelt himself attended the dedication of Techwood Homes in the fall of 1936. Techwood opened its doors to its first residents the next year, and University Homes followed suit in 1938.

Tensions

The charges of communism surrounding Palmer's public housing proposal reflected a common concern of local officials and police that the economic distress of the Depression might lead to a communist insurrection and increased calls for black political, economic, and social equality. A small group of communists actually were present in the city during this period and undertook efforts to organize both black and white workers. The police, who frequently raided suspected gatherings of communists, pacifists, and other groups that met on an interracial basis, arresting the participants and charging them with violation of an 1866 state anti-insurrection law, did their best to stifle those causes. These activities led the American Civil Liberties Union in 1937 to label Atlanta one of the nation's ten worst centers of repression.

One of the people arrested and jailed in these raids was Angelo Herndon, a nineteen-year-old black communist who had come to Atlanta to organize the unemployed. After being charged with trying to overthrow the government, Herndon went on trial before a packed Atlanta courthouse in 1932. The jury found him guilty and recommended a sentence of eighteen to twenty years in prison. Herndon's arrest and conviction was challenged and publicized by the Communist Party, the International Labor Defense, and the Provisional Committee for the Defense of Angelo Herndon, and the case soon became an international *cause célèbre* and a symbol (much like the famous Scottsboro Boys case) of southern injustice. Finally, in 1937 the U.S. Supreme court ruled that Georgia's anti-insurrection law was too vague, and Herndon and others arrested under this statute regained their freedom.

Members of the Columbians, one of several white supremacy groups in Atlanta, stand trial for incitement to riot, 1946.

The economic and social tensions associated with the Depression also led to the emergence of several white supremacist organizations, including the American Order of Fascisti, or "Black Shirts," as they were commonly known. The Black Shirts grew quickly in number during the early 1930s and undertook a campaign to pressure Atlanta employers to fire their black workers and replace them with unemployed whites. Many employers complied with the organization's demands, but weaknesses within the movement (including the lack of a developed organizational structure and the absence of any program beyond a simple demand for white employment) soon led to its downfall.

As the rise of the Black Shirts suggests, employment opportunities for African Americans in Atlanta during the 1930s were severely restricted. Nevertheless, black workers in the city could sometimes find jobs with federal programs. (Unfortunately, this did not hold for those in the state's rural areas.) In fact, Mayor Hartsfield went so far as to veto a city council resolution that proposed that only white Atlantans be eligible for jobs on the city's WPA-funded sewer construction project. Nonetheless, services and relief provided to the black communities of Atlanta during the depression remained far below those offered whites. In May 1935 the average general relief was $32.66 per month for whites in Atlanta versus $19.29 for African Americans.

By the late 1930s the severity of the Depression in Atlanta had begun to wane. With private business picking up, the federal government trimmed the number of WPA workers in the city. The banks all reopened, and aviation continued to grow as an industry. It would take World War II and the industrial development and expenditures associated with that effort, however, to fully return Atlanta to its earlier prosperity and launch the city into a new era of growth and transformation.

CHAPTER IV

City Without Limits: 1940–Present

A B-29 leaves the final assembly line at the Bell bomber plant during World War II.

We stand, not so much as a gateway to the South, but as a gateway to a new time, a new era, a new beginning for the cities of our land.

—Maynard H. Jackson, Jr.
first African-American mayor
of Atlanta, 1974

IN 1940, ATLANTA WAS HOME to about three hundred thousand residents—two-thirds of whom were white and one-third African American. While the city had aspirations of becoming one of the nation's largest and most influential urban centers, it operated primarily as a regional hub for transportation and commerce. Connections to outlying suburban developments and communities in Fulton, DeKalb, and Cobb counties existed via trolley lines, roads, and early highways, but most areas outside the city limits consisted of rural stretches of fields, woods, and farms, interrupted by the occasional small town and city.

Sixty years later, at the turn of a new century, the picture was vastly changed. While the population within Atlanta's city limits had grown by less than 115,000, the surrounding metropolitan area had mushroomed to include more than twenty counties with a population of over four million. Within the city, a dramatic demographic and racial change also had taken place with African Americans now comprising the majority population (sixty-one percent). In the outlying suburbs, the ratios were reversed with whites in the majority (sixty-six percent). Also present in greater numbers than ever before in this changing population and residential mix was an increasing number of foreign-born and immigrant groups and communities. In census year 2000, for example, foreign-born residents made up about ten percent of the total Atlanta metropolitan population—more than double the percentage of any previous census year.

The event that began the dramatic growth and transformation of Atlanta in the last half of the twentieth century was World War II. But the engines that continued to drive this change were the same histor-ical forces and elements that had done so much to shape the growth and development of the city in earlier eras—transportation, race rela-tions, and the Atlanta Spirit. In the decades following World War II, the city borders would once again expand through annexation and settle-ment in surrounding unincorporated counties; Atlanta's air and rail connections would be augmented by important links to the nation's emerging interstate highway system; and the city's central core would be reshaped through extensive highway construction and urban renewal programs.

Along the way, the city reached a new level of national stature reflected in the maturation of Atlanta's cultural institutions, the arrival of "Big League" professional sports teams, the vertical expansion of the city's skyline through the addition of towering new skyscrapers, and the growth of a thriving convention and hospitality industry. By the turn of the twenty-first century, Atlanta was, in all senses of the word, a "metropolis"—the main city or capital of its region. Atlanta's "region," however, was no longer simply the South, or even for that matter, the nation. Beginning in the 1960s, the city sought to set itself apart from other race-torn areas of the South by adopting the slogan "A City Too Busy to Hate." Later, Atlanta would set its sights even higher, abandoning regional and national limitations altogether as it sought acclamation as an international player and the "World's Next Great City."

These catchy slogans, so characteristic of the Atlanta Spirit of promotion and boosterism, reflect on one level some of the dramatic changes that have occurred in Atlanta during the last sixty years. At the same time, they also obscure or downplay some of the important ties and connections that Atlanta continued (and continues) to main-tain with the South and with its earlier history.

WORLD WAR II

The city's dramatic late twentieth-century growth and transformation began, by almost all accounts, with World War II—a watershed event for the South in general and Atlanta in particular. Between 1940 and 1945, the federal government invested over $10 billion in war indus-tries and military bases located in the South. It expended millions more on related projects such as public housing, health-care facilities, and aid to schools in the communities where the military buildup was the greatest. The addition of a million new civilian jobs region-wide through government projects and war industries helped curb high unemployment rates and sent wages and per capita income soaring in those areas where the industries and bases were located. The enlistment of large numbers of southern men and women into the armed forces (nearly one-third of the eleven million white men, more than two-thirds of the one million black men, and a high percentage of the quarter-million women who served in uniform were from the South) increased employment opportunities at home and spurred an exodus of rural southerners to cities in the South and North in search of good wages and more stable incomes.

World War II had an equally dramatic impact on Atlanta. It ended the Depression, swelled the city's population, spread a broad net of federal installations throughout the metropolitan area, enlisted black and white men and women in the armed forces and in war-related industries, and brought to the forefront forces that would dramatically affect the city's race relations and politics in the post-World War II era. For better and worse, Atlanta would never be the same again.

THE MILITARY PRESENCE

Atlanta's most obvious connection to World War II was through the many military bases and support institutions that ringed the city. Camp Gordon, an army training base during World War I that was located in nearby Chamblee, became the site during the second world war of a flight training station and Lawson General Hospital—a large medical complex that treated some thirty-three thousand army personnel and war casualties (including some German POWs) during the period from 1941 to 1945. Fort McPherson in southwest Atlanta, which had served as a federal military barracks following the Civil War and as a training camp during World War I, was also enlarged during World War II and utilized as an induction center. The Atlanta General Depot (later Fort Gillem), an enormous army supply depot, was established on a fifteen-hundred-acre tract of land in Clayton County about fifteen miles southeast of downtown Atlanta. Federal defense funds also supported the expansion of the rail yards in Clayton County and the Atlanta municipal airport in Hapeville.

The clustering of these bases, supply depots, and military airfields in Atlanta, coupled with the city's traditional role as a railroad transportation center, meant that thousands of soldiers and military support personnel passed through or were stationed in Atlanta during the war, and their presence had both immediate and far-ranging consequences for the city. Soldiers from Fort McPherson, most of whom were white, and from Fort Benning in Columbus, Georgia, most of whom were black, frequently came to the city in search of entertainment and recreation, and Atlanta welcomed both groups—although on a strictly segregated basis. African-American soldiers passed through a separate "colored" entrance when they arrived in Atlanta at Terminal Station, and their activities, while they were in the city, were confined primarily to black-owned and -operated institutions. Representatives of the black United Services Organization (USO) or Traveler's Aid greeted the visitors at the railroad station and directed them to the Butler Street YMCA, where they could play basketball, ping pong, or checkers; swim; or attend dances; or to nearby Auburn Avenue, where a wide spectrum of black businesses, restaurants, nightclubs, hotels, and social activities were available. When the Butler Street YMCA became too crowded, a USO unit was also established at Booker T. Washington High School. Facilities and recreational opportunities for white soldiers were more widespread throughout the city, but essentially they provided the same services as those in Atlanta's black communities. Unlike black businesses, however, which occasionally served white servicemen, these white facilities were strictly off-limits to black soldiers.

As might be expected, Atlanta's entertainment and service industries, both black and white, benefited from the presence of the military population. But the impact of the military buildup in the city had its negative effects as well. Housing was increasingly in short supply, as building materials were reserved for military projects and civilian housing construction in Atlanta ground to a halt. The conservation of materials for the war effort also led to a rationing among the civilian population in Atlanta (as elsewhere in the nation) of scarce items such as meat, sugar, coffee, tires, and gasoline. And finally, the presence of large numbers of soldiers on leave in the city led, on occasion, to disturbances of the peace and contributed to a near-epidemic outbreak of venereal disease in Atlanta. To combat these problems, black and white military police patrolled the city's entertainment districts, and local officials clamped down hard on violators of the city's moral codes. (It was against the law in Atlanta, for example, for an unmarried man and woman to be alone together in a room with the door closed.) These actions, coupled with the widespread availability of penicillin (which the government dispensed for free), eventually helped bring venereal disease rates under control.

WAR INDUSTRIES

The preparations for war also spurred the growth of war-related industries within the Atlanta metropolitan area and offered increased employment opportunities for the city's residents. Chevrolet's Lakewood plant, for example, converted its operations during the war to the production of munitions. The largest war industry to locate in

Employees at the Bell bomber plant work on the fuselage of a B-29 during World War II.

the area, however, was the Bell Aircraft plant, which built B-29 bombers. At its peak, the Bell plant, which was located in Cobb County, employed about thirty thousand workers, including a sizable number of women and a growing number of African Americans.

The inclusion of these two groups in the workforce was primarily the result of an increasing shortage of employable white males (due to the induction of most able-bodied men into the armed forces) and President Franklin Roosevelt's issuance in 1941 of Executive Order 8802, which outlawed racial discrimination in defense plants. As white women moved into defense work and received promotions, and as more and more African-American men were drafted into the military, positions began to open up in the defense plants for African-American women. For the most part, these openings were confined to the lower-paying, more menial positions. Nonetheless, an important precedent had been set. For one of the first times in the city's history, blacks and whites, males and females, were all working together in an industrial setting.

COCA-COLA GOES TO WAR

Another famous Atlanta company—Coca-Cola—also became involved in the war and, in fact, ended up accompanying servicemen and women overseas. When Coca-Cola realized that sugar rationing would be extended to soft drinks, the company successfully lobbied to exclude the military from rationing and then obtained the soft drink contract with the armed forces. Bottling plants, which were technically under the supervision of the military, were established at numerous locations overseas, and Coca-Cola literally followed the military onto three continents. Technicians were sent out to the various plants to make sure that the product remained consistent, and portable backpacks that could dispense the soft drink were even carried to the front lines. In the process, Coca-Cola not only became a favorite drink among American GIs, but increased its international presence and influence as well. By the end of the war, Coca-Cola was well poised to expand its production and distribution throughout the world.

THE USS ATLANTA

Atlanta's support for the war extended beyond the involvement of local industries and companies in the war effort and the induction of many of its young men into the service. Atlanta's civilian population also supported the war effort through participation in volunteer organizations like the Red Cross and the Civilian Defense and through the purchasing of war bonds. The greatest single indicator of Atlanta's commitment to the war effort, however, may have been the city's campaign to underwrite the cost of building a new navy warship named for Atlanta.

Launching of the USS Atlanta IV, *February 1944.*

On September 6, 1941, the USS *Atlanta*, a naval cruiser, was christened by Margaret Mitchell (author of the novel *Gone With the Wind*) and launched into action. A little over a year later, the ship was torpedoed and sunk off Guadalcanal. Mayor William B. Hartsfield spearheaded a war bond drive in Atlanta to raise the necessary funds to replace the ship, and the campaign succeeded in raising almost enough money for two ships. On February 6, 1944, a second USS *Atlanta* was christened (again by Mitchell) and sent into action. After engagements in the Far East theater, the ship was decommissioned on July 1, 1949, and placed in the Pacific Reserve Fleet. (It was later sunk during an explosives test off San Clemente Island, California, in 1970.) The first *Atlanta* earned five battle stars for service during World War II; the second ship was awarded two battle stars for accomplishments during the war.

FIGHTING FOR DEMOCRACY AT HOME

Although there was widespread support for the war in Atlanta, the experience of some soldiers, especially African-American veterans, caused them to rethink and to challenge the assumptions and restric-

Margaret Mitchell christens the USS Atlanta IV, *February 1944.*

tions of Jim Crow. Southern blacks who served in the war resented the fact that they were being asked to risk their lives to fight racism abroad at the same time that they were segregated and discriminated against in the armed forces and at home. The black press seized on this issue during the war and emphasized to its readers time and time again the importance of fighting a two-front war for democracy at home and abroad.

African-American veterans were not the only southerners whose traditional views of race and race relations were challenged during the war. Harold C. Fleming, a young white Georgian who served as a company commander of black soldiers in World War II, became aware of the injustices of Jim Crow as a result of his wartime experiences. "It did more to change my life," he later related, "than any other experience I've ever had." When he returned to Georgia in 1947, Fleming moved to Atlanta where he became involved in and later served as executive director of an organization dedicated to fighting racial discrimination—the Southern Regional Council (SRC).

The SRC was born on August 5, 1943, at a meeting held at Atlanta University. Here, an interracial group of prominent black and white leaders (including Ralph McGill, editor of the *Atlanta Constitution*; Methodist Bishop Arthur J. Moore; Benjamin Mays,

The USS Atlanta III (foreground) *at the Battle of Midway, June 1942.*

Major General Frederick Uhl on Armistice Day in downtown Atlanta, 1944.

president of Morehouse College; and Rufus E. Clement, president of Atlanta University) met to respond to a challenge issued by an earlier conference of black leaders that had met in Durham, North Carolina. The signatories of the "Durham Manifesto," as it came to be known, had declared that they were "fundamentally opposed to the principle and practice of compulsory segregation in our American society" and had further concluded "that it is possible to evolve in the South a way of life, consistent with the principals for which we as a nation are fighting throughout the world, that will free us all, white and Negro alike, from that, and from throttling fears." The forty delegates who met in Atlanta concurred with these statements and resolved to create a "strong, unified Southern Regional Council" that, unlike its predecessor, the Commission on Interracial Cooperation (CIC), would include and involve African Americans on an equal basis with whites. Like the CIC and the Durham Manifesto, however, the council reluctantly agreed to postpone a direct attack upon segregation and concentrate instead on achieving "equal opportunity for all peoples of the region." On January 6, 1944, the SRC was granted a charter and began what would be a long campaign to achieve racial justice and equality in Atlanta and throughout the South. Initially the council sought to improve race relations through programs of research and education and through behind-the-scenes negotiations and discussions with politicians and civic leaders promoting racial moderation. By 1951, however, the council's board of directors concluded that this course of action had not proven fruitful and endorsed instead racial desegregation as the organization's primary goal.

POSTWAR GROWTH AND EXPANSION

World War II in Atlanta had been a period of deprivation and shortages, but it was also an era of impressive growth for the metropolitan region and its industries. The postwar period continued and extended this growth. In 1947, a new Ford assembly plant was opened in Hapeville, and the following year, General Motors opened a new factory in Doraville. Bell Aircraft, the Atlanta area's biggest wartime industry, shut down in 1946 but was taken over by the Lockheed Aircraft Corporation five years later (during the Korean War). By 1954 there were eight hundred new industries in Atlanta and almost twelve hundred national corporations with offices in the city.

Atlantans commemorate Armistice Day, 1944.

ANNEXATION AND GOVERNMENT REORGANIZATION

Atlanta's civic and political leaders welcomed this growth and made efforts to support and sustain it through an aggressive annexation drive, urban renewal projects, and changes and improvements in the city's transportation systems, its water supply, and its government structure. The 1951 Plan of Improvement, drawn up by a citizens' study commission, brought about several of these changes. One of the major elements of the plan was a proposal to restructure the government responsibilities of the City of Atlanta and Fulton County to eliminate duplicate services. Under this plan, the city would take over park and recreation duties and police and fire protection, and the county would assume responsibility for health and welfare services and tax collection. In addition to these changes, the 1951 Plan of Improvement also called for the annexation of some densely populated areas north and south of the city. Similar annexation plans had been rejected in 1938, 1943, and 1947, but this time the referendum passed. As a result, the size of the city tripled in 1952 from 37 to 118 square miles, and almost 100,000 new residents were added to the city's population, bringing the total to 428,299.

HIGHWAYS AND AIRWAYS

Important changes and improvements also occurred in the city's highways and airways. In 1946 (some ten years before the federal interstate

The Ford Motor plant in south Atlanta.

The downtown I-75/I-85 connector under construction, 1948.

highway program was established), white business leaders in Atlanta pushed for the adoption of the so-called Lochner report—a plan prepared by national traffic consultant H. W. Lochner—that called for, among other things, the construction of a north-south, limited-access expressway through downtown Atlanta, additional viaducts or elevated streets over the railroad tracks, and a circular highway ringing the downtown. City voters approved a $16 million bond campaign to begin buying the right-of-way, and in 1949, with assistance from the federal and state governments, the highway construction project was begun. By 1956, when the federal government launched its national interstate highway construction project (providing ninety percent of the necessary funding), the Atlanta expressway was already handling levels of traffic projected for 1970. Atlanta's early preparedness allowed the city to eventually link up with three major interstate highways (I-75, I-85, and I-20) and to construct an outer-ring expressway (I-285) to encircle the city and provide connections between the major transportation arteries.

Air traffic also continued to be an important growth industry in the postwar period, and Atlanta effectively strengthened and extended its connections in this field as well. Atlanta had pioneered several firsts in aviation. It was the first city, for example, to have an air traffic control tower (1938) and the first to utilize an instrument approach system (1942).

This early commitment to the air industry, coupled with the expanded use of Atlanta's air facilities during World War II, put the city

The new and expanded Grady Memorial Hospital opened in 1958.

in a competitive position to capture regional control of air passenger service following the war. By the end of World War II, two major airlines, Eastern and Delta, were already headquartered in and operating out of the Atlanta municipal airport, and city hall, under the leadership of Mayor Hartsfield, was committed to an expansion of the facilities and services offered at Candler Field. In 1948, Atlanta opened a new passenger terminal at the airport—a large metal, Quonset hut-style facility that cost the city $180,000 to construct. This was followed in 1961 by another brand-new terminal (built at a cost of $21 million, but outmoded within twenty years). By 1971, as a result of rapidly increasing flights and passenger totals, Hartsfield International Airport was already the second busiest terminal in the United States (Chicago's O'Hare was first) and the fourth busiest in the world.

CITY SERVICES

The remarkable growth and expansion that occurred in Atlanta during the postwar period also necessitated changes and improvements in the city's water systems, its public education facilities, and its medical services.

The first problem was addressed by the construction of Buford Dam in 1956 by the Army Corps of Engineers. This dam, which had been enthusiastically supported by Mayor Hartsfield, Georgia senators Walter George and Richard Russell, and area congressmen, reserved enough water from the Chattahoochee River to supply two million Atlanta-area residents and also created a very popular recreational lake with 540 miles of shoreline (Lake Lanier).

Atlanta's public schools were also upgraded and expanded during this period, and the practice of sexually segregating the city's high schools was ended and replaced by a system of coeducational neighborhood schools. Racial segregation in the city's public schools did not end at this time, however, and remained strictly in force until 1961.

Medical services and institutions in the city also grew during this period, although they remained segregated as well. In 1958, a new and expanded Grady Memorial Hospital opened under the aegis of the Fulton-DeKalb Hospital Authority. Black patients in the city, however, continued to be treated and hospitalized at the associated Hughes Spaulding Pavilion.

The construction of the new Grady Hospital provides a good example of the increased postwar cooperation among Atlanta's urban counties. Another indication of the recognized need for planning at the larger multi-county or metropolitan level was the establishment of the Metropolitan Planning Commission (MPC) by Georgia's General Assembly in 1974. The MPC was originally a two-county planning body with authority to recommend (but not enact) plans for the orderly growth and development of the Atlanta metropolitan area. Later, the MPC would evolve into the Atlanta Regional Commission (ARC), which oversaw a much larger seven-county area (Fulton, DeKalb, Cobb, Clayton, Gwinnett, Rockdale, and Douglas). Like its predecessor, however, the ARC would continue to function primarily as a regional advisory board.

HOUSING AND URBAN RENEWAL

One of the first problem areas that the Metropolitan Planning Commission attempted to address was Atlanta's pressing postwar housing shortage. The Depression of the 1930s had slowed housing construction in the city, and building efforts during World War II had largely been reserved for war-related projects. As a result, much of the city's housing supply was overcrowded and deteriorating by the war's end.

The housing problem was particularly acute in Atlanta's African-American communities, where overcrowding and structural deterioration were typically at their worst. Despite the presence of a sizable and growing black middle class, housing options for African Americans in Atlanta were severely limited by a combination of forces, including discriminatory lending practices, restrictive covenants and deeds (private property restrictions written into deeds and neighborhood ordinances that declared certain neighborhoods off-limits to African Americans and Jews), zoning regulations, terrorism and violence, and strategically placed and strengthened barriers within the city (such as industrial zones, railroads and highways, cemeteries, and dead-end or unpaved streets), which served to divide whites and blacks into separate neighborhoods. Except for the limited residential expansion that had occurred on the city's west side during the 1920s and 1930s, Atlanta's black population was largely confined to older sections of the city surrounding the central business district. By 1950, Auburn Avenue—the pride of black Atlanta, the birthplace of Martin Luther King Jr., and a showcase in the early twentieth century for black business and residential wealth—contained over twenty-five thousand persons per square mile. Black communities also were burdened by aged and deteriorating housing. In 1950, for example, over two-thirds of the black dwelling units in the city, according to the U.S. census, were "dilapidated." (By way of contrast, only fourteen percent of the white dwelling units were similarly classified.) Ten years later, almost three-fourths of all the dilapidated residential structures to be found in Atlanta were located in black communities.

The city's urban renewal programs and highway construction projects of the 1950s and 1960s threatened to make the situation even worse. The route of the north-south expressway, for example, bisected Auburn Avenue and wiped out areas of inner-city neighborhoods. Similarly, urban renewal projects, which resulted in the construction of a new civic center and a stadium, also destroyed homes and displaced residents in the process. In the period from 1956 to 1966 alone, almost sixty-seven thousand persons—the vast majority of them poor and black—were uprooted by these governmental activities. And while urban renewal programs eventually included provisions for the relocation of those displaced, only about eleven percent of the displacees who qualified for public housing during this ten-year period were actually relocated to public housing projects.

In response to this worsening housing problem, African-American leaders and organizations quickly mobilized to negotiate with city hall over replacement housing and agreed-upon areas for black residential expansion. In 1946, the same year that the Lochner report was released, the Atlanta Urban League called a meeting of representatives from business, government, and social agencies to discuss the issue. A Temporary Coordinating Committee on Housing was created with Walter H. Aiken, a leading black contractor, as chairman. The coordinating committee in turn established three other committees: a land committee, chaired by realtor T. M. Alexander, "to investigate further

Developer Walter Aiken supervising construction of homes in south Atlanta.

the possibility of getting outlet areas for Negro expansion"; a corporation committee composed of representatives from Atlanta Mutual Building and Loan Association, the Atlanta Life Insurance Company, and Citizens Trust to study the feasibility of setting up a corporation to build on the selected sites; and a third committee which was charged with working closely with and influencing county planners, the Atlanta Chamber of Commerce, and other governmental housing organizations and agencies.

In 1947 the coordinating and land committees enlarged their membership to include representatives from the Community Planning Council, the Empire Real Estate Board (of black realtors), and the land planning and racial relations units of the local Federal Housing Administration. This expanded committee, which became known as the Atlanta Housing Council, subsequently issued a report identifying six areas of Atlanta in which the committee felt the black population could and should expand. In each area, the report emphasized, some African Americans were already residing, and land (much of it owned by African Americans) was readily available for residential development.

Although city officials had no public involvement in the housing council's deliberations, the Hartsfield administration privately endorsed both the general concept of black residential expansion areas and the specific sites suggested by the council. Five years later, the Metropolitan

Planning Commission identified its own proposed black expansion areas in a document entitled *Up Ahead*. In this planning report, the commission acknowledged a "serious concentration of Negroes in unhealthy and inadequate downtown neighborhoods," resulting from the inability of African Americans to secure either enough available used housing or enough open development land to meet the group's growing needs. The solution, according to the commission's report, was "to find outlying expansion areas to be developed for new colored housing." The document then went on to identify several possible expansion sites.

Up Ahead received severe criticism both from whites who owned land in the proposed expansion areas and from some African Americans who felt that the commission's plans would help to preserve and even intensify the already rigid residential segregation patterns within the metropolitan area. The immediate need of blacks for greater housing space, however, eventually overcame the objections of both groups, and by 1955 all six areas named by the Atlanta Housing Council as expansion areas in 1947 and four of those identified in *Up Ahead* had been developed as black residential communities.

African-American leaders also succeeded in gaining new public housing for the poor in their communities. Carver Homes, for example, opened in 1953 on the south side, and Perry Homes opened two years later on the west side. By one account, some 1,990 new public housing units, 3,100 new private apartments, and 3,450 new owner-occupied homes were built for black residents in Atlanta during the period from 1945 to 1956. This new construction helped ease the housing shortage somewhat for Atlanta's African-American communities, but it did little to end or diminish residential segregation in the city. Instead, new housing, including public housing, tended to be located in already existing black communities. As a result, public housing in Atlanta during this period tended not to disperse the black population throughout the metropolitan area, but instead to confine it to those areas of the city where African Americans were already present in sizable numbers.

THE GOVERNING COALITION

That Atlanta's black communities could exercise any voice in the city's policies during the post-World War II period was testimony both to their growing political strength and Mayor William B. Hartsfield's political acumen and racial progressiveness.

Early in his political career, Hartsfield had been a traditional southern segregationist. He had fought the creation of the Fair

Employment Practices Commission in the 1930s and had even asked the House Un-American Activities Committee in 1944 to investigate the NAACP. Mayor Hartsfield, however, was no typical racial demagogue. As African American political and economic power began to grow in the postwar period, Hartsfield realized that the black middle class could provide support for his reform-style politics.

This black political support was essential to Hartsfield since he was losing much of his earlier political base with the exodus of educated and affluent whites to the Atlanta suburbs. After African-American protestors marched on city hall demanding fairer law enforcement and the hiring of black police officers, Hartsfield met with leaders of the group to discuss the issue. This meeting set the precedent for what would become a Hartsfield administration trademark—quiet, behind-the-scenes negotiations with black leaders to resolve difficult racial issues. This was an approach that Hartsfield later would label "go slow, go easy, but go."

Such meetings would never have happened, of course, if black Atlantans had not succeeded in the 1940s in dramatically increasing their percentage of the total city electorate. Several events and forces contributed to this increase. The repeal of the poll tax by the Georgia legislature in 1945 and the invalidation of the white primary by the U.S. Supreme Court the following year, for example, removed two very important barriers to black political participation in the state and local elections. But the greatest impetus to increase black voter registration in Atlanta was a very successful and well-organized voter registration drive that was conducted in 1946 by the All-Citizens Registration Committee (which included representatives of the NAACP, the Urban League, the Atlanta Civic and Political League, and other black political and civic organizations). As a result of this drive, almost eighteen thousand new black voters were added to the registration books in a period of only fifty-one days, and by the end of the year there was a total of twenty-one thousand registered African-American voters in Atlanta. (By way of contrast, there were only about three thousand registered black voters in 1945). In 1949, in an effort to better coordinate and concentrate their new-found political strength, black Republicans and Democrats joined together to form the Atlanta Negro Voters' League—a body that was soon openly courted by the mayor and other white candidates for public office.

Despite their growing electoral strength, African Americans were still, at best, a minority partner in the governing coalition of early postwar Atlanta. The group that had the most influence and impact on city hall's policies and plans at this time was the white busi-

Atlanta's first African-American police officers were hired in 1948.

ness elite of Atlanta (what one observer later termed the city's "power structure"). This alliance of city hall and white business interests was nothing new for Atlanta. The New South creed espoused by Henry Grady after the Civil War, the Forward Atlanta campaign of the 1920s, and most of the city's other promotional campaigns during the first one hundred years of its history were clearly based on this relationship. In the post–World War II years, however, this co-mingling of business and political interests would have additional long-term effects and a dramatic impact both on race relations in Atlanta and the shape and layout of an expanding city.

In 1941, downtown merchants, businessmen, and major property owners formed the Central Atlanta Improvement Association (CAIA)—an organization that would play a critical role in developing and designing the highway construction and urban renewal programs that reshaped the city's core. CAIA and its membership endorsed the Lochner plan, which proposed a route for the north-south expressway that would curve around the edge of downtown, forming a buffer between the white central business district and black neighborhoods to the east. The organization also worked closely with the Metropolitan Planning Commission in laying out plans for the rejuvenation and expansion of the central business district. In general, the CAIA and the city's business elite endorsed urban renewal projects that would create new public facilities (but not public housing) in the central city and pushed for the relocation of displaced black residents to outlying areas on the west and south sides of the city.

While the goals and objectives of the white business elite frequently did not take into full account the wishes and interests of Atlanta's black communities, they were nonetheless very concerned about the image that Atlanta projected in national business circles. As a result, the white business elite generally supported the efforts of Hartsfield and Atlanta's black leadership to remove or weaken some of the most glaring and easily-remedied inequalities under Jim Crow. And it was the support and influence of business leaders such as Coca-Cola C.E.O. Robert Woodruff that would prove crucial in later efforts to peacefully desegregate the city's schools and public facilities.

CIVIL RIGHTS AND DESEGREGATION

Voter registration, c. 1946.

Although African Americans continued to play a minor role in local governance until the 1970s, the growing political strength and influence of African Americans in postwar Atlanta was reflected in a number of areas. In 1946, black votes proved critical to the election of Helen Mankin Douglas as a congressional representative from the Fifth District. And in 1953, Atlanta University president Rufus Clement became the first African American to hold citywide office in the twentieth century when he was elected to the Atlanta school board.

Negotiated settlements and behind-the-scenes discussions between black leaders and city hall also led to an easing of Jim Crow restrictions in some areas. In return for black electoral support for the 1951 Plan of Improvement, for example, Mayor Hartsfield privately promised to help remove some of the more glaring and irritating symbols of racial segregation. Accordingly, he instructed clerks at city hall to begin addressing mail to black citizens using the titles "Mr." and "Mrs." rather than just their first names as was common under Jim Crow. And in Atlanta's airport, the signs on the facility's segregated restrooms were left unpainted until they eventually faded from view. In 1958, after long negotiations with key black ministers, the mayor also agreed to help stage a test case of the state's bus segregation laws. Similar laws in other states had already been declared by federal courts to be unconstitutional, and African Americans in Atlanta were anxious to challenge these statutes. An earlier protest organized and led by Reverend William Holmes Borders of Wheat Street Baptist Church, however, had proven unsuccessful and had elicited promises from Governor Marvin Griffin and the state

Segregated water fountains at Kress Department Store in downtown Atlanta.

attorney general to call out the National Guard to ride the city's buses and arrest protestors for disturbing the peace. To avoid this showdown and the attendant bad publicity for the city, Mayor Hartsfied and the city's black leadership worked out a plan whereby a preselected group of African American protesters would be arrested for violating state segregation laws. After their arrest, the protesters were immediately released on bond, the state law was challenged in federal court, and Atlanta's buses were eventually integrated (sparing the city the long and costly demonstrations that had gripped Montgomery, Alabama, three years earlier). The desegregation of municipal golf courses was similarly negotiated behind the scenes and achieved with a minimum of unrest and publicity.

Outside city hall, in some of Atlanta's largest companies, important changes were also beginning to take place in the structure and composition of their work forces. Lockheed, for example, had all-black crews working alongside all-white crews and at Scripto, the pen and pencil manufacturer, an increasing number of African-American women began working on the factory's assembly line.

The most notable success in desegregation during Hartsfield's administration, however, was not the disappearance of "white" and "colored" signs in the city's airport terminal, the integration of Atlanta's buses or golf courses, or even the gradual desegregation of the work force. It was instead the widely publicized and peaceful desegregation of Atlanta's public school system in 1961.

The local impetus for desegregation was a suit filed against the Atlanta school system by the NAACP in 1958. The black plaintiffs in

The desegregation of Murphy High School, August 1961.

this suit won their case, and the court ordered Atlanta to submit a desegregation plan by December 1959. Although Mayor Hartsfield and many of his business allies advocated abiding by the decision, it was by no means certain at the time that this process could be carried out peacefully and without incident. The U.S. Supreme Court's 1954 decision in *Brown* v. *Board of Education* that called for the desegregation of the nation's schools had been met with vociferous and, at times, violent protest in the South. Attempts to integrate public schools in Little Rock, Arkansas, and New Orleans had resulted in civil disturbances, and white political leaders throughout the region issued the call for "massive resistance" to efforts to desegregate the South's institutions and submitted a wide spectrum of plans to resist, delay, or circumvent the edict of the high court. In Georgia, the state legislature had already passed a law that required that schools close before submitting to desegregation and had also made it a felony (punishable by up to two years in jail) for any state or local official in Georgia to expend funds for the benefit of a racially integrated school. Similarly, the Georgia Association of County Commissioners went on record as being opposed to "any race mixing in any Georgia schools anywhere, at any time, under any circumstances."

The image-conscious Mayor Hartsfield and his allies in the business community not only wanted to avoid violence but to make the city look good in the process. Hartsfield had coined the description of

Atlanta in the 1950s as "The City Too Busy to Hate," and he was determined that Atlanta continue to project this image. The image was tested, however, in 1958 when a bomb ripped a huge hole in the side of the Temple, Atlanta's oldest and most prominent Jewish synagogue. No one was injured in the attack, but Mayor Hartsfield, the police, and the city's prosecutors worked aggressively to find the guilty parties and bring them to justice. Four suspects were arrested the next day, and although no one was ever convicted of the crime, President Eisenhower publicly praised Mayor Hartsfield for his decisive response, telling him, "You have set an example for the entire nation."

The good will and positive national publicity that Atlanta received for its response to the Temple bombing was not lost on the mayor as he and his administration prepared to accede to the court-ordered desegregation of Atlanta's public schools. Once again, Hartsfield's preferred response was to move forward, but move slowly. "I have often said to my Negro citizens," he stated during testimony to a federal Commission on Civil Rights in 1959, "that the important thing is the direction in which we are moving, and not always the speed with which we are moving." But even moving slowly did not guarantee that the rest of Atlanta would go along with the plan. Many white Atlantans still remained adamantly opposed to the desegregation of the city's schools and pro-segregation forces established two organizations to present and publicize their views—the Metropolitan Association for Segregated Education (MASE) and Georgians Unwilling to Surrender (or GUTS, led by Atlantan and future governor of Georgia Lester Maddox).

Fortunately for Mayor Hartsfield, a growing number of Atlanta citizens, institutions, and organizations began to endorse the idea of abiding by the court's desegregation decision in an effort to avoid the violence that frequently accompanied massive resistance and to keep the city's schools open. In 1957, for example, eighty white Atlanta Protestant ministers signed a "manifesto" that urged obedience to the law and called for the preservation of the public school system. (Two years later, 311 ministers signed a second similar manifesto.) Another grouping of mothers of school-aged children, worried that the city's schools might be closed rather than integrate, formed an organization called Help Our Public Education, and Jane Hammer (wife of the first director of the Metropolitan Planning Commission) chaired an organization called Organizations Assisting Schools in September (OASIS), that was made up of all the major local organizations that supported peaceful desegregation.

The city's business elite and civic boosters also garnered support for the gradual and peaceful desegregation of Atlanta's schools. John

Sibley, former chairman of Trust Company of Georgia (and a member of Robert Woodruff's inner circle) chaired a commission that conducted hearings throughout the state on the school desegregation issue. Sibley denounced the 1954 *Brown* v. *Board* decision as "devoid of legal reasoning" but emphasized that it was now the law and that the law needed to be obeyed.

Although a majority of witnesses at these hearings (by a margin of three to two) took the stand that the state's schools should close rather than integrate, the Sibley commission recommended that the schools remain open in favor of slow and limited integration. The Atlanta Chamber of Commerce also endorsed this view and continued to hammer home the important lessons to be learned from the experiences of Little Rock and New Orleans. (Statistics were prepared, for example, to show how costly—in economic terms—Little Rock's 1957 riots had been.) Eventually, the Atlanta Board of Alderman, the business community, the *Atlanta Constitution*, the League of Women Voters, the Board of Education, the Georgia Education Association, and other local civic organizations all came together in opposition to the principals and goals of massive resistance.

Despite this growing public and organizational support, it was by no means certain that school desegregation would occur without incident. Relations between the black community and white business leaders were already strained by an aggressive sit-in campaign launched by black college students in 1960 to desegregate downtown restaurants and other public facilities, and in December of the same year, the English Avenue Elementary School in Atlanta (a black public school) and a dozen nearby houses were severely damaged by a bomb explosion. The governing coalition was eventually able to negotiate a "cooling-off period" with the student demonstrators so the public school desegregation could go forward, but tensions remained high as segregationists and white supremacy organizations fanned the fires of local emotion and discontent.

In response to these perceived threats to public safety, the Atlanta police department initiated an elaborate surveillance program of racial agitators and white supremacy organizations such as the Ku Klux Klan, and a law-and-order week was organized during which churches and synagogues offered special prayer meetings for peaceful desegregation. These extraordinary efforts proved successful, and on August 30, 1961, nine black students (chosen from a pool of 133 candidates) peacefully integrated four Atlanta public high schools—Brown, Henry Grady, Murphy, and Northside.

Hartsfield and his business allies made the most of this momentous occasion and all its public relations benefits. The huge press corps attending the event (including two hundred out-of-town reporters) was briefed in an elaborate pressroom set up at city hall, given a handbook prepared by OASIS, driven from school to school to witness the peaceful integration, offered a bus tour of the city, and treated to an integrated cocktail party at the Biltmore Hotel that evening. Hartsfield labeled the occasion Atlanta's "finest hour," and many in the city and throughout the nation agreed. President John F. Kennedy called a press conference to praise the city and urged other communities throughout the region and the nation "to look closely at what Atlanta has done and to meet their responsibility, as the officials of Atlanta and Georgia have done, with courage, tolerance and, above all, respect for the law." Most of the national news media in attendance also lauded the city for its accomplishment. In reality, the integration that the national press and local citizens witnessed was little more than token, but the significance of the event was nonetheless momentous. Atlanta had proved to itself and to the world that racial desegregation could be achieved peaceably, and in the process the city earned for itself a reputation for racial progressivism and moderation in a region known for neither.

BIG LEAGUE CITY

The close alliance between private business and public government continued during the administration of Atlanta's next mayor, businessman Ivan Allen Jr. While president of the Atlanta Chamber of Commerce, he had helped formulate a six-point plan for city progress that included the speeding up of expressway construction; increased urban renewal; the construction of a new civic center and stadium; the development of a rapid transit system; a continued plan of gradual but steady school desegregation; and a call for additional low-income housing. Mayor Allen made this six-point program the priority of his administration and the means by which he hoped to make Atlanta into a "big league city" with public facilities, sports and cultural offerings, and a public transportation system to match those of other national urban centers. Within ten years, all of the projects outlined by Allen had been implemented, but not without some attendant discord and a fundamental restructuring of the city's spatial and racial configuration.

FORWARD ATLANTA: PART II

One of the first efforts of Mayor Allen to promote Atlanta's potential and promise involved the reintroduction of the "Forward Atlanta" campaign, a national advertisement blitz that his father had successfully utilized during the 1920s to bring new industries and business to the city. The second Forward Atlanta campaign was launched in 1961 by the chamber of commerce and succeeded in raising $1.5 million from local businesses. These funds allowed the chamber to hire a professional staff, publish economic research data, and actively solicit new business through national advertisements that emphasized Atlanta's racial moderation, pro-business environment, prominence as a regional transportation and distribution center, and beautiful homes and neighborhoods.

Like its predecessor, the second Forward Atlanta campaign succeeded in attracting new businesses to the city. For much of the early twentieth century, Atlanta had been a branch office town. In the 1960s it became a national headquarters city, as homegrown businesses attained national corporate status and other national businesses relocated to Atlanta. Job rolls expanded by tens of thousands each year during the decade, unemployment levels fell as low as 1.9 percent, and Atlanta continued to rank in the top ten cities in terms of downtown construction, bank clearings, and employment. The regional capital with aspirations of national prominence now had the businesses and the economic statistics to support its claim.

BIG LEAGUE SPORTS

One of the hallmarks of a "big league city" is the presence of major league sports teams, and in the 1960s Mayor Allen aggressively pursued his dream of bringing professional sports to Atlanta. In 1963 Allen met privately in Atlanta with Charles O. Finley, owner of the Kansas City Athletics of the American Baseball League. Finley offered to move his team to Atlanta if the city would build him a new stadium, and Allen agreed to the proposal. The site that the two men eventually agreed upon for the stadium was in an area to the immediate south of the central business district that had been cleared through an earlier urban renewal project. While the land at the time lay vacant, the city did not own the property (it was controlled by the Atlanta Housing Authority).

Nevertheless, Allen went ahead with the plan. He met with Mills B. Lane, head of the Citizens and Southern Bank, and the two came up with a proposal to reconstitute the old Stadium Authority with Lane as treasurer and Coca-Cola Bottling Company executive Arthur Montgomery as chairman. Lane also agreed to pledge the full credit of his bank to the project.

While this plan was being put into effect, the American League informed the mayor that Finley did not have enough league votes to

move his team to Atlanta. Arthur Montgomery received word, however, that stockholders of the Milwaukee Braves of the National Baseball League were interested in relocating their team, and a lunch meeting of Braves stockholders and Atlanta executives was arranged. A favorable response from the luncheon convinced Allen and his allies to continue with the project, and Lane supplied money for architects to begin plans for the stadium even though there was not yet formal approval of the deal from the Braves, the city, or the county. As Mayor Allen later recounted, he and his friends were planning a stadium on "land we didn't own, with money we didn't have, for teams that didn't exist."

A handshake deal with the Milwaukee Braves representatives and their commitment that they would move the team to Atlanta in 1965 finally brought about the public announcement of the deal, and local government officials quickly swung into step to get the project under way and completed on time. The board of aldermen and the Fulton County Commission approved the plan, and the state legislative delegation from Atlanta rushed through the necessary authorization of the funding. To meet the tight construction deadline, the stadium authority agreed to pay an additional $600,000 premium to ensure that the stadium would be built within a year, and fifty-one weeks later the Atlanta–Fulton County Stadium was completed and ready for big league baseball.

Ironically, the stadium had to wait an additional year for its new baseball team while the Milwaukee Braves were ensnarled in litiga-

Alexander Calder's "Three Up, Three Down" (1973) is installed in front of the High Museum of Art, designed by Richard Meier (1980–1983).

tion with the city of Milwaukee. In the meantime, the stadium secured yet another tenant—a professional football team.

As before, Allen relied upon the assistance of his business peers to bring off the deal, convincing Cox Broadcasting executive Leonard Reinsch that he should seek ownership of the new team. Reinsch concluded that the city's best bet would be to solicit the awarding of an American Football League (AFL) franchise since the National Football League (NFL) had earlier turned the city down, and he succeeded in securing an AFL franchise contract. Before Reinsch could present his contract to the Stadium Authority, however, NFL commissioner Pete Rozelle changed his mind and decided that Atlanta would be a good market for an expansion team. As a result, Atlanta got a new NFL football team owned, not by Reinsch, but by insurance executive Rankin Smith, who had been introduced to Rozelle by Georgia Governor Carl Sanders.

As a result of all these hurried and complex negotiations, Atlanta became the first city ever to obtain major league baseball and football teams in a single year. The city also succeeded in adding a professional basketball team to its roster in 1968 when the St. Louis Hawks of the National Basketball Association relocated to Atlanta. At first, the Hawks played in Georgia Tech's Alexander Memorial Coliseum, but in 1972 they moved to a new home in the Omni, a $17 million entertainment and sports facility built on the old railroad gulch west of downtown. The first big league sports team to play in the new structure, however, was not the Hawks but the Atlanta Flames of the National Hockey League, who opened their inaugural season in the fall of 1972. (The team moved to Calgary, Alberta, Canada, in 1980).

THE "HIGH" ARTS

Arts and culture are another measure of urban prominence, and in the 1960s Atlanta cultural institutions also grew in stature and size. Unfortunately, their growth was spurred in large part by a tragic event. On June 3, 1962, 106 Atlantans, most of them members of the Atlanta Art Association, boarded a charter flight in Paris as a part of their tour of European museums. The members of the group, as Mayor Allen later described them, were "the backbone of Atlanta's cultural society, the city's leading patrons of the arts."

As the Air France 707 jet roared down a runway at Orly Airport, something went wrong, and the pilot tried to abort the takeoff. The plane skidded off the end of the runway, plowed through a field, and crashed into a small stone cottage, where the jet burst into flames. All of the people on board (except for two flight attendants) were killed in the accident, and Atlanta's arts community was dealt a heavy blow.

Earlier in the year, Atlanta citizens had rejected a bond issue that included funding for an arts center in Piedmont Park. In the aftermath of the tragedy, however, $13 million was raised through private donations (including a $4 million gift from Robert W. Woodruff) to build a new arts center dedicated to the memory of those who died at Orly. The Atlanta Memorial Arts Building (now the Robert W. Woodruff Arts Center) was completed in 1968 and initially housed not only the High Museum, but also the Atlanta Symphony Orchestra, the Atlanta College of Art, the Alliance Theatre, and the Atlanta Children's Theatre.

Other cultural institutions that grew and matured during this period included the Center for Puppetry Arts, the Atlanta Ballet, and the Atlanta Historical Society (which moved its headquarters in 1966 from Peachtree Street to the elegant Swan House mansion in Buckhead).

MASS TRANSIT

Another hallmark of a big league city and a major element of Mayor Allen's six-point plan was the development of a rapid mass-transit system for the city and its surrounding environs, and in his second term of office, Allen succeeded in laying the foundations for the creation of the Metropolitan Atlanta Rapid Transit Authority (MARTA). The actual financing and startup of MARTA would not occur, however, until after Allen had retired from office.

The campaign for a modern transit system began in 1964 when voters approved an amendment to the state constitution that authorized the establishment of a regional transit authority and provided limited planning funds. A MARTA board was subsequently appointed to represent Atlanta and the surrounding suburban counties. In keeping with Atlanta's tradition of strong links between government and business, the city's representatives to the board consisted of four business executives—three whites (including department store owner Richard Rich, who became MARTA chairman) and one African American (L. D. Milton, president of Citizens Trust Company).

Despite this promising start, plans for MARTA and its rapid rail system quickly ran into difficulty. In 1968, Atlanta area voters rejected a proposal to underwrite the local cost of rail construction with property taxes. The measure was defeated not only in the suburban communities that took part in the election, but in the city as well, with Atlanta black voters comprising a significant portion of those opposed

Downtown Atlanta, mid-1960s.

to the measure. African-American leaders, including Jesse Hill (the president of Atlanta Life Insurance) criticized the project for excluding African Americans from the planning process, for neglecting to hire enough black workers, and for focusing too exclusively on the needs and wishes of white downtown interests.

Mayor Allen retired before these issues could be resolved, but his successor, Sam Massell, garnered the necessary votes to allow MARTA to proceed with its plans. Before this could be achieved, however, MARTA had to go back to the drawing board and redesign both its proposed routes and its funding source. In place of a property tax increase, the Massell administration suggested a one-percent sales tax to underwrite the local share of construction costs (the remaining amount would be picked up by the federal government). Even with these changes, opposition to the rapid transit system remained strong, especially among black voters, many of whom argued that the proposed sales tax was regressive and that it would hit the city's poor the hardest. Mayor Massell undercut this criticism to some extent by extracting a promise from the MARTA board that it would set the fare for the system at fifteen cents and hold it there for seven years. In 1971 the proposal was submitted to the voters, and by a slender margin the referendum was approved.

OTHER MEASURES OF SUCCESS

As the 1960s drew to a close, Mayor Allen saw many of his dreams for the city realized. Atlanta had a new stadium hosting big league baseball and football. A new civic center had been constructed on land cleared through urban renewal. The city had established itself as the regional center of a rapidly expanding rail, air, and highway transportation system. The influx of new businesses and the growth of local ones had spurred the economy and made Atlanta the headquarters for many national corporations. And the city's many cultural arts institutions were growing, maturing, and becoming increasingly well known throughout the nation.

There were other indicators that Atlanta was becoming a major urban center. The metropolitan population, for example, reached the million mark in 1959, and continued to grow quickly during the following decade. The city's skyline was expanding as well. In the period from 1930 to 1960, only one high-rise building—the twenty-two-story Fulton National Bank building—was constructed in downtown Atlanta. In the 1960s, however, a number of new skyscrapers began to appear. One of the individuals most responsible for this trend was Atlanta architect John Portman. The first of Portman's downtown creations, the million-square-foot Merchandise Mart, was completed in 1961 and became the nucleus of a complex of office towers, hotels, retail shops, restaurants, and merchandise space known as Peachtree Center. Portman's innovative design features—such as his large open atriums (including the twenty-story floor-to-roof atrium in the Hyatt Hotel)—dramatically influenced hotel architecture and were imitated throughout the United States and the world. Portman's success also spawned a flurry of construction in downtown Atlanta (seventeen skyscrapers of at least fifteen floors were built during the 1960s) and helped pull the commercial center of the city farther north along Peachtree.

Growth and construction during this period was not just restricted to the downtown, however. In fact, the 1960s also saw the emergence of the city's earliest suburban malls and office parks. In 1959, Lenox Square, metropolitan Atlanta's first regional shopping center, opened in Buckhead, some seven miles north of the central business district. Richard Rich, the chief executive officer of Rich's department store, had made the decision to resist establishing any suburban stores until the interstate highway system was nearer completion and until the Atlanta metropolitan population reached the one million mark. When both of these conditions were met in 1959, Rich's became one of the anchor stores of Lenox Square and helped launch the beginnings of suburban mall development in the metropolitan area. By 1972 there were twenty-four major outlying shopping areas in the Atlanta region and eleven regional shopping centers.

While Atlanta may have lagged somewhat behind other cities in the construction of suburban retail centers, the city was a pioneer in the development of office parks. Between 1965 and 1971, new office parks in the Atlanta area accounted for the construction of over 5.2 million square feet of additional office space. Most of these new office parks were located in the northern suburbs of the city, where space for expansion was available and less costly and where an increasing percentage of the workforce (mostly white) now resided. Suburban industrial parks (which numbered over seventy by 1973) and trucking facilities, which were tied to the metro area's expanding freeway system, offered additional suburban employment and helped draw an increasing number of jobs and workers away from the central business district.

By 1970, despite a decade of impressive construction and development in downtown Atlanta, the city's suburbs were already outpacing the central city in population growth and housing construction. The city of Atlanta's population, for example, grew by less than two percent during the 1960s, and began to decline in numbers following its peak in 1970. The suburban population, on the other hand, mushroomed, accounting for over eighty-six percent of the total population increase in the Atlanta metropolitan area during the 1960s.

Housing figures for this same period reflect a similar trend. In 1960, for example, housing within the city accounted for almost one-half of all the dwelling units in the metropolitan area. Ten years later, the city's share had fallen to thirty-eight percent as dramatic suburban growth overshadowed inner-city housing construction, and the destruction of some thirty-four thousand homes within the city limits through urban renewal and highway construction contributed to yet another Atlanta housing shortage. From 1970 on, much of the impressive growth and development that would establish Atlanta as one of the nation's most important urban centers would take place in the expansive suburban regions beyond the city's borders.

RACE, POLITICS, AND CHANGES IN THE GOVERNING COALITION

At the same time that Atlanta was acquiring all the characteristics of a major city, dramatic changes were also taking place in the makeup and goals of Atlanta's governing coalition. For much of the postwar period, city hall and the white business elite had been allied in a common cause to promote city growth and economic development. The black leadership of Atlanta had been content during this period to make use of their limited but well-coordinated political power and influence to negotiate the gradual relaxation of Jim Crow and to push for the desegregation of the city's public institutions. In the decade of the 1960s, however, a new leadership came to the fore in Atlanta's black communities—a leadership that was younger and less patient with the results and pace of the behind-the-scenes negotiations and "gentlemen's agreements" of the earlier era. By the end of the 1960s, the old biracial agreements were no longer in place, and African Americans had assumed control of the city's governing structure for the first time in Atlanta's history.

Cracks in the Coalition

One of the first major challenges to the governing coalition occurred in 1961 when black college students organized sit-ins to desegregate Atlanta's downtown restaurants. This campaign, as noted earlier, threatened to upset relationships and alliances forged between black leaders and the white business elite and exposed generational cleavages within the black community. Martin Luther King Jr., who had returned to Atlanta following the Montgomery bus boycott and who had personally participated in one of the sit-in demonstrations, soon found himself in the unenviable position of mediating between radical college students and older black leaders such as his father, "Daddy" King, who favored a less confrontational approach. The junior King was able to bridge the generational divide and convince students to halt their protests in return for a promise from white business leaders that after a cooling-off period, the downtown stores would be desegregated. The coalition had held, but the cracks and divisions remained.

One year later, changes in black leadership and tactics became even more apparent in the response to what became known as the Peyton Road barricade incident. In that year, as African Americans moved into the formerly whites-only subdivision of Peyton Forest in southwest Atlanta, the city responded, much as it had in the past, by erecting street barriers to slow and contain further black residential expansion. (Whites apparently continued to enter the subdivision from the south, where housing remained all-white at the time.) The previous year, Mayor Hartsfield had put up a similar barricade in the same section of the city without much damaging reaction. This time, however, the response from the black community was quite different. Black leaders rejected newly-elected Mayor Allen's offer to rezone 250 acres of nearby industrial land to allow the construction of low- to middle-income housing for African Americans and even declined his invitation to meet with representatives of the Atlanta Negro Voters League, the Empire Real Estate Board, and white homeowners to discuss the situation. The newly-formed Citizens Committee for Better City Planning (which included representatives of the Southern Christian Leadership Conference, the Student Non-Violent Coordinating Committee, and the Committee on Appeal for Human Rights) kept up pressure on city hall to remove the barricades, and two suits were filed in court to challenge the city's actions.

In addition to the hostile reaction from Atlanta's black communities, the Peyton Forest barricade attracted the attention of the national press in articles, reports, and editorials that questioned the city's racial progressivism and compared the barricade to the Berlin Wall. This publicity embarrassed the city and forced city hall to finally recognize that the days of a tightly segregated housing market in Atlanta, kept in place by overt discrimination and racial barriers, were over. When a Fulton County Superior Court judge ruled that the barricade was unconstitutional, the mayor did not appeal the decision, but instead moved as quickly as possible to have the barriers taken down.

Riots broke out in the Summerhill neighborhood, summer, 1966.

This public acknowledgement of the right of African Americans to housing on an equal opportunity basis was an important turning point in Atlanta's history. It paved the way for black residential expansion into new areas of the city (particularly in southwest Atlanta). It also accelerated "white flight" out of the city and into the suburbs. During the decade of the 1960s, the city's white population would decline by 60,000 while its black population increased by 70,000. Neighborhoods in southwest Atlanta were transformed, seemingly overnight, from all-white to majority-black communities. In the process, residential segregation within the city actually increased. In effect, the residential color line had finally been broken in Atlanta, only to be redrawn even more dramatically in the boundary between city and suburb.

In 1964, the city was presented with an opportunity to repair the strained relations between its black and white leaders when native son Martin Luther King Jr., was presented with the Nobel Peace Prize. At first, the awarding of this prestigious honor presented Atlanta's white leadership with a dilemma. Some resented the role he had played in the sit-in campaign to desegregate downtown facilities and his involvement in other local protests (including labor union demonstrations at the Scripto Company factory). Still, to ignore the Nobel award would sully the city's national image and call into question its commitment to racial progress. King was honored in Washington and New York after his return to the United States, but when he arrived in Atlanta there was no official welcome from city hall. After persistent pressure and persuasion from Mayor Allen and Coca-Cola executive Robert W. Woodruff, however, the business community and its leadership reluctantly agreed to honor King with a biracial formal dinner (the first in the city's history), held at the Dinkler Hotel on January 27, 1965. More than fifteen hundred blacks and whites—including most of Atlanta's business leaders attended the event.

In 1966, racial problems again surfaced in Atlanta when a riot broke out in Summerhill, a black community that Mayor Allen later described as a "tinderbox of poverty, disease, crime, frustration and unrest, sitting in the very shadow of our new stadium." The immediate cause of the unrest was the shooting and wounding of a black auto-theft suspect, but the underlying roots of the disturbance were unaddressed and unresolved neighborhood problems, including overcrowded housing, the absence of recreational facilities, and high unemployment. By five o'clock in the afternoon on September 6, 1966, hundreds of protesting residents were in the streets, cars had been overturned and burned, and windows shattered. Mayor Allen arrived in the community along with some police and twenty-five black ministers he had summoned and tried to calm the crowd, but neither his nor the ministers' pleas were effective. Instead, as Allen got on top of a police car with a bullhorn to address the crowd, bricks were thrown, the car was rocked, and the mayor was forced to dive for safety into the arms of accompanying policemen. The crowd was finally dispersed with tear gas, and the unrest eventually subsided the following evening—but not before sixteen people had been injured and seventy-five arrested.

Less than a week later, racial violence again broke out—this time when a white man driving through the Boulevard area of the Bedford Pine community shot and killed a sixteen-year-old black. The incident set off a three-day riot in the area with police battling firebombs and bricks. About 20 people were injured and 140 arrested during the melee.

Initially, both the mayor and some of the media blamed the riots on the militant activities and agitating language of Stokely Carmichael and other members of the Student Non-Violent Coordinating Committee, who were present at both disturbances decrying police brutality

Andrew Young Jr. (center) was elected to the U.S. House of Representatives in 1972. Vice Mayor Maynard Jackson (applauding) *celebrated the win.*

and city neglect. Later, however, city hall came to accept the assessment of the Council on Human Relations of Greater Atlanta, which concluded that "the basic responsibility lies with Atlanta's lack of concern over miserable conditions in slum areas." Two months after the riots, Allen called a Mayor's Conference on Housing that set a two-year goal of 9,800 units of low- and moderate-income housing and a five-year goal of 16,800 new units, and also set up a Community Relations Commission to hear complaints and recommendations of residents in low-income neighborhoods. Although the new housing goals were not met by the promised deadlines (due, in large part, to neighborhood factionalism and conflict, distrust of the city officials, and disagreements over the location of subsidized housing), the dissatisfaction and unrest present in Atlanta's low-income black communities and violently expressed in these riots forced the city to reexamine and reshape its housing and urban renewal policies.

The New Power Structure

In April 1968, the city leadership again convened to honor Martin Luther King Jr. This time, however, it was on the occasion of his assassination. More than 200,000 mourners (including well-known national politicians and celebrities) assembled in King's hometown to pay tribute to the civil rights leader. And in the tradition of Atlanta's history of tragedy and rebirth, a commitment to black political progress emerged in the wake of King's death. Colleagues, as well as followers and admirers of King, turned to the ballot box to secure black political gains and representation, and they were successful.

In 1969, Maynard Jackson was elected as the city's first African-American vice mayor (along with Sam Massell, the city's first Jewish mayor), and in 1972, Reverend Andrew Young (a colleague and aide of King) became the first black Georgian to be elected to Congress since Reconstruction. Black community representation in the Georgia legislature also increased during these years, and in 1973, Maynard Jackson became Atlanta's first African-American mayor. That same year, blacks gained equal representation on the city council for the first time and a slight majority on the school board.

Another indication of the changing political climate in Atlanta in 1973 was the adoption of a new city charter that changed the selection process for most city council members from at-large elections (which had traditionally been used to restrict minority representation) to district elections and that mandated the involvement of intown neighborhoods in the preparation of one-, five-, and fifteen-year comprehensive development plans. That same year, a long-standing fight over city school desegregation was brought to a close by a negotiated settlement that, in effect, granted greater African-American input in administrative and staff assignments in the school system and approved a student assignment plan that ensured that each city school would be at least thirty percent black. (In return for these assurances, the local NAACP dropped demands for busing and a metropolitan-wide end to racial imbalance in the schools.)

Maynard Jackson, Atlanta's new mayor, was sailing into unchartered governmental waters when he took office in 1974. Not only was Atlanta a majority black city for the first time in its history, but its charter had been fundamentally changed, and the old governing coalition that had ruled the city for decades was no longer in place.

Jackson was in many ways, however, the perfect man for the job. Only thirty-five years of age when he was elected, Jackson was nonetheless very familiar with Atlanta, its politics, and its many economic, cultural, social, and political coalitions. Though born in Dallas, Texas, Jackson had strong Atlanta connections. His maternal grandfather was John Wesley Dobbs, a black community and fraternal leader who had championed voter registration in Atlanta (and who is credited with nicknaming Auburn Avenue "Sweet Auburn"), and his father was pastor of Atlanta's historic and influential Friendship Baptist Church from 1945 until his death in 1953.

Jackson's election signaled more than simply a racial change in the governing coalition of Atlanta. It also represented a fundamental transformation in the priorities and socio-economic makeup of local government itself. Before assuming office, Jackson announced his intention to create a new environment at city hall where "grassroots leaders, white and black, will be sitting alongside of persons who are quite wealthy, quite influential, and sometimes not as attuned as they need to be to what it is really like to be living close to disaster." The new mayor hoped to bring new people and new groups to the bargaining table, and the composition and policies of his administration reflected that orientation.

The number of women and minorities employed by the city shot up during Jackson's two terms in office, and his administration implemented a sweeping program to guarantee the black community and black businesses a substantial share of city business. Affirmative-action hiring policies were soon required of all city suppliers, and joint-venture arrangements were negotiated in situations where minority businesses were nonexistent or too small to handle the projects by themselves.

The new mayor's interest in involving grassroots organizations in the government, planning, and development of the city was also reflected in the development of Atlanta's neighborhood planning unit (NPU) system. To carry out the new city charter's mandate for increased citizen participation, Atlanta was divided into twenty-four neighborhood planning units. Each unit was composed of a cluster of inner-city neighborhoods and was designed to bring together area community leaders and involve them in important decision-making processes. The new ordinance setting up the NPU system required that all planning and zoning proposals go before the affected NPUs for their reaction and comments, and Mayor Jackson created a Division of Neighborhood Planning to give the NPUs assistance in developing their priorities and in expressing their opinions.

These actions by the Jackson administration to involve grassroots organizations in government and to increase participation by minority businesses in city projects alarmed and angered some members of Atlanta's white business elite. Particularly galling to these businessmen were Jackson's insistence that twenty percent of the contracts awarded to companies working on Atlanta's new $400 million airport go to minority firms, his suggestion that he might deposit the city's money in Birmingham banks if Atlanta's financial institutions did not name women and minorities to their boards and implement plans for members of these groups to progress up the corporate ladder, and his dramatic expansion of the powers and personnel of the mayor's office.

In response to these developments, Harold Brockey, the chairman of Central Atlanta Progress, an organization composed mainly of downtown business leaders and major property holders in the area, sent a letter to Mayor Jackson in which he outlined concerns about the lack of access to the mayor, the deterioration of the close historical relationship between business and government, and the growing perception within Atlanta's white business community that Jackson was anti-white. When the local and national press caught wind of the letter and publicized it, both Jackson and white business leaders closed ranks to deny allegations that a rift was developing between the city and its white businesses and that these businessmen were making plans to abandon the city for the suburbs.

While the Brockey letter did not alter Maynard Jackson's priorities, it did lead to better communication between city hall and the business community. And in the process, Jackson and the white business elite succeeded in working out a set of accommodations that included an agreement that joint ventures would be encouraged, but not required, in airport construction contracts; the establishment of regular meetings between city hall and business leaders; the creation of an independent agency (the Atlanta Economic Development Corporation) to oversee and evaluate economic development projects; and Jackson's promise to make trips with members of the chamber of commerce to promote Atlanta and its investment potential. Jackson's election to office and the change in the racial composition of the city had forever transformed the local power structure, but biracial negotiations and cooperation were still an important part of Atlanta's governing style. Jackson's willingness to listen to and address business concerns and priorities ensured that these processes and the economic development of the region would continue to move forward.

Black control of the local political process was demonstrated anew in 1981, when Andrew Young defeated a well-financed white opponent, Sidney Marcus, in the race for mayor. Unlike Maynard Jackson, Andrew Young was already a well-known figure (both nationally and internationally) when he took office. He had been one of Martin Luther King Jr.'s most trusted lieutenants during the civil rights movement, had been elected to Congress in 1972, and had served as President Jimmy Carter's ambassador to the United Nations. During his stint as U.N. ambassador, Young had earned the admiration of Third World nations and the criticism of some Western leaders and politicians for his sometimes unguarded and candid comments about the nature and priorities of Western diplomacy. Despite this reputation, Young was less an agitator than a conciliator. It was during his administration as mayor that the relationship between city hall and the white business elite was strengthened and restored, and the power and influence of the neighborhood planning units was diminished.

Economic development was an important part of Young's plans for the city, and shortly after he took office he arranged a luncheon with downtown business leaders, most of whom had supported his opponent in the mayoral race. At this luncheon, Young opened his address to the businesspeople by declaring that "I didn't get elected with your help," then followed with the admission that "I can't govern without you." In one short conciliatory meeting, Young had succeeded in cementing an alliance between city hall and business leaders that would remain strong throughout his terms in office.

At the same time that Young was solidifying his relationship with business leaders, he was working to diminish the influence of neighborhood groups by undermining the power of the NPU system. Under Young's administration, the NPU staff was reduced to one person, and in a series of stand-offs between business interests and neighborhood organizations, Young consistently weighed in on the side of business. In issues as diverse and as divisive as a proposal to create a "residential parkway" in northeast Atlanta, a plan to establish an intown "piggyback" facility to connect trucks (from I-20) with a CSX Transportation rail yard and line near the neighborhoods of Cabbagetown, Reynoldstown, and Grant Park, and the creation of a domed football stadium in the Vine City area, Mayor Young eventually supported the proposed projects despite the active and vocal opposition of neighborhood groups.

By the end of Young's first term of office, the relationship between business and city hall had been strengthened, and downtown business leaders once again had easy access to the mayor's office. But while this biracial coalition continued, the makeup of the local political power structure remained very different from that found in Atlanta during the early postwar decades. The office of the mayor, the presidency of the city council, and a large majority of Atlanta's elective and appointive offices were now held by African Americans, and the city that had been two-thirds white in 1950 was now two-thirds black.

City hall remained pro-business and pro-development in its orientation, but the nature of those business connections was also changing. Andrew Young, for example, promoted Third World investment in the city and welcomed and encouraged an increasingly international business presence in Atlanta. This pro-business focus and approach was also evident in the administrations of the African-

American mayors who would follow Young into office—Maynard Jackson (who returned for a third term in 1990), Bill Campbell (a long-time city council member who served as mayor from 1994 to 2002), and Shirley Franklin (Atlanta's first woman mayor, who took office in 2002).

Another Atlanta group whose growing political strength found expression in the latter decades of the twentieth century was the city's growing gay and lesbian population. Political activism in Atlanta's gay community began in the early 1970s, in part as a reaction and response to the famous Stonewall Riots of 1969 in New York City in which gays engaged in protests and street battles with police for five days following the raid of a Greenwich Village gay bar called the Stonewall Inn. In 1970, on the anniversary of the riots, about one hundred gay activists marched down Peachtree Street in what would become the annual Gay Pride celebration. The following year, the Gay Liberation Front was formed, and in 1972 the Atlanta Lesbian Feminist Alliance was established.

An increase in gay activism and political involvement in the 1980s and 1990s resulted in new local laws and statutes on sexual discrimination, including a 1986 city council resolution banning discrimination against employees based on sexual orientation and a 1993 statute extending benefits to same-sex domestic partners of Atlanta city employees. This increased political clout was also reflected in the election of gays and lesbians to local and state office. In 1997, Cathy Woolard became Georgia's first openly gay elected official, winning an Atlanta City Council seat. Four years later she was selected as council president. That same year (2001) Karla Drenner of Avondale (an Atlanta suburban community) became the first openly gay state legislator in the South when she was elected to the Georgia House of Representatives.

Other emerging political groups and coalitions include Atlanta's rapidly-growing ethnic and cultural communities. Latinos, the state's and Atlanta's largest and fastest-growing immigrant group, for example, are already represented in public office, ranging from the metropolitan area's first Hispanic police chief—John King in Doraville—to two unopposed Latino candidates in 2002 running for the Georgia House of Representatives—Pedro Marin, who was born in Puerto Rico, and David Casas, of Cuban descent. As the number of registered voters in other immigrant groups continue to rise, this increasing ethnic diversity will also likely be reflected in Atlanta's governing coalition. For the present, however, the city and metropolitan region's political structure remains largely biracial.

TOURISM AND CONVENTIONS

At the same time that the composition of Atlanta's governing coalition was changing in the 1970s, so too was the local economic mix. During that decade, the tourism and convention trade emerged as the growth industry for Atlanta and the surrounding region. In the downtown area alone, hotel room inventories increased from four thousand in 1965 to fourteen thousand a decade later as more and more highrise hotels were built to handle the rapidly increasing demand. By 1972, Atlanta already ranked third among cities in terms of its convention business, with only Chicago and New York handling more delegates per year.

This dramatic growth in tourism was due to a number of factors. The Atlanta Convention and Visitors Bureau's aggressive marketing of the city, for example, certainly helped, as did Atlanta's strategic transportation connections—including Hartsfield International Airport (which handled an average of 2,400 flights to 135 U.S. cities in 1980), links to three major interstate highways, and the city's long-established rail connections. But perhaps the biggest boost to the growth of the convention and tourist trade in the 1970s was the construction of a number of support facilities to accommodate large conferences and trade shows. Chief among these new convention buildings were the Merchandise Mart (which opened in 1961 and was expanded in 1968); the Civic Auditorium (1965); the Apparel Mart (1979, expanded in 1989); the Omni International (an office-hotel megastructure that was completed in 1972); and the World Congress Center (which, when it opened in 1976, featured the nation's largest single-floor exhibition space, as well as a large auditorium with built-in simultaneous interpretation facilities). This concentration of convention support facilities in Atlanta (coupled with the presence of downtown sports arenas and stadiums) made the city an attractive locale for large conferences, conventions, concerts, and trade shows and also helped Atlanta secure a number of high-profile gatherings during the following decades, including the 1988 Democratic National Convention and the 1994 Super Bowl.

THE GOVERNMENT PRESENCE

Another factor contributing to the growth of the local economy during this period was the wide spectrum of governmental agencies and institutions based in the metropolitan area. On the local level, Atlanta operated as the seat of municipal and county government. On the state level, of course, it served as Georgia's capital city and the headquarters of many of the state's departments and agencies. On the federal level, Atlanta hosted the largest regional concentration of national governmental agencies (including the rapidly growing Centers for Disease Control and Prevention) to be found outside Washington, D.C. Finally, as noted earlier, the metropolitan area also included a number of military bases and installations, including Dobbins Air Force Base, Fort McPherson, and the Atlanta Naval Air Station.

Taken as a whole, these governmental bodies constituted one of the metropolitan area's largest employers and a force that exerted considerable influence on Atlanta's development and changing economy in the last half of the twentieth century. With the increasing movement of jobs, retail industries, and office buildings to the urban perimeter, for example, the local, state, and federal government presence in downtown proved to be one of the area's few stabilizing influences, keeping a sizeable workforce in place during the 1980s and 1990s and even expanding, in the case of the federal government, to occupy one of downtown Atlanta's most important commercial institutions—Rich's department store.

THE INTERNATIONAL CITY

As Atlanta's metropolitan area continued to grow and its economy became more diversified in the latter decades of the twentieth century, the city once again reinvented and redefined itself—this time as an "international" city. Throughout its history, as this book has demonstrated, Atlanta's political, business, and civic leaders invented slogans and concepts to announce both the city's contemporary orientation and importance, as well as its future aspirations. In the nineteenth century, for example, the city advertised itself as "The Gateway to the South," and during the height of the Civil Rights Movement, the mayor and the business elite promoted an image of Atlanta as "The City Too Busy to Hate." In the early 1970s, the city elevated its status and its sights yet again when it began billing itself as "The World's Next Great City." And like the slogans of earlier eras, this latest proclamation at first consisted of one-part reality and two-parts exaggeration.

In the years that followed, however, Atlanta gained additional support for its self-description as a city of international importance. The construction of the massive Hartsfield International Airport, as noted earlier, provided the city with international flight connections. The opening of the World Congress Center and the construction of growing numbers of high-rise hotels in downtown Atlanta and in the suburban periphery strengthened the city's hold on a rapidly increasing international convention business. International economic

ties to Atlanta were also furthered through the arrival of foreign companies and investors in the metropolitan area. By 1995, there were already more than one thousand foreign companies from thirty-five foreign countries located in the Atlanta metropolitan statistical area, as well as forty-two foreign consulates (career and honorary) and twenty-seven trade and tourism offices.

The international presence in Atlanta also increased through the arrival of new ethnic and immigrant groups. In March 1995, for example, there were an estimated 105,000 Hispanic residents in metropolitan Atlanta, some 25,000 Jamaicans, 13,000 Koreans, and almost 20,000 immigrants and refugees from southeast Asia.

At the same time that international groups and businesses were establishing a presence in Atlanta, local businesses, organizations, and even sports teams were also increasing their visibility abroad. Coca-Cola, for example, built upon its World War II overseas expansion to become one of the best known beverage products in the world; Cable News Network (CNN), a locally based unit of Turner Broadcasting, emerged as the world's most-watched news channel; and Atlanta's first major league professional sports team—the Atlanta Braves—became the World Baseball Champions in 1995 (forever erasing the sports image of Atlanta as "Loserville").

President Jimmy Carter, a longtime member of the faculty of Emory University, further expanded Atlanta's international visibility through the Carter Center's efforts to negotiate for peace and to eradicate the crippling effects of poverty and disease in countries all over the globe. The Nobel Foundation awarded Carter its Peace Prize for 2002 for "his decades of untiring effort to find peaceful solutions to international conflicts, to advance democracy and human rights, and to promote economic and social development." In his Nobel Lecture given in Oslo, Carter accepted the award "not . . . as a public official, but as a citizen of a troubled world who finds hope in a growing consensus that the generally accepted goals of society are peace, freedom, human rights, environmental quality, the alleviation of suffering, and the rule of law."

Perhaps the greatest indication of Atlanta's rising international status, however, occurred when the city hosted the 1996 Centennial Olympic Games. Like the Cotton States and International Exposition a century earlier, the Olympic Games drew attention and crowds to the city and made Atlanta one of the select group of twenty-one cities that have been chosen to present the Olympic summer games since their rebirth in 1896. Competing with Atlanta for the prize in 1990 were Toronto, Canada; Melbourne, Australia; Manchester, England; Belgrade, Yugoslavia; and Athens, Greece (the first city to host the modern Olympics a century earlier.) Some of the strengths that helped promote Atlanta's bid were the same forces that had propelled the city's rapid growth and development during the second half of the twentieth century—a large international airport, ample hotel rooms, an extensive rapid rail and bus transportation system, experience handling large masses of people because of the city's large convention industry, and a strong international corporate presence. Leading the charge to capture the Games was Atlanta businessman and attorney Billy Payne.

The resulting 1996 Atlanta Olympic games were one of the largest sporting events ever held. More athletes (10,788) participated than ever before in Olympic history, including more than forty percent more women than in the preceding 1992 Olympics. More international delegations (197) were also present, and for the first time since the modern games began, every delegation that was invited by the International Olympic Committee to participate accepted the invitation. The Centennial Olympic Games in Atlanta also featured more sports (26) and more events (271) than ever before, spread out over 29 competition venues (most of which were located in the Atlanta metropolitan area). It is estimated that 5 million people attended the Olympics in Atlanta, while an additional 3.5 billion watched worldwide via television. An incredibly large force of staff and volunteers (over 100,000) was also involved in preparations for and the presentation of the Atlanta Olympic Games.

Although the Games were considered a success by Atlanta residents and most of the visitors and athletes who attended, there were complaints, lodged most frequently by the international press, about the city's inadequate lodging and public transportation facilities. The greatest stumbling block for the Centennial Olympic games, however, was a tragedy that occurred midway through the events on July 27, 1996. On that day, a pipe bomb left in an abandoned backpack exploded in Centennial Olympic Park (a popular gathering place where hundreds of thousands of people came each day to shop for official Olympics merchandise or to enjoy the concerts and performances of the Southern Crossroads Festival). One person was killed directly by the blast, another died later of a heart attack, and 110 others were injured. The park was closed for three days while the sporting competitions continued, but reopened with a moving ceremony that both marked the tragedy and reaffirmed the public's and the athletes' resolve that the Games continue.

The Centennial Olympic Games in Atlanta ended on August 4, 1996, but their impact continued to be felt in many areas. The Games contributed, for example, to the construction of a number of sports or competition venues on the campuses of local colleges and universities, including an aquatic center at Georgia Tech, a fifteen hundred-seat stadium at Morris Brown College, a five thousand-seat stadium at Clark Atlanta University, and a gymnasium at Morehouse College. Many of these facilities, as well as other competition venues constructed for the Atlanta Olympics, were also utilized for the Tenth Paralympic Games—the premiere competition event for physically impaired athletes that took place in Atlanta shortly after the Olympic Games concluded. For ten days from August 15 to August 25, 1996, over 3,300 Paralympic athletes from 104 countries competed in seventeen full medal and two demonstration sports. In the process, 268 world or Paralympic records were set or broken as an estimated fifty million spectators watched in person or on television.

When the Olympic and Paralympic Games were concluded, three facilities and sites that had played a key role in these events found new adaptive uses. The Olympic Stadium, where most of the track and field events for both Games had taken place, was reconfigured to become Turner Field (home of the Atlanta Braves baseball team). The Olympic Village, which housed the athletes during the Games, was converted to student housing for both Georgia Tech and Georgia State Universities. And the twenty-one-acre Centennial Olympic Park, a focal point for the Olympic and Paralympic experience, was transformed into a new public park—the first large public park to be developed in a major U.S. city in more than twenty-five years.

The impact of the 1996 Olympics was also clearly reflected in Atlanta's and the state's economies, which profited from an infusion of some $5 billion. But the greatest long-term impact associated with Atlanta's Olympic experience may have actually resulted from the intense national and international scrutiny the city received both during and after the Games. Critics during the Games, as noted earlier, often drew attention to the city's inadequate public transportation system and its unrestrained commercialism (witnessed in the corporate and vendor environments surrounding Centennial Olympic Park). After the Games and following a bid scandal associated with the 1998 Winter Olympics in Salt Lake City, Utah, the press, Congress, and the International Olympic Committee (IOC) took a closer look at Atlanta's campaign to capture the 1996 Olympics and its financing of those Games. Although Atlanta emerged from this experience relatively unscathed, the IOC was forced by press attention and public pressure to alter many of its policies and procedures for reviewing and selecting host cities. In the end, despite the criticisms, Atlanta Olympic leaders achieved many of their goals, including gaining increased international recognition for the city, and Atlanta took its place among an elite list of global cities which have successfully hosted and presented the Olympic Games.

THE PROMISES AND CHALLENGES OF A NEW MILLENIUM

As Atlanta prepared to face its second turn-of-the-century and a new millennium, the forces and trends that had shaped the city and the surrounding metropolitan area in the decades following World War II were still at work and clearly evident. Suburban growth and development that began in the 1960s, for example, accelerated towards the turn of the century as the total number of residents in the metropolitan area grew from 2,233,000 in 1980 to 4,112,200 in 2000. During the 1990s, Atlanta outpaced all other metropolitan areas in the United States (except Phoenix) in its rate of population growth and by 2000 it was number one in the nation. The absence of geographical or topographical barriers to expansion in the Atlanta metropolitan area also contributed to a very dispersed population pattern. In fact, Atlanta at the turn of the twenty-first century had the smallest population density of all major metro regions in the United States. (In 1999, for example, Atlanta's population density was 1,370 per mile, compared with 5,400 per mile for Los Angeles.)

A significant trend worth noting, however, was the movement of almost 9,000 new residents into the city of Atlanta between 2001 and 2002—the largest single-year increase since the 1950s. This back-to-the-city movement not only represents a reversal of the white flight or suburban exodus of the 1960s, but may also represent the beginnings of the economic rejuvenation of downtown Atlanta.

As throughout most of its history, the populations residing in the city of Atlanta and the surrounding metropolitan area at the turn of the century were primarily African American and white—with the city retaining a majority black population (61.4 percent) in 2000, while the suburbs remained majority white (66.3 percent). Also contributing to this population mix and distribution, however, were an increasing number of new ethnic and cultural groups. By the year 2000, Hispanics constituted 4.5 percent of the Atlanta city population and Asians another 3.2 percent. In the larger metropolitan area, a similar change was taking place, as 10 percent of the population (more than double the number in any preceding census year) were now categorized as foreign-born. Almost 80 percent of these immigrant groups came from Latin America and Asia, including an increasing number of newcomers from Mexico, Jamaica, Korea, Vietnam, Cambodia, China, and a wide range of countries in Africa and Central and South America.

In the transportation sector, airplanes and automobiles continued to have a tremendous impact on the metropolitan region. The deregulation of the airline industries in the late 1970s and the adoption of a hub-and-spoke system enabled Hartsfield International Airport to gain an increasing number of international and European routes in the following decades. By 2001, Hartsfield was the busiest passenger airport in the world, serving almost seventy-six million people a year. Twenty-one airlines operated out of this airport, flying to destinations all over the world (including fifty-five non-stop flights to cities outside the United States). Today, as a result of the increased passenger and flight load, Hartsfield International Airport is pursuing the building of a fifth runway at a projected cost of some $5 billion.

Automobiles, the transportation mode that had done so much to shape the city in the first half of the twentieth century, also continued to have a major impact on the layout and lifestyles of metropolitan Atlanta as the city neared the turn of the century. As the numbers of residents in the outlying areas continued to grow in the 1980s and 1990s, the state Department of Transportation responded by increasing the number of passenger lanes on interstates I-85, I-75, and I-20 (including, most recently, the construction of high-occupancy vehicle lanes to encourage carpooling) and also on I-285, the high-speed, limited-access highway that encircles the city. Georgia 400—a toll road connecting suburban communities north of Atlanta to the city—was also constructed. By the turn of the century there were 2.5 million vehicles registered in the metro area, and motorists were driving approximately 100 million miles every day on Atlanta highways and roads.

In the area of mass transit, MARTA, once envisioned as a cure for both Atlanta's dependence upon automobile travel and the city's non-pedestrian orientation, failed to completely fulfill either of these goals. Suburban counties—particularly Cobb and Gwinnett—resisted the expansion of MARTA rail and bus lines into their jurisdictions and right-of-ways for rail expansion in other areas proved extremely costly. New rail stations and track were added, however, to the main north/south line, resulting in a rapid rail route that stretched from the Chamblee Dunwoody area in north Dekalb County through downtown Atlanta to the airport on the south side of the region. By the turn of the century, despite county opposition and financial restrictions, MARTA was transporting an estimated 155 million passengers annually by bus and rail.

The changes in Atlanta's transportation sectors, especially at Hartsfield International Airport, also supported the city's bid during the latter decades of the twentieth century to increase its convention and tourism business. In year 2000, there were over three million people attending conventions in Atlanta and staying in the metropolitan area's 88,000 hotel rooms. The on-going enlargement of the Georgia World Congress Center (for a projected total of 1.4 million square feet of exhibit space and 105 meeting rooms), the revitalization of Underground Atlanta, and the construction of new sports facilities—Turner Field for the Atlanta Braves baseball team, the Georgia Dome for the Atlanta Falcons football team, and Phillips Arena for the Atlanta Hawks basketball and Atlanta Thrashers hockey teams—contributed to this effort as well. These downtown facilities provided residents and tourists with increased options for entertainment and also slowed somewhat the movement of many major retail and commercial enterprises and industries to the outlying suburbs. The announcement in 2002 that the world's largest aquarium, an enlarged World of Coca-Cola museum, and a new children's museum will be located on the grounds of Centennial Olympic Park should further anchor and serve the growing downtown entertainment and convention business.

These important trends and developments in population growth, residential distribution and makeup, transportation, and business and commerce at the turn of the century appear, on the surface, to describe a city and a metropolitan region that is vibrant, growing, and economically strong. There are some troubling signs and problems, however, associated with some of these trends that must be addressed and corrected in the twenty-first century. Unchecked suburban sprawl and widespread automobile usage, for example, have contributed to difficult traffic problems and a host of environmental issues, including the loss of trees and greenspace and increased air and water pollution. The Atlanta metro area lost some 190,000 acres of tree cover from 1988 to 1998 to residential and commercial development in the suburban metropolis. The following year, the region produced a record sixty-nine days of smog alerts, and the average traffic commute of thirty-two miles, already the longest in the nation, became one of the slowest as well, as interstates and highways filled up with cars. In 1998, the Environmental Protection Agency ruled that Atlanta did not comply with the 1990 Clean Air Act, a decision that threatened to halt $1 billion in federal highway funds and an additional $700 million that had already been approved for highway projects before the ruling. The state government of Georgia responded with urgent appeals to workers to telecommute and/or ride-share and the establishment of a Greater Regional Transportation Authority (GRTA) with the power to create a regional public transit system and the ability to compel metro counties to pay for it. Plans for a great "northern arc"—a superhighway to connect interstates I-85 and I-75 further north of Atlanta—also began to be considered and promoted.

The significant racial divide between city and suburb actually lessened somewhat at the turn of the century, as black suburbanization continued to increase and a small, but growing back-to-the-city movement among white Atlantans gained momentum. In addition, an increasing number of Atlanta-area residents, both black and white, according to polls and surveys, are now more willing to live in integrated neighborhoods. This change in attitude was also borne out in a recent Brookings Institution study which noted that the number of metro Atlanta residents living in the most integrated neighborhoods rose by 2,500 percent during the 1990s (while the number in the most segregated areas dropped by 39 percent). Residential segregation of the races, however, is still very evident, and, according to an Associated Press analysis of 1990 and 2000 black-white housing patterns, Atlanta remains the most segregated city in Georgia and the second most segregated city in the nation (behind Chicago).

Comparisons between the city of Atlanta and its suburbs at the

Buildings along Peachtree Street dominate the present-day skyline.

turn of the century also reveal significant and continuing differences in income and job opportunities. The poverty rate for the entire metro area in 2000, for example, was only 7.9 percent, while within the city it was 25 percent. Similarly, from 1980 to 1990, the central city's share of jobs in the region dropped from 40 to 30 percent, while northern suburbs' share rose from 40 to 52 percent.

WHAT THE FUTURE HOLDS

As this book has demonstrated, problems, as well as opportunities associated with urban growth, race, and transportation have long been a part of Atlanta's history, and they are likely to influence the development and character of this city and region for years, and perhaps decades, to come. Atlanta's ability to bridge the racial, economic, political, and geographical divisions that have historically separated the city from its outlying regions and metro Atlanta's success in establishing intraregional processes and agencies to plan, develop, and shape future metropolitan growth and to control the use and pollution of the region's land, air, and water may well determine whether Atlanta survives or thrives in the twenty-first century. It is difficult to imagine or predict what new image and vision the Atlanta Spirit will invent for this new age, but if it succeeds in meeting these challenges, Atlanta may become as Mayor Maynard Jackson once described it thirty years ago, "a gateway to a new time, a new era, a new beginning for the cities of our land."

RESOURCES AND SUGGESTED READINGS

GENERAL RESOURCES ON ATLANTA

Blass, Kimberly S., and Michael Rose. *Atlanta Scenes: Photojournalism in the Atlanta History Center Collection.* Dover, N.H.: Arcadia Publishing, 1998.

Garett, Franklin M. *Atlanta and Environs: A Chronicle of Its People and Events.* 2 vols. Athens: University of Georgia Press, 1954.

Mason, Herman "Skip." *Going Against the Wind: A Pictorial History of African-American Atlanta.* Atlanta: Longstreet Press, 1992.

———. *Politics, Civil Rights, and Law in Black Atlanta, 1870–1970.* Charleston: Arcadia Publishing, 2000.

Newman, Harvey K. *Southern Hospitality: Tourism and the Growth of Atlanta.* Tuscaloosa: The University of Alabama Press, 1999.

Metropolitan Frontiers: Atlanta, 1835–2000. Signature exhibition. Atlanta History Center. Opened 1993.

Rose, Michael. *Atlanta Then and Now.* San Diego, California: Thunder Bay Press, 2001.

Roth, Darlene. *Greater Atlanta: A Shared Destiny.* Carlsbad, California: Heritage Media Corp., 2000.

Roth, Darlene, and Andy Ambrose, *Metropolitan Frontiers: A Short History of Atlanta.* Atlanta: Longstreet Press, Inc., 1996.

Rutheiser, Charles. *Imagineering Atlanta: The Politics of Place in the City of Dreams.* New York: Verso, 1996.

Shavin, Norman, and Bruce Galphin. *Atlanta: Triumph of a People.* Atlanta: Capricorn Corp., 1982.

White, Dana F., and Timothy J. Crimmins, eds. *Atlanta Historical Journal* (Summer/Fall 1982). Special issue on the physical development of the city and surrounding areas.

I. BEGINNINGS: 1800–1865

Castel, Albert. *Decision in the West: The Atlanta Campaign of 1864.* Lawrence, Kansas: University Press of Kansas, 1992.

Davis, Robert S., Jr. *Requiem for a Lost City: Sallie Clayton's Memoirs of Civil War Atlanta.* Macon, Ga.: Mercer University Press, 1999.

Davis, Stephen. *Atlanta Will Fall: Sherman, Joe Johnson, and the Yankee Heavy Battalions.* Wilmington, Delaware: SR Books, 2001.

Dyer, Thomas G. *Secret Yankees: The Union Circle in Confederate Atlanta.* Baltimore: The John Hopkins University Press, 1999.

Ehle, John. *The Trail of Tears: The Rise and Fall of the Cherokee Nation.* New York: Anchor Books/Doubleday, 1998.

Hill, Sarah. *Weaving New Worlds: Southeastern Cherokee Women and Their Basketry.* Chapel Hill: The University of North Carolina Press, 1997.

Hill, Sarah, and Sue Evans Vrooman. *Native Lands: Indians and Georgia.* Atlanta: Atlanta History Center, 1999. (Exhibit catalogue)

Hudson, Charles. *The Southeastern Indians.* Knoxville: University of Tennessee Press, 1976.

Kennett, Lee. *Marching Through Georgia: The Story of Soldiers and Civilians During Sherman's Campaign.* New York: HarperCollins Publishers, 1995.

McMurry, Richard M. *Atlanta 1864: Last Chance for the Confederacy.* Lincoln, Neb.: University of Nebraska Press, 2000.

Rose, Michael. *Atlanta: A Portrait of the Civil War.* Charleston, S.C.: Arcadia Publishing, 1999.

Williams, David. *The Georgia Gold Rush: Twenty-Niners, Cherokees, and Gold Fever.* Columbia, S.C.: The University of South Carolina Press, 1993.

II. A NEW SOUTH CITY: 1865–1900

Atlanta Exposition and South Illustrated. Chicago: Adler Art Publishing Co., 1895.

Carter, Rev. E. R. *The Black Side: A Partial History of the Business, Religious and Educational Side of the Negro in Atlanta.* Atlanta: n. p., 1894.

Cooper, Walter G. *The Cotton States and International Exposition and South, Illustrated.* Atlanta: The Illustrator Co., 1896.

Davis, Harold E. *Henry Grady's New South: Atlanta, A Brave and Beautiful City.* Tuscaloosa, Alabama: The University of Alabama Press, 1990.

Doyle, Don H. *New Men, New Cities, New South: Atlanta, Nashville, Charleston, Mobile, 1860–1910.* Chapel Hill: University of North Carolina Press, 1990.

Duncan, Russell. *Entrepreneur for Equality: Governor Rufus Bullock, Commerce, and Race in Post-Civil War Georgia.* Athens: University of Georgia Press, 1994.

Garrett, Franklin. *Yesterday's Atlanta.* Miami: E. A. Seemann Publishing, Inc., 1977.

Hertzberg, Steven. "The Jewish Community of Atlanta from the End of the Civil War Until the Eve of the Frank Case." *American Jewish Historical Quarterly.* 62 (March 1973): 250–85.

———. *Strangers Within the Gate City: The Jews of Atlanta, 1845–1915.* Philadelphia: Jewish Publication Society of America, 1978.

Hunter, Tera W. *To 'Joy My Freedom: Southern Black Women's Lives and Labors After the Civil War.* Cambridge: Harvard University Press, 1997.

Jones, Jacqueline. *Labor of Love, Labor of Sorrow: Black Women, Work and the Family, From Slavery to the Present.* New York: Vintage Books, 1985.

King, Augusta Wylie. "Atlanta's First Ball Park and Baseball Team, 1866." *Atlanta Historical Bulletin.* 8 (December 1947): 12–17.

Lewis, David Levering. *W. E. B. Du Bois: Biography of a Race, 1868–1919.* New York: Henry Holt and Company, 1993.

Merritt, Carole. *The Herndons: An Atlanta Family.* Athens: University of Georgia Press, 2002.

Mixon, Gregory. "The Political Career of Henry A. Rucker: A Survivor in a New South City," *Atlanta History: A Journal of Georgia and the South.* 45 (Summer 2001): 4–26.

Orr, N. Lee. *Alfredo Barili and the Rise of Classical Music in Atlanta.* Atlanta: Scholars Press, 1996.

Rabinowitz, Howard N. *Race Relations in the Urban South, 1865–1890.* Athens: University of Georgia Press, 1996.

Russell, James Michael. *Atlanta, 1847–1890: City Building in the Old South and the New.* Baton Rouge: Louisiana State University Press, 1988.

Sheehan, C. J. "Atlanta's Public Schools, 1873–1883." *Atlanta Historical Bulletin.* 2 (November 1936): 5–12.

Thornberry, Jerry John. "The Development of Black Atlanta, 1865–1885." Ph.D. diss. University of Maryland, 1977.

III. FORWARD ATLANTA: 1900–1940

Bauerlein, Mark. *Negrophobia: A Race Riot in Atlanta, 1906.* San Francisco: Encounter Books, 2001.

Brownell, Blaine A. "The Commercial-Civic Elite and City Planning in Atlanta, Memphis and New Orleans in the 1920s." *Journal of Southern History.* 41 (August 1975): 339–68.

Bryant, James C. "Yaarab Temple and the Fox Theatre: The Survival of a Dream." *Atlanta History: A Journal of Georgia and the South.* 39 (Summer 1995): 5–22.

Burrison, John A. "Fiddlers in the Alley: Atlanta as an Early Country Music Center." *Atlanta Historical Bulletin.* 21 (Summer 1977): 59–87.

Crimmons, Timothy J. "Bungalow Suburbs: East And West." *Atlanta Historical Journal.* 26 (Summer/Fall 1982): 83–94.

Crowe, Charles. "Racial Massacre in Atlanta, September 22, 1906." *Journal of Negro History.* 54 (April 1969): 150–73.

Daniel, Wayne W. *Pickin' on Peachtree: A History of Country Music in Atlanta, Georgia.* Chicago: University of Illinois Press, 1990.

Darnell, Tim. *The Crackers: Early Days of Atlanta Baseball.* Athens, Ga.: Hill Street Press, 2003.

Davis, Leroy. *A Clashing of the Soul: John Hope and the Dilemma of African American Leadership and Black Higher Education in the Early Twentieth Century.* Athens: University of Georgia Press, 1998.

Dinnerstein, Leonard. *The Leo Frank Case.* New York: Columbia University Press, 1968.

Dittmer, John. *Black Georgia in the Progressive Era.* Urbana: University of Illinois Press, 1977.

Fink, Gary M. *The Fulton Bag and Cotton Mills Strike of 1914–1915.* Ithaca, N.Y.: ILR Press, 1993.

Fleming, Douglas L. "The New Deal in Atlanta: A Review of the Major Programs." *Atlanta Historical Journal.* 30 (Spring 1986): 23–45.

Goodson, Steve. *Highbrows, Hillbillies and Hellfire: Public Entertainment in Atlanta, 1880–1930.* Athens: University of Georgia Press, 2002.

———. "This Mighty Influence for Good and Evil: The Movies in Atlanta, 1895–1920." *Atlanta History: A Journal of Georgia and the South.* 39 (Fall/Winter 1995): 28–47.

Grantham, Dewey W. "Regional Claims and National Purposes: The South and the New Deal." *Atlanta History: A Journal of Georgia and the South.* 38 (Fall 1994): 5–17.

Hall, Jacquelyn Dowd. "Private Eyes, Public Women: Images of Class and Sex in the Urban South, Atlanta, Georgia, 1913–1915." *Atlanta History: A Journal of Georgia and the South.* 36 (Winter 1993): 24–39.

———. *Revolt Against Chivalry: Jessie Daniel Ames and the Women's Campaign Against Lynching.* New York: Columbia University Press, 1979.

Herring, Neill, and Sue Thrasher. "UAW Sit-Down Strike, Atlanta, 1936." *Southern Exposure.* 1 (Winter 1974): 63–83.

Hertzberg, Steven. *Strangers Within the Gate City: The Jews of Atlanta, 1845–1915.* Philadelphia: Jewish Publishing Society of America, 1978.

Hickey, Georgina. *Hope and Danger in the New South City: Working-Class Women and Urban Development in Atlanta, 1890–1940.* Athens: University of Georgia Press, 2003.

Jackson, Kenneth T. *The Ku Klux Klan in the City.* New York: Oxford University Press, 1967.

Kuhn, Clifford M., Harlon E. Joye, and E. Bernard West. *Living Atlanta: An Oral History of the City, 1914–1948.* Athens: University of Georgia Press, 1990.

Kuhn, Clifford M. *Contesting the New South Order: The 1914–1915 Strike at Atlanta's Fulton Mills.* Chapel Hill: University of North Carolina Press, 2001.

Maclachlan, Gretchen E. "Atlanta's Industrial Women, 1879–1920." *Atlanta History: A Journal of Georgia and the South.* 36 (Winter 1993): 16–23.

MacLean, Nancy. "The Leo Frank Case Reconsidered: Gender and Sexual Politics in the Making of Reactionary Populism." *Jumpin' Jim Crow: Southern Politics from Civil War to Civil Rights.* Eds. Jane Dailey, Glenda Elizabeth Gilmore, and Bryant Simon. Princeton, N.J.: Princeton University Press, 2000.

Martin, Charles H. *The Angelo Herndon Case and Southern Justice.* Baton Rouge: Louisiana State University Press, 1978.

Melnick, Jeffrey. *Black-Jewish Relations on Trial: Leo Frank and Jim Conley in the New South.* Jackson: University Press of Mississippi, 2000.

Moseley, Charlton. "William Joseph Simmons: The Unknown Wizard." *Atlanta History: A Journal of Georgia and the South.* 37 (Spring 1993): 17–32.

Preston, Howard L. *Automobile Age Atlanta: The Making of a Southern Metropolis.* Athens: University of Georgia Press, 1979.

Pomerantz, Gary. *Where Peachtree Meets Sweet Auburn.* New York: Scribner, 1996.

Roth, Darlene. *Matronage: Patterns in Women's Organizations, Atlanta, Georgia, 1890–1940.* New York: Carlson Publishing Inc., 1994.

Rouse, Jacqueline Anne. *Lugenia Burns Hope: Black Southern Reformer.* Athens: University of Georgia Press, 1989.

Watson-Powers, Lynn. "Southern Bases: Baseball Before the Braves." *Atlanta History: A Journal of Georgia and the South.* 37 (Summer 1993): 25–40.

White, Dana F. "The Black Sides of Atlanta: A Geography of Expansion and Containment, 1870–1970." *Atlanta Historical Journal.* 26 (Summer/Fall 1982): 199–225.

Wiggins, Gene. *Fiddlin' Georgia Crazy: Fiddlin' John Carson, His Real World and the World of His Songs.* Urbana: University of Illinois Press, 1987.

IV. CITY WITHOUT LIMITS: 1940–PRESENT

Abrams, Ann Uhry. *Explosion at Orly: The Disaster that Transformed Atlanta.* Atlanta: Avion Press, 2002.

Allen, Fredrick. *Atlanta Rising: The Invention of an International City, 1946–1996.* Atlanta: Longstreet Press, 1996.

Allen, Ivan, Jr., and Paul Hemphill. *Mayor: Notes on the Sixties.* Athens: University of Georgia Press, 1978.

Ambrose, Andy. "Redrawing the Color Line: The History and Patterns of Black Housing in Atlanta, 1940–1973." Ph.D. diss. Emory University, 1992.

Bayor, Ronald H. *Race and the Shaping of the Twentieth-Century Atlanta.* Athens: University of Georgia Press, 1996.

Berge, Gunnar. 2002. Nobel Peace Prize presentation address, 10 December, Oslo, Norway.

Branch, Taylor. *Parting the Waters: America in the King Years, 1954–1963.* New York: Simon and Schuster, 1988.

Bullard, Robert D., and E. Kiki Thomas. "Atlanta: Mecca of the Southeast." *In Search of the New South: Black Urban Experiences in the 1970s and 1980s.* Ed. Robert D. Bullard, 75–97. Tuscaloosa: University of Alabama Press, 1989.

Carter, Jimmy. 2002. Nobel Lecture, 10 December, Oslo, Norway.

Egerton, John. *Speak Now Against the Day: The Generation Before the Civil Rights Movement in the South.* New York: Knopf, 1994.

Fairclough, Adam. *To Redeem the Soul of America: The Southern Christian Leadership Conference and Martin Luther King, Jr.* Athens: University of Georgia Press, 1987.

Ferguson, Karen J. *Black Politics in New Deal Atlanta.* Chapel Hill: University of North Carolina Press, 2002.

Garreau, Joel. "Atlanta: The Color of Money." *Edge City: Life on the New Frontier.* 139–78. New York: Doubleday, 1991.

Garrow, David J. *Bearing the Cross: Martin Luther King, Jr. and the Southern Christian Leadership Conference.* London: Vintage Books, 1993.

Greene, Melissa Faye. *The Temple Bombing.* Reading, Mass.: Addison-Wesley Publishing Company, 1996.

Goldfield, David R. *Black, White, and Southern: Race Relations and Southern Culture, 1940 to the Present.* Baton Rouge: Louisiana State University Press, 1990.

Hampton, Henry, and Steve Fayer. *Voices of Freedom: An Oral History of the Civil Rights Movements from the 1950s through the 1980s.* New York: Bantam Books, 1990.

Hein, Virginia H. "The Image of a City Too Busy to Hate: Atlanta in the 1960s." *Phylon.* 33 (Fall 1972): 205–21.

Heys, Sam and Allen B. Goodwin. *The Winecoff Fire: The Untold Story of America's Deadliest Hotel Fire.* Atlanta: Longstreet Press, 1993.

Hornsby, Alton, Jr. "The Negro in Atlanta Politics, 1961–1973." *Atlanta Historical Bulletin.* 21 (Spring 1977): 9–11.

King, Coretta Scott. *My Life with Martin Luther King, Jr.* New York: Holt, Rineholt, and Winston, 1969.

Lewis, John. *Walking With the Wind: A Memoir of the Movement.* New York: Simon and Schuster, 1998.

"The Making of Modern Atlanta." (8-part television series). Atlanta: WPBA, Channel 30, 1991.

Rice, Bradley R. "If Atlanta Were Dixie." *Sunbelt Cities: Politics and Growth Since World War II.* Eds. Richard R. Bernedad and Bradley R. Rice, 31–57. Austin: University of Texas Press, 1993.

Schwartz, Janet, and Denise Black. *Ethnic Atlanta.* Atlanta: Longstreet Press, 1993.

Silver, Christopher, and John V. Moeser. *The Separate City: Black Communities in the Urban South, 1940–1968.* Lexington: University Press of Kentucky, 1995.

Sjoquist, David L., ed. *The Atlanta Paradox.* New York: Russell Sage Foundation, 2000.

Spritzer, Lorraine Nelson and Jean B. Bergmark. *Grace Towns Hamilton and the Politics of Southern Change.* Athens: University of Georgia Press, 1997.

Stone, Clarence N. *Regime Politics: Governing Atlanta, 1946–1988.* Lawrence: University Press of Kansas, 1989.

Teel, Leonard Ray. *Ralph Emerson McGill: Voice of the Southern Conscience.* Knoxville: The University of Tennessee Press, 2001.

Thompson, Robert A., Hylan Lewis, and Davis McEntire. "Atlanta and Birmingham: A Comparative Study in Negro Housing." *Housing and Minority Groups.* Eds. Nathan Glazer and Davis McEntire, 13–83. Berkeley: University of California Press, 1960.

Von Hoffman, Alexander. *House by House, Block by Block: The Rebirth of America's Urban Neighborhoods.* New York: Oxford University Press, 2003.

Young, Andrew. *An Easy Burden: The Civil Rights Movement and the Transformation of America.* New York: HarperCollins Publishers, 1996.

Zhao, Jianli and Franklin Ng, eds. *Strangers in the City: The Atlanta Chinese, Their Community, and Stories of Their Lives.* New York: Routledge, 2002.

INDEX

Numbers in *italic* denote illustrations.

Adair, Forrest, 85
Adair, George, 85
Adair, Perry, 118, 119
Adairsville, 36
African Americans: enslaved, 13, 17, 27, 29–32, 34; free persons of color, 30; and politics, 56, 58–61, 169–71, 185–94; nineteenth-century elite, 61–68; and education, 62–63, 126–28, 173–79; orphanages, 64, 97; in workforce, 64–65; businesses of, 65–66; and benevolent societies, 96; in sports, 115–16; and residential segregation, 131–32, 147, 168–69, 187, 203. *See also* Civil rights movement
African Methodist Episcopal (AME) Church, 30
Agnes Scott College, *89, 90*
Aiken, Walter H., 167, *168*
Air transportation, 147–49, 164–65, 201, 202
Alexander, William D., 144
Alexander Memorial Coliseum, 180
All-Citizens Registration Committee, 170
Allen, Ivan, Jr., 177, 178, 180, 181, 183, 186–87, 188
Allen, Ivan, Sr., 104
American Order of the Fascisti, 153
Ames, Jesse Daniel, 132
Andrews, Sidney, 52, 53
Anthony, Susan B., 138
Anticommunism, 152–53
Anti-Defamation League, 136
Apparel Mart, 195
Arkwright, Preston, 85
Army of the Cumberland, 38
Army of the Ohio, 38
Army of the Tennessee, 38
Ashby Theater, 110
Asian immigrants, 197, 201
Association of Southern Women for the Prevention of Lynching (ASWPL), 132
Atkinson, Henry M., 85
Atlanta Agricultural and Industrial Association, 74
Atlanta and Charlotte Railroad, 50
Atlanta and Edgewood Street Railroad Company, 83, 142
Atlanta and Richmond Railroad, 50

Atlanta and West Point Railroad, 24, 38, 42
Atlanta Art Association, 107, 180
Atlanta Baptist Female Seminary, 62, 63. *See also* Spelman College
Atlanta Baseball Club, 91
Atlanta Birmingham and Atlantic Railroad, *144*
Atlanta Black Crackers, 115–16
Atlanta Braves, 178–80, 202
Atlanta Campaign, 35–46
Atlanta Children's Home, *87*
Atlanta Civic and Political League, 170
"Atlanta Compromise," 100
Atlanta Constitution, 47, 48, 69, 131
Atlanta Convention and Visitors Bureau, 195
Atlanta Cotton Factory, 73
Atlanta Crackers, 91, 113, 114. *See also* Atlanta Black Crackers
Atlanta Cubs, 115
Atlanta Daily World, 105
Atlanta Deppens, 115
Atlanta Economic Development Corporation, 192
Atlanta Enterprise, 27
Atlanta Equal Suffrage Association, 92
Atlanta Falcons, 180, 202
Atlanta Female Academy, 27
Atlanta Female Institute, *36*
Atlanta Flames, 180
Atlanta Free Kindergarten Association, 87
Atlanta-Fulton County Stadium, 179
Atlanta General Depot, 157
Atlanta Hawks, 180, 202
Atlanta Historical Society, 107, 181
Atlanta Housing Council, 168
Atlanta Independent, 105, 106
Atlanta Intelligencer, 27, 105
Atlanta Journal, 131
Atlanta Kindergarten School, 87
Atlanta Lesbian Feminist Alliance, 194
Atlanta Life Insurance Company, 66, 105, 168
Atlanta Luminary, 27
Atlanta Manufacturers' Association, 74, 78, 81
Atlanta Medical College, 27, *28, 36*
Atlanta Municipal Airport, 148. *See also* Candler Field
Atlanta Music Club, 107
Atlanta Music Festival, 90

Atlanta Mutual Building and Loan Association, 168
Atlanta National Bank, 50
Atlanta Negro Voters League, 170, 186
Atlanta Normal Training School, 87
Atlanta Railway and Power Company, 85
Atlanta Rapid Transit Company, 85
Atlanta Regional Commission (ARC), 166
Atlanta Rolling Mill, 26, 32, *41*
"Atlanta Spirit," 24, 48, 103, 156, 204
Atlanta Thrashers, 202
Atlanta Tribune, 27
Atlanta University, 61, 62–63, *89*
Atlanta University Center, 62–63
Atlanta Woman's Club, 91
Auburn Avenue, 75–76, 167
Austell, Alfred, 50
Automobile, 146–47. *See also* Interstate highway system
Ayer, Frederic, 62

Bailey, Tom, 110
Baltimore Block, 82, *83*
Barili, Alfredo, 90–91
Baseball, 91, *92,* 115, 179–80
Battle Hill Tuberculosis Hospital, 125
Bell, John, 32
Bell Bomber plant, 159, 163
Bell Johnson Opera Hall, 90
Benevolent societies, 34, 96
Bentley, Moses, 66
Berry, Carrie, 42, *43*
Big Bethel AME Church, 62, 63, 64, 105, 125
Biltmore Hotel, 177
Birth of a Nation (film), 110, 136–37
"Black Mecca," 61
Black Shirts, 153
Bleckley, Haralson, 145
Bleckley Plan, 145
Bomb proofs, 42, *43*
Booker T. Washington High School, 86, 126–27, 128, 129
Borders, William Holmes, 172
Boudinot, Elias, *14, 16*
Boutell, John: house of, *37*
Boy's High School, *86,* 128. *See also* Henry W. Grady High School

Breckinridge, John C., 32
Brockey, Harold, 192
Brothers of Aid, 96
Brown High School, 176
Brown v. *Board of Education,* 176
Buford Dam, 165
Bullock, Rufus B., 58, 59, 99
Burnett, Tom, 91, 113
Buzzards Roost, 7, *8*

Cabbagetown, 73, 139, 193
Cable News Network (CNN), 197
Calhoun, James Montgomery, 38, *40,* 45
Calhoun, Moses, 66
Calhoun, William L., 73
Campbell, Bill, 194
Campbell County, 16
Camp Gordon, 143, 157
Candler, Asa, 76, 85, 131, 136, 142, 145
Candler, Warren, 130
Candler Building, 101
Candler Field, 147, 165
Candler Park/Edgewood, 146–47
Capital City Club, 91, 109
Carmichael, Stokely, 188–89
Carrie Steele Orphanage, 64
Carroll County, 16
Carson, Fiddlin' John, 108, 136
Carter, Jimmy, 192, 197–98
Carver Homes, 169
Carver Theater, 110
Cassville, 36
Centennial Olympic Park, 199, 202
Centers for Disease Control and Prevention
    (CDC), 196
Central Atlanta Improvement Association
    (CAIA), 171
Central Atlanta Progress (CAP), 192
Central of Georgia Railroad, 19, 81
Chattahoochee River, 4
Cherokee County, 16
Cherokee Indians, 4–17
Christian Association Mission School, 96
Citizens Committee for Better City Planning, 186
Citizens Trust Bank, 105, 168
City Hall, *54*
"City Too Busy to Hate," 156, 174–75, 196

Civic Auditorium, 195
Civil rights movement, 112, 160–63, 170,
    172–77, 187–88
Civil War, 32–46
Civil Works Administration (CWA), 150
Clark University, 62, 63
Clark Atlanta University, 199
Clarke, E.Y., 78
Clement, Rufus E., 167, 172
Cleveland, Grover, *71, 72,* 81
Cobb County, 17
Coca-Cola, 76, 77, 159–60, *202*
Cole Opera House, 90
Colquit, Alfred H., 73
Columbia Theological Seminary, 130–31
Commercial High School, 128
Commission on Interracial Cooperation
    (CIC), 108, 132, 162–63
Committee on Public Safety, 32
Communism, 152–53
Community Chest, 125–26
Community Planning Council, 168
Concordia Association, 96
Concordia Hall, 90
Cone, Reuben, 24
Confederate Veterans Home, 125
Conley, Benjamin F., 59, 73
Conley, James, 135
Connally, Temperance, *18*
Connally, Thomas, *18*
Cotton, 72–73
Cotton States and International Exposition, 48,
    69, 96–100
Coweta County, 16
Cox College and Conservatory, *129*
Crawford, Frazier and Co., *31*
Creek Indians, 3–17
Crumbley, Floyd, 65
Cunningham, Nancy, *42*
Cyclorama, 151

Daughters of the American Revolution (DAR),
    91
Davis Hall, 90, 106
Decatur, 17
Decatur Street, 27
DeGive, Laurent, 90

DeGive Opera House, 90, 106, 110
DeKalb County, 2, 16, 29
Delta Air Lines, 165
Democratic Executive Committee of Atlanta, 138
Democratic National Convention (1988), 195
Dobbins Air Force Base, 196
Dobbs, John Wesley, 190
Domestic partners, 194
Douglas, Helen Mankin, 172
Douglas, Stephen A., 32
Drenner, Karla, 194
Druid Hills, 85, 130, 142
Du Bois, W. E. B., 63, 100
Durham Manifesto, 162

East Atlanta Land Company, 83, 142
East Tennessee Railroad, 51
Eastern Airlines, 165
Ebenezer Baptist Church, 64, 105, 125
Education, 126–31
81 Theater, 108, 110
Ellis Street, *37*
Elsas, Jacob, 73, 139–40
Emory University, 130
Empire Building, 101
Empire Real Estate Board, 168, 180
English American Building, 75, 77, 101
English Avenue Elementary School, 176
Equitable Building, 75, *78,* 83, *101*
Etowah Mounds, 2
Executive Order 8802, 159
Exposition Cotton Mills, 73
Ezra Church, 40

"Factory Lot," The. *See* Cabbagetown
Fair Employment Practices Commission
    (FEPC), 169–70
Fairlie-Poplar district, 104
Fayette County, 16, 17
Fayetteville, 17
Federal Emergency Relief Administration
    (FERA), 149
Federation of Negro Women's Clubs, 92
Fifteenth Amendment, 58–59
Finch, William, 58, 59
Fire of 1917, 123, *124*
First Congregational Church of Atlanta, 64, 125

Flatiron Building, 75, 77, 101
Fleming, Harold C., 161
Flipper, Festus, 30
Flipper, Henry O., 30
Flipper, Joseph S., 30
Football, 116–18, 180, 202
Fort Benning, 157
Fort Gillem, 157
Fort McPherson, 116, 157, 196
Fort Standing Peachtree, 5, 18, 19
"Forward Atlanta," 102, 104, 171, 177
Fourteenth Amendment, 54–55
Fox Theatre, 108, 110
Frank, Leo, 133, *134,* 135–36
Franklin, Shirley, 194
Fraternal organizations, 125
Freedmen's Bureau, 62
Free persons of color, 30
Friendship Baptist Church, 62, 63, 64, 190
Fulton, Hamilton, 19
Fulton Bag and Cotton Mills, 73, *74,* 134, 139–40
Fulton County, 29, 34
Fulton-DeKalb Hospital Authority, 166
Fulton National Bank Building, 183

Gaines, Frank H., 90
Gate City Free Kindergarten Association, 87
Gate City Nine, 91, 113
"Gate City of the South," 2
"Gateway to the South," 196
Gay Liberation Front, 194
Gay Pride, 194
General Motors, 104, 141, 163
George, Walter, 165
Georgia Capitol, *57*
Georgia Dome, 202
Georgia Equal Suffrage League, 138
Georgia Institute of Technology (Georgia Tech), 48, 69, 88, *89,* 116, 199
Georgia Men's League for Woman Suffrage, 138
Georgia Military Academy, 129
Georgia National Bank, 50
Georgia National Guard, 140
Georgians Unwilling to Surrender (GUTS), 175

Georgian Terrace Hotel, 101
Georgia Pacific Railroad, 50, 65, 81
Georgia Power, 142
Georgia Railroad and Banking Company, 19, 38, *44*
Georgia Railway and Electric Company, 85
Georgia Railway and Power Company, 85, 142
Georgia Real Estate Loan and Trust Company, 61
Georgia Relief Commission, 150
Georgia Tech, *See* Georgia Institute of Technology
Georgia Western Railroad, 50
German immigrants, 96. *See also* Jews
German Immigration Society, 74
German Manufacturing Society, 74
German prisoners of war (POWs), 157
German Turnverein, 96
Ghioni's and Sussini's Grand Italian Opera Company, 90
Girl's High School, 128
Gold, discovery of, 14
Gone With the Wind (book), 111
Gone With the Wind (film), *110,* 111–13
Gordon, John B., 58
Graham, George, 58, 59
Grant, Lemuel P., *24,* 24, 37, 82, 120
Grant Park, 37, 67, 82, 91, 193
Greater Regional Transportation Authority (GRTA), 203
Great Fire of 1917, 123, *124*
Griffin, Marvin, 172
Griffith, D. W., 110, 136–37
Gwinnett County, 16, 17

Haas, Aaron, 134
Hammer, Jane, 175
Hammond, O. S., 49
Hanson, George W., 144
"Hanson Six," 144
Harlem Theater, 110
Hartsfield, William B., *110,* 147, 148, 153, 165, 169, 172–75, 176–77

Hartsfield International Airport, 148, 165, 201, 202
Hawkins, Benjamin, 11
Hebrew Orphans Home, 94, 126
Heisman, John, 116, 117
Help Our Public Education (HOPE), 175
Henry County, 16
Henry W. Grady High School, 176. *See also* Boy's High School, Tech High School
Herndon, Alonzo F., *66,* 105, 152
Herndon, Angelo, 152–53
Herndon Building, 105
Herring, Rudolf, 94
Hibernian Benevolent Society, 96
Hibernian Hall, 90
Hicks, Barbecue Bob, 107
High, Harriett (Mrs. Joseph), 107
High Museum of Art, 181
Hill, Jesse, 183
Hispanics, 194, 201
Home for the Friendless, 96
Home Park, 147
Hood, John Bell, 38, *40,* 42
Hope, John, 151
Hope, Lugenia Burns, 122, 138
Hopkins, Harry, 150
Housing, Mayor's Conference on, 189
Houston Street Kindergarten, *88*
Howard, David T., 65
Howard, W. S., 49
Howell, Clark, 131
Howell, Evan P., *70*
Howell's Mill, *20*
Hughes Spalding Pavilion, 166
Humphries, Charner, 18
Hurt, Joel, *82,* 83, 85, 142

Immigration, 47, 74, 96, 197, 201
Immigration Association of the State of Georgia, 74
Indian Removal Act, 13–14
Indians, 4–17
Industry, 26, 32–33, 34, 50, 72–75, 158–60, 163
Inman, Samuel M., 75
Inman Park, 83, 143
Integration, school, 173–77
Interdenominational Seminary, 62

Internal Improvements, Board of, 18
International Cotton Exposition, 73, 79, 120
Interstate highway system, 164, 203
Irish immigrants, 96

Jacobs, Thornwell, 130
Jackson, Andrew, 5, 13
Jackson, Maynard, *189,* 190, 192, 194, 204
Jews, 73, 75, 94, 96, 109, 133–36, 175
Jim Crow, 66–68
Johnson, Andrew, 54
Johnston, Joseph E., 35, *38*
Jones, Robert Tyre (Bobby), 118–120

Key, James, 150
Kennedy, John F., 177
Kennesaw Mountain, 36
Kimball, Hannibal Ingalls, 56, 59, 73, 79
Kimball House Hotel, *52,* 56, 86, *95*
Kimball Opera House, *56,* 59
King, Martin Luther, Jr., 111, 185, 187–88,
     189–90
King, Martin Luther ("Daddy"), Sr., 112, 186
Knights of Mary Phagan, 136
Kress Department Store, *173*
Ku Klux Klan, 68, 102, 135–37, 176

Labor strikes, 138–141
Ladies Soldier Relief Society, 34
Lakewood General Motors plant, 104, 141,
     158. *See also* General Motors
Lakewood Park, *121,* 122
Lane, Mills B., 178
Lanier, Lake, 166
Latinos, 194, 201
Lawrenceville, 17
Lawson General Hospital, 157
Lee, George W., 32, 35
Lenox Square, 184
Lincoln Monument Association of Atlanta, 55
Lincoln Theater, 110
Lochner Report, 164
Lockheed Aircraft Corporation, 163, 173
Loew's Grand, 110, 111
Logan, Carrie Steele, 97, 125
Long, Stephen D., 1
Louisville and Nashville Railroad, 51, 142

Luckie, Solomon, *42*
Lumpkin, Martha Atalanta, *25*
Lumpkin, Wilson, 19, 26

MacIntosh, William, *10,* 12, 13
Macon and Western Railroad, 38, 39
Maddox, Lester, 175
"March to the Sea," 46
Marcus, Sidney, 192
Margravate of Azilia, 4
Marietta and North Georgia Railroad, 81
Marist College, *129*
Markham, William, 32
Markham House, 66
Marshall, John, 14
Marthasville, 25–26
Massell, Sam, 183
Mayfair Club, 109
Mays, Benjamin, 161–62
McClellan, George B., 35
McElreath, Walter, *108*
McGill, Ralph, 161
McKinley, Jacob, 65–66
McPherson, James B., 38, 40
McTell, Blind Willie, 107
Meade, George Gordon, 55
Mechanic's Institute, 72
Men and Religion Forward Movement, 140
Merchandise Mart, 184, 195
Metropolitan Association for Segregated
     Education (MASE), 175
Metropolitan Atlanta Rapid Transit Authority
     (MARTA), 181, 183, 202
Metropolitan Planning Commission (MPC),
     166, 168–69, 171
Micco, Yoholo, 16
Militia, state, 132
Milwaukee Braves, 179
Mims, John E., 27
Mississippian Era, 2–3
Mitchell, Alexander Welden, *29*
Mitchell, Isaac Green, *18*
Mitchell, Margaret, 18, 111, *161*
Mitchell, Samuel, 24
Monroe Railroad, 19
Montag, Sigmund, 136
Montgomery, James McC., 18

Montgomery, Robert, 4
Moore, Arthur J., 161
Moral and Reform Party, 27
Morehouse College, 62, 63, 199
Morris Brown College, 30, 62, 63, 199
Moss, Buddy, 107
Murrell, John A., 27
Murrell's Row, 27
Murphy High School, 176
Murphy, Willis, 65
Mutual Federal, 105

National Association for the Advancement of
     Colored People (NAACP), 170, 173–74
National American Woman Suffrage
     Association (NAWSA), 138
National Basketball Association (NBA), 180, 202
National Football League (NFL), 180. *See also*
     Atlanta Falcons
National Hockey League, 180. *See also* Atlanta
     Thrashers
National Negro Business League, 131
National Pencil Company, 135, 136
Native Americans, 4–17
Naval Air Station, 196
Negro Anti-Emigration Club, 74
Negro Building, 96–97
Neighborhood planning units (NPU), 191, 193
Neighborhood Union, 122, 125
Nelson's Ferry, 18
"New Deal," 149–52
"New South," 48, 54, 69
Newspapers: *See Atlanta Constitution, Atlanta
     Daily World, Atlanta Enterprise, Atlanta
     Intelligencer, Atlanta Journal, Atlanta
     Luminary, Atlanta Tribune*
Nineteenth Amendment, 138
Norcross, Jonathan, 27, 73
North Avenue Presbyterian School, 129
Northside High School, 176

Oakland Cemetery, 27, 67, 91
Odd Fellows Building, 105, 109
Office parks, 184
Oglethorpe University, 88, 139
Old Fourth Ward, 62, 131
Olmsted, Frederick Law, 83, 85, 142

Olympic Games (1996), 198–200
Omni, 180
Omni International, 195
Organizations Assisting Schools in September (OASIS), 175
Orly Airport: plane crash at, 180–81
Orphanages, 64, 97, 109

Paces Ferry, 18
Palmer, Charles F., 151
Peachtree Center, 184
Peachtree Street, 27, *37,* 194
Pemberton, John Stith, 76
Perry, Herman, 147
Perry Homes, 169
Peters, Richard, house of, *1*
Peyton Road barricade, 186
Phagan, Mary, 135
Phillips Arena, 202
Piedmont Chautauqua, 69
Piedmont Driving Club, 91, *93, 108,* 109, 118
Piedmont Exposition of 1887, 69, 80, 120
Piedmont Hotel, 101
Piedmont Park, 67
Piedmont Sanitorium, 134
Pittcairn Aviation, 148
Plan of Improvement, 163, 172
Ponce de Leon Ball Park, 91, 114
Ponce de Leon Park, *121,* 122
Ponce de Leon Springs, 67, *84, 91,* 122
Ponder, Ephraim, 30; house of, *41*
Pope, John, 55
Portman, John, 183, 184
Powers Ferry, 18
Proctor, Henry Hugh, 64, 125
Progressive Club, 110
Public housing, 151–52, 169
Public Works Administration (PWA), 150–51

Quartermaster's Depot, 33

Railroads, 18–19, 22–24, 33, 38, *39, 42, 44, 46,* 47–48, 50–51, 65, 81, 141–42
Rawson, Edward Everett, *26;* house of, *28*
Rawson sisters (Mary, Carrie, Laura, and Eunice), *45*
Reconstruction, 49–61

Republican Party, 48, 54, 56, 58–61
Resaca, 36
Reynoldstown, 193
Rice, Frank D., 78
Rich and Brothers Dry Goods, *75*
Rich, Morris, 75
Rich's Department Store, 184
Richmond and West Point Railroad, 51
Ridge, John, *14,* 15, 16
Ridge, The (aka Major Ridge), *14,* 15, 16
Riots: Civil War widows, 34; Race, of 1906, 131–33; Summerhill, *187,* 188; Bedford Pine, 188
Robert W. Woodruff Arts Center, 181
Robinson, Jackie, 114
Roosevelt, Eleanor, *150*
Roosevelt, Franklin, 149, 159
Ross, John, *14,* 15
Ross's Landing, 23
Rowdy Party, 27
Royal Theater, 110, 112
Rucker, Henry Allen, *60,* 76, 105, *106*
Russell, Richard, 165

Saint Andrew's Benevolent Society, 96
Salvation Army, 96
Sanders, Carl, 180
Sandy Springs Methodist Episcopal Church, 27
Schofield, John M., 38
Schofield, Lewis, 32
Schools, 126–31
Scott, George Washington, 90
Scripto Company, 173, 188
Seaboard Air-Line, 142
Secession, 32
Segregation, 66–68, 131–32, 147, 168–69, 187, 203
Sexual orientation: discrimination based on, 194
Settlement Home Kindergarten, *87*
Sheltering Arms Nursery, 87, 96
Shepperson, Gay B., 150
Sherman, William Tecumseh, 35–46, *36*
"Shinplasters," 34
Shopping malls, 184
Sibley, John, 175–76
Sibley commission, 176

Simmons, William J., 137
Sims, Walter, 147
Sisters of Honor, 96
Slaton, John M., 135
Slave market, *31*
Slavery, 29–32
Smith, Hoke, 131
Smith, James M. , 59
Smith, Rankin, 180
Smith, W. R. C. , 104
Snake Nation, 27
Social clubs, 91, *93, 108,* 109, 110, 118
Southeastern Fair, 122
Southeastern Freight Association (SFA), 51
Southeastern Passenger Association (SPA), 51
Southern and Central Railroad, 51
Southern Christian Leadership Conference (SCLC), 186
Southern League, 91
Southern Regional Council (SRC), 161–63
South View Cemetery, 67
Spelman College, 62, *89. See also* Atlanta Baptist Female Seminary
Spiller and Burr Pistol Factory, 33
Sports, 113–20, 178, 180, 202
Spring Street Viaduct, 145
Stadium Authority, 178
Standard Club, 109
Standard Life Insurance, 105
Standing Peachtree, *7, 19*
Steele, Carrie. *See* Logan, Carrie Steele
Sterling, Alexa, 118
St. Louis Hawks, 180
Strand Theater, 110
Streetcars, 82, 141, 142, 146
Student Non-Violent Coordinating Committee (SNCC), 184, 188–89
Suburbs, 146–47, 187, 203–4
Summer Hill School, 62
Super Bowl (1994), 199
Sutton, Willis A., 128
"Sweet Auburn." *See* Auburn Avenue

Talmadge, Eugene, 150
Tanner, Gid, and the Skillet Lickers, 108
Tate, James, 65
Taylor, Samuel B., 117

Tech High School, 128. *See also* Henry W.
  Grady High School
Techwood Homes, 151–52
Telegraph, *95*
Temple, The, 175
Terminal Station, 142
Terminus, 1, 24, 25
Textile mills, 72–73, *74,* 134, 139–40
Theaters, 90, 108–9, 110–11
Third Military District, 55
Thomas, George H., 38
Top Hat Club, 108, 109
Tourism, 195
Trail of Tears, 16
Traveler's Aid, 158
Treaty of New Echota, 15
Turner Broadcasting System (TBS), 197
Turner Field, 199, 202

Unionists, 32
Union Station, 142, *144*
United Automobile Workers Union (UAW),
  Local 34, 141
United Daughters of the Confederacy (UDC),
  91
United Textile Workers Union of America
  (UTW), Local 886, 140
University Homes, 151–52

Up Ahead (planning commission document),
  169
Urban League, 167, 170
United Services Organization (USO), 158
USS *Atlanta* III, 160, *161*
USS *Atlanta* IV, *160, 161*

Vann, David, *17*
Vann, Joseph, 16
Varieties Theater, 90
Vigilance Committee, 32
Vine City, 193
Virginia and Georgia Railroad, 51
Virginia-Highland, 147
Voter registration, 170

Ward, William T., 45
Ware, Gertrude, 87
Washington, Booker T., 97, 99–100. *See also*
  Booker T. Washington High School
Washington Park, 147
Washington Seminary, 87
Water supply, 93
Watson, Tom, 135
Webster, Robert, 45
Wesley Chapel, 27, *28*
Western and Atlantic Railroad, *22,* 23, 24, 33,
  38, *39, 46, 51*

Westminster School, 129
Westview Cemetery, 67
Wheat Street Baptist Church, 64, 105, 125, 172
Wheeler, Joseph, 42
"White flight," 187
Wilson, J. S., 78
Winecoff Hotel, 101
Woman's Building, 98
Woman suffrage movement, 92, *93,* 137–38
Wood, Leonard, 116
Woodruff, Robert, 114, 172, 181, 188
Woodward Academy, 129
Woolard, Cathy, 194
Worcester v. *Georgia,* 14
Works Progress Administration (WPA), 150,
  153
World Congress Center, 195, 196, 202
World of Coca-Cola, *202*
"World's Next Great City," 156, 196
WSB radio, 108

Yaarab Temple, 110–11
Yazoo Land Fraud, 7, 11
Young, Andrew, *189,* 190, 192–93
Young Men's Christian Association (YMCA),
  Butler Street, 158